THE
CULTURE
OF
YOUTH

VOLUME 7
1960-1973

THE
CULTURE
OF
YOUTH

INTRODUCTION BY
ASA BRIGGS

Project editor Peter Furtado

Project art editor Ayala Kingsley

Text editors Robert Peberdy, Mike March, Sue Martin

Cartographic manager Olive Pearson

Cartographic editor Zoë Goodwin

Designers Frankie Wood, Janet McCallum, Wolfgang Mezger, Gill Mouqué, Niki Overy, Linda Reed, Nicholas Rous, Tony de Saulles, Dave Sumner, Rita Wütrych

Picture research manager Alison Renney

Picture research Jan Croot, Diane Hamilton, Rebecca Hirsh, Angela Murphy, Diana Phillips, Linda Proud, Christine Vincent, Charlotte Ward-Perkins

Editorial assistants Elaine Welsh, Monica Byles

AN EQUINOX BOOK

Devised and produced by
Andromeda Oxford Ltd
11–15 The Vineyard
Abingdon Oxfordshire OX14 3PX
England

This edition published by
Hamlyn, part of Reed
Consumer Books Ltd,
Michelin House,
81 Fulham Road,
London SW3 6RB

ISBN 0-600-57995-6

Printed in Germany by
Mohndruck Graphische Betriebe
GmbH. Gutersloh.

ADVISORY EDITORS

Alan Borg
Imperial War Museum,
London

Asa Briggs
Worcester College, Oxford

Carlo Cipolla
University of California,
Berkeley, USA

Sir Napier Crookenden
Formerly Lieutenant of Her
Majesty's Tower of London

Andrew J. Goodpaster
US Army (retired)

Wolfgang Krieger
Ebenhausen, Germany

David Landes
Harvard University, USA

William McNeill
University of Chicago, USA

Peter Pulzer
All Souls College, Oxford

**Hartmut Pogge von
Strandmann**
University College, Oxford

Philip Waller
Merton College, Oxford

Geoffrey Warner
Open University

M.L.H.L. Weaver
Linacre College, Oxford

Charles Webster
All Souls College, Oxford

EDITORS

John Campbell
Freelance writer, London

John Harriss
London School of Economics

Richard Maltby
University of Exeter

C. S. Nicholls
St Antony's College, Oxford

Sidney Pollard
Formerly of University of
Bielefeld, Germany

J. M. Winter
Pembroke College,
Cambridge

CONTRIBUTORS

Gerold Ambrosius
University of Bremen,
Germany

Duncan Anderson
Royal Military Academy,
Sandhurst

Ian Beckett
Royal Military Academy,
Sandhurst

Geoffrey Best
Formerly of University of
Sussex

Robert Bideleux
University of Swansea

Simon Boughey
Corpus Christi College,
Cambridge

Gail Braybon
Freelance writer

Sir Julian Bullard
All Souls College, Oxford

Kathleen Burk
Imperial College, London

Angus Calder
Open University

Peter Carey
Trinity College, Oxford

Jane Carmichael
Imperial War Museum,
London

Malcolm Cooper
Formerly of Newfoundland
University, Canada

P. L. Cottrell
University of Leicester

Robert Dare
University of Adelaide,
Australia

Martin Dean
Formerly of University of
Cambridge

Anne Deighton
University of Reading

John Erickson
University of Edinburgh

David Fletcher
The Tank Museum, Wareham

CONTENTS

James Foreman-Peck
University of Hull

Brian Foss
Freelance writer

Michael Geyer
University of Chicago, USA

Robert Gildea
Merton College, Oxford

Anthony Glees
Brunel University

Roger Griffin
Oxford Polytechnic

Jennifer Hargreaves
Roehampton Institute,
London

Nathaniel Harris
Freelance writer

Nigel Harris
University College, London

Gundi Harriss
Birkbeck College, London

David Horn
University of Liverpool

Julian Jackson
University College of
Swansea

Keith Jeffrey
University of Ulster

Matthew Jones
St Antony's College, Oxford

Paul Kennedy
Yale University, USA

Ghislaine Lawrence
National Museum of Science
and Industry, London

Peter Lowe
University of Manchester

Keith Lyons
London School of Economics

Dermott MacCann
Brunel University

Peter Martland
Corpus Christi College,
Cambridge

Roger Morgan
London School of Economics

Lucy Newton
Leicester University

A. J. Nicholls
St Antony's College, Oxford

David Penn
Imperial War Museum,
London

Brian Holden Reid
King's College, London

Catherine Reilly
Freelance writer

Denis Ridgeway
Formerly of Royal Navy
Scientific Service

Gowher Rizvi
University of Warwick

Keith Sainsbury
University of Reading

Harry Shukman
St Antony's College, Oxford

Penny Sparke
Royal College of Art, London

Jill Stephenson
University of Edinburgh

Stanley Trapido
Lincoln College, Oxford

T.H.E. Travers
University of Calgary,
Canada

S.B. Whitmore
Formerly British Army of the
Rhine, Germany

Paul Wilkinson
University of Aberdeen

Elizabeth Wilson
North London Polytechnic

Roger Zetter
Oxford Polytechnic

Ronald Tamplin
University of Exeter

Ruth Pearson
University of East Anglia

Peter Lambert
University of East Anglia

INTRODUCTION

The keynote of the 1960s, a decade with a strong sense of identity, was change, change that could excite or repel or, more often, bewilder. In consequence it was a decade that made much of the generation gap. Young people complained that the old could not understand them, and held them back; the old argued that the young were subverting many of the values that had been fought for, with much bloodshed, over the previous 50 years. The focus was on the new. Old institutions, political economic, educational, religious, were under review or just as often attack. So also were established conventions, moral and social. Yet most institutions and conventions survived, if often partially reformed or reshaped.

There were sharp contrasts of mood – even contradictions – at different times during the 1960s, particularly between the early and late years of the decade, and at no one single point in time were society, politics or culture all of one piece even in one place. By 1973, however, the whole decade, often characterized as the "swinging sixties," already seemed to be part of history. Its excesses were remembered more than its achievements.

In Western Europe and the United States this was a period of affluence, with consumption levels rising to unprecedented heights; and the numbers of people there to share it seemed to have become subject to regulation as the new contraceptive pill now gave women the key to control their own fertility. Brought into Europe from the United States in 1960 and made commercially available in 1961, the pill was widely distributed before there was talk of radical and militant "women's liberation". It was resisted in many countries as immoral, and condemned, like other forms of "artificial" contraception, in a Papal encyclical of 1968, *Humanae vitae*. The population of the Third World, where birth control, if available at all, was more rudimentary, continued to "explode". In the face of that and increasing pressure on food and other resources there was increasing talk about "the limits to growth" – in sharp contrast to the positive and dynamic futurology of the early years of the decade.

Among the many human rights asserted during the decade, women's rights were the most universally demanded. Feminism found many new voices in the West, as did ethnic rights. Opposition grew, in the West as well as in Africa, to South Africa's policy of *apartheid*, while in 1964 Martin Luther King, the American black civil rights leader, won the Nobel Peace Prize: in 1968, though, he was shot and killed while campaigning in Memphis, Tennessee.

Memphis figured also in the cultural mythology of the 1960s, as the home of Elvis Presley, who dominated rock music until 1963. By then, however, the Beatles had appeared on the pop music scene, the first of many British groups who started obscurely and won international acclaim. It was to the sound of pop music that the claims of a permissive society were advanced during the 1960s, a society permissive in its attitudes not only to sex but, as the decade went by, to mind-changing drugs. By the end of the decade, "flower power", most conspicuous in California, the key place on the map of change, offered a gentle challenge to what militant students and some of their professors called "the military, capitalist, imperialist complex". The hippies or the flower people, mainly drawn from the middle classes, lived in a psychedelic world of their own.

By far the largest section of the community remained "mainstream", and there was as much resistance to permissiveness as there was acceptance of it. Moreover, while the nonconformist and the rebellious were involved in their diverse forms of challenge, some of them focussing on the structures of their own educational establishments as microcosms of the structural faults of society at large, American military and capitalist power was growing. By the end of the decade this military and economic might was being employed imperially – and far away – in a country of which few Americans had heard in 1960 – Vietnam, formerly a part of French-controlled Indochina.

After the expulsion of the French in the 1950s, Vietnam was a divided country politically and ideologically: like Korea, it was under the sway of two governments, the north resolutely Communist, the south predominantly anti-Communist, with the anti-Communism taking different forms. For this reason foreign intervention was inevitable. From 1965 the United States greatly increased the scale of its intervention in Vietnamese affairs. The main justification at the time was that if North Vietnam, backed by both the Soviet Union and by the People's Republic of China, defeated the south there would be a "domino effect" throughout southeast Asia and beyond, and country after country sympathetic to the west would fall into Communist hands.

The American Democrat president, Lyndon B Johnson, who had taken office after the assassination of JF Kennedy in November 1963, found himself increasingly embroiled in the Vietnamese conflict after having committed himself to a vigorous domestic campaign to extend black civil rights. And with increasing embroilment in the conflicts of southeast Asia there was increasing division at home. Protests against the military draft fueled other forms of youth protest, while television, thought of throughout the decade as the major force generating change, brought the agonizing realities of the war into the home as never before.

As a result of the continuing impact of the war and the failure to reach any settlement, Johnson decided not to run for the presidency in 1968. This was a year of dramatic events on both sides of the Atlantic, and the Republican Richard Nixon, who had been defeated by Kennedy in 1960, was the new victor in the US elections. Yet Nixon also became embroiled in southeast Asia, despite having begun his presidency by withdrawing some American troops and calling for reduced American commitments in Asia as a whole. The upshot of his campaign was to spread the conflict to neighboring countries such as Cambodia and Laos. It was not until 1973 that the United States suspended hostilities in Vietnam by which time Nixon, re-elected to the presidency in 1972, was in the deepest of trouble on the home front in the aftermath of the Watergate scandal. In 1974 he was to become the first American president to resign, shamed in the eyes of the world.

European change

Western Europe felt the impact of the Vietnamese war only indirectly, though opposition to the war remained high on the

▶ Vietnamese civilians displaced by war.

agenda of radical and youth politics. There were other dramas. In May 1968 student riots began in Paris, followed by strikes and disturbances throughout France which led General de Gaulle, who had been president since 1959, to quit his own capital without warning, and the following year he also resigned after being defeated in a referendum on the reform of the Senate. He had been a dominating figure in the politics of the European Economic Community and had vetoed Britain's attempt to enter it in 1963.

There was a change of government in Britain in the following year, with the Labour party under Harold Wilson winning power for the first time since 1951. Wilson, too, had distant embroilments – notably in Africa where Ian Smith, prime minister of Rhodesia, declared independence "unilaterally" in November 1965 – and there were soon to be embroilments nearer home in Northern Ireland, to which British troops were sent following civil rights disturbances in 1969. These were influenced by movements in the United States, and asserted the rights of the Catholic, nationalist minority. In the ensuing conditions of civil war and repeated terrorist attacks on the state, in Northern Ireland and on the mainland, the death of the first British soldier in Ulster took place in 1971.

Political change remained difficult or impossible in eastern Europe, where there were student riots in Warsaw in 1968 and where Czechoslovakia, under a new liberal leader, Alexander Dubček, enjoyed a brief "Prague spring" in 1968. Warsaw was subdued from within: Czechoslovakia was to suffer a grim Moscow winter: Russian tanks occupied the country in August 1968. Dubček was ousted, and a long grey period of Communist rule followed.

The Soviet Union was then led by Leonid Brezhnev, who had become Secretary of the Communist party in 1964 after the fall of Nikita Khrushchev. He was to remain in power until 1982, presiding over a period of stagnation. This was in sharp contrast to the "Cultural Revolution" in China, a period of violent disturbance, inaugurated from the top by China's leader Mao Zedong in 1966. Maoist influence stretched far in the late 1960s, although the full facts of the terror in the Cultural Revolution were not known to many of the Western radicals who proclaimed themselves Maoist.

In 1972 Nixon, interested like his Secretary of State, Henry Kissinger, in the realities of global power politics, visited both Moscow and China. Despite all the crises, the Cold War had given way to a period of coexistence. There had been one moment of great danger for the world, however, in 1962. It centered geographically neither on Asia or the Soviet Union but on Cuba, where Fidel Castro, a charismatic leader who had taken over in 1959, had been drawn into the Communist camp. In September 1962 the Soviet Union, then led by Khrushchev, agreed to provide arms for Cuba, and in October 1962 Kennedy announced the discovery of Soviet rocket bases there, aimed at the United States. For a time the world seemed on the brink of nuclear war. The threat receded, and in the middle of January 1963 Kennedy announced to the relief of the watching world that the crisis was over. Kennedy's assassination in November 1963 removed him from the world scene, and in October 1964 Khrushchev was removed also, deposed while on holiday. Three months later the death of Churchill removed from the scene the last of its great wartime leaders.

One world
That for all its political and ideological divisions the planet was a single entity was illuminated when astronauts orbited the

Moon in 1968, discovering its dark side, and when a year later the first man, an American, actually walked on the Moon. "That's a small step for a man", he said, but "one great leap for mankind". American and Russian rivalry in space provided the impetus for this adventure; it was expensive, but less alarming to mankind than rivalry on the ground. By 1973, however, the environmental problems of the whole planet, global in scale and in their interrelationships, were beginning to receive more attention than outer space.

The organization Friends of the Earth was brought into being in 1971, and a year later a United Nations Conference in Stockholm agreed on a Declaration beginning with the words "Man is both creator and molder of his environment... In the long and tortuous evolution of the human race on this planet a stage has been reached when, through the rapid acceleration of science and technology, man has acquired the power to transform his environment in countless ways and on an unprecedented scale. Both aspects of man's environment, the natural and the manmade, are essential to his well-being and to the enjoyment of basic life itself." The impending threat and immediate effects of the continuing environmental damage wreaked in the course of the blinkered pursuit of technological sophistication and worldwide consumerism were to menace the planet for the rest of the century.

No part of the planet has figured more prominently in "the tortuous evolution of the human race" than "the Middle East" and this area, with rich cultural treasures, remained a center of political conflict during the 1960s and 1970s as well as one of the main sources of a commodity on which the world had come to depend – oil. It was a commodity which affected almost all aspects of the environment.

The short Arab-Israeli war of June 1967, launched by president Nasser of Egypt and supplied by a coalition that included Syria and Jordan, was won decisively by Israel after six days of fighting. Arab territories far greater in extent than the existing state of Israel were captured. Total casulties were estimated at at least 100,000. The result, however, could not be a lasting peace, and tension – and terrorism – persisted after the war and after the death of Nasser in September 1970. In September 1972 Arab guerrillas broke into the Olympic village at Munich, where the Olympic Games were being held; all nine Israeli hostages they captured were killed, along with two other Israeli team members, five Arabs and one policeman. A year later, in October 1973, Israel was placed on the defensive on its own territory when Egypt launched a shock attack across the Suez Canal on the day of Yom Kippur, the holiest day in the Jewish calendar. Supported by Syria, the Egyptians made small territorial gains, but the military power of Israel was once again demonstrated and a ceasefire agreement was signed on 11 November, by coincidence the same day as that of the signing of the armistice at the end of World War I.

The 1970s had begun with a change of government in Britain, and with Edward Heath as Conservative prime minister Britain at last entered the European Community (in face of strong Labour opposition) in October 1972. "We have shown this is a Europe for the people", Heath declared. Yet Heath's government faced great difficulties with large sections of the British people, particularly militant trade unionists, in 1972 and 1973 and at the end of 1973 a three-day working week was threatened because of the failure of power supplies. It was also arranged that television was to close down at 10.30 pm each evening. That itself was now deemed a privation, for television, not long before feared as the motor for social decline, was now regarded everywhere as the major purveyor both of entertainment and of news.

◄ Andy Warhol and friends enjoy 15 minutes of fame.

THE VIETNAM YEARS

Time Chart

	1961	1962	1963	1964	1965	1966	1967
Europe/Mediterranean	• 22–26 Apr: Rightwing military rebellion in Algeria defeated. Later attempt by OAS (Secret Army Organization) to assassinate De Gaulle also failed • Aug: Border closed between E and W Berlin • 31 Oct: Stalin discredited (USSR)	• Mar: Conclusion of Evian agreements ended Algerian guerrilla conflict • 11 Oct: 21st Ecumenical Council (Vatican II) opened by Pope John XXIII – largest ever gathering of RC hierarchy with Protestant observers	• 14 Jan: De Gaulle (Fr) blocked UK entry to EEC • 22 Jan: French and W German treaty pledging cooperation in foreign policy, defense and cultural affairs • 30 Aug: Hotline telephone link opened between US and USSR presidents	• 15 Oct: Khrushchev replaced by Leonid I. Brezhnev as party leader and Aleksei N Kosygin as premier (USSR) • 15 Oct: In UK, Labour government elected under Harold Wilson after 13 years of Conservative rule	• 12 May: 10 Arab nations cut ties with W Germany after it established diplomatic relations with Israel	• 29 Mar: 23rd Soviet Union Communist Party congress marked by absence of Chinese • July: France withdrew military support from NATO: HQ moved to Brussels. 7 Sep, French announced their share of NATO military expenses to be halted from Dec 31	• 21 Apr: "Greek colonels'" regime imposed. 13 Dec, King Constantine exiled after failure to restore democracy. Col. George Papadopoulos became premier; "regent" appointed • 16 May: UK membership of EEC blocked by De Gaulle (Fr)
The Middle East	• 29 Sep: Declaration of Syrian independence after revolt of army officers against Egyptian domination of UAR under Nasser • 18–19 Dec: Portuguese colonies of Goa, Damoa and Diu invaded by Indian troops	• 3 Jul: Algerian independence won through referendum. Socialist Mohammed Ahmed Ben Bella elected first premier after 20 Sep elections following power struggle • 20 Oct: Mass Chinese invasion of India – partial withdrawal on 7 Nov	• 8 Feb: Premier Kassem killed in pro-Nasser military coup (Irq)	• April: UN peacekeeping force sent to Cyprus. 10 Aug, Turkey and Cyprus accepted UN cease-fire, ending threat of Mediterranean war • 27 May: Death of Nehru, prime minister for 17 years. Succeeded by Lal Bahadur Shastri	• 19 June: Algerian President Ben Bella deposed by army-supported socialist nationalists under Col. Houari Boumédienne	• 19 Jan: Indira Gandhi, daughter of Nehru, elected prime minister of India • Nov–Dec: Continuing Middle East conflict – border clashes between Israel and Jordan, backed by Arab League. Israel censured by UN Security Council	• 5–10 Jun, Six-Day War: Israeli air force destroyed almost entire Arab air forces on the ground. By the time of the UN cease-fire on 10 June, 4 times its own size had been captured by Israel in sweep toward Suez canal • mid-Nov: Pact signed by Greece, Turkey, Cyprus averted threatened Greco–Turkish war
Africa	• 31 May: S Africa declared an independent republic • 13 Sep: "Congo Problem": UN forces attacked the seat of the Katangan secessionist regime	• 17 Jun: African common market established (Mor, Gha, Gui, Mali and UAR) • 9 Oct: Uganda gained independence within British Commonwealth under Dr Milton Obote • 9 Dec: Tanganyika became republic within British commonwealth under Julius K. Nyerere	• 15 Jan: After UN campaign President Moise Tshombe agreed end of 30-month secession of Katanga from Congo • May: Organization for African Unity formed by 30 states, Addis Ababa, to maintain solidarity and abolish colonialism	• 26 Apr: Zanzibar merged with Tanganyika to form Tanzania • 12 Jun: Life sentence for Nelson Mandela for "sabotage" (S Afr) • 26 Jun: Moise Tshombe, ex-president of Katangan secessionist state called out of exile to help form new Congolese government	• 11 Nov: Rhodesia's illegal Unilateral Declaration of Independence (UDI) from Britain: sanctions imposed by Britain and UN	• 6 Sep: Prime Minister H.F. Verwoerd, originator of apartheid, assassinated (S Afr) • Oct: End of S African mandate in Namibia (SW Afr) voted by UN General Assembly	• 13 Mar: Ex-Premier Moise Tshombe sentenced to death in absentia for treason by military court (Congo) • 30 May: Majority Christian Ibo Eastern region of Nigeria seceded as Biafra: civil war lasted in this region 2½ years
The Americas	• 3 Jan: US severed diplomatic and consular links following Cuban request to cut personnel in Havana • 20 Jan: John F Kennedy inaugurated as 35th and youngest President • 17 Apr: Failed invasion by CIA-backed anti-Castro Cuban exile force at Bay of Pigs. US internationally criticized for intervention	• 30 Sep: US race riots as 1st black student enrolled at southern university under military escort • 28 Oct: "Cuban missile crisis" ended as US agreed to end naval blockade in return for dismantling of USSR missile bases	• Continuing racial unrest focused in Alabama (US) • 22 Nov: Kennedy assassinated, Dallas, Texas. Lyndon B Johnson sworn in as next President	• 9–10 Jan: Panama crisis with clashes over disputed rights in Panama Canal. Relations briefly severed by Panama when US refused to renegotiate treaties • 2 Jul: Civil Rights Act signed by Johnson (US) • 7 Aug: Gulf of Tonkin Resolution passed by US Congress, enabled Pres. Johnson to commit large forces to Vietnam	• 21 Feb: Malcolm X, founder of proviolence Black Nationalist group, assassinated (US) • 28–29 Apr: US military aid sent to stall Communist takeover in Dominican Republic • 15–16 Oct: Mass antiwar demonstrations held (US) • 1 Dec: start of US airlift of Cuban refugee exodus	• International protest over US involvement in Vietnam war	• 12 Jul: Huge race riots, Newark, NJ. US Federal troops first used to quell riots, Detroit, 23–30 Jul • 23 Jul: Puerto Ricans voted to remain in US commonwealth rather than become federated or independent • 8 Oct: Death of Cuban guerrilla Che Guevara, shot after capture (Bol)
Asia and Pacific	• 16 May: S Korea – anticommunist military junta deposed government and arrested president • 11 Dec: After Kennedy's undertaking to massively increase number of US advisors, arrival in Saigon of 2 US Army helicopter companies with 400 troops (S Vnm)	• 8 Feb: US Defense Dept. created Military Assistance Command (MAC) in S Vietnam • May: Hong Kong erected barrier to deter illegal immigration from China • 12 May: US and other forces sent to Thailand to counter Communist threat in Laos	• 16 Sep: Malaysia created from federation of Malaya, Singapore, Sarawak and North Borneo • 1–2 Nov: President Diem killed in US-supported military coup (S Vnm)	• 30 Jan: S Vietnamese government ousted – 3 more changes within a year • 16 Oct: China, after 1st successful nuclear test, called for world summit to ban nuclear weapons and destroy stockpiles	• 2 Mar: US declared its combatant status (S Vnm) • 9 Aug: Singapore left Federation of Malaysia • 2 Sep: Start of Chinese cultural revolution • 5 Dec: China entered Vietnam conflict • 30 Dec: Ferdinand Marcos became President (Phi)	• End of Robert Menzies' 17 years in government (Aus) • 1 May: 1st intentional shelling by US in Cambodia • 29 Jun: N Vietnamese capital, Hanoi, first bombed by US	• Jan: People's Liberation Army mobilized to support worker-peasants against Red Guard (Chn) • Mar: Thailand allowed US bomber bases for closer access to Communist targets (N Vnm) • 11–14 Sep: Border clashes between Chinese and Indian troops
World	• 7 April: UN voted unanimously to censure S Africa's apartheid policy • 18 Sep: UN Secretary-general Hammarskjöld's death in plane crash precipitated UN crisis; succeeded by U. Thant of Burma	• International nuclear weapons disarmament talks fail with main lack of agreement from USSR and France • 14 Dec: Signing by 5 states of San Salvador Charter to establish Organization of Central American States	• 19 Mar: Declaration of San José called for Central American Common Market • 5 Aug: Signing of nuclear test-ban treaty by UK, US and USSR: a permanent ban on nuclear testing in the atmosphere, outer space or under-water	• 21 Jan: 6th session of disarmament conference with participation of 17 nations, Geneva (till 17 Sep)	• 2 Mar: W Germany, France, Italy and Benelux nations agreed merger of EEC, Euratom and ECSC (effective 1 Jan 1966)	• 24–25 Oct: Manila Conference – Australia, New Zealand, Philippines, Thailand, South Korea, South Vietnam – pledged political self-determination and aid to S Vietnam also withdrawal of troops 6 months after N Vietnam's end of aggression	• 27 Jan: Treaty limiting use of outer space for military purposes signed by 62 nations • 12–14 Apr: 19 countries met to form economic program for the Americas • May: Bertrand Russell's "International Tribunal on War Crimes" condemned US for Vietnam. Australia, New Zealand and S Korea named accomplices

1968	1969	1970	1971	1972	1973
● 8–9 Mar: Clashes between students and police spread to other workers (Tch). 20–21 Aug: invasion by Soviet forces to restore strict communism ● 2 May: Student protest spread to civilian population and threatened stability of regime (Fr). De Gaulle announced reform program	● 28 Apr: De Gaulle replaced as president by Georges Pompidou following referendum defeat (Fr) ● 23 Jul: Prince Juan Carlos was selected to succeed Generalissimo Franco as ruler of Spain on his retirement ● 15 Aug: UK army given control of Ulster security ● 21 Oct: Willy Brandt became Chancellor of W Germany	● 18 Jun: Conservative Edward Heath became UK prime minister ● 12 Aug: Soviet and W German leaders signed nonaggression treaty ● 7 Dec: W Germany and Poland signed pact renouncing force to settle disputes and agreeing border	● 3 Sep: 1st postwar Berlin accord signed by UK, France, US, USSR, E and W Germany: freedom of Western traffic to cross Eastern territory to West Berlin; Wall to remain; border to remain closed ● 24 Sep: UK expelled 105 Russian officials on evidence from USSR defector	● 30 Jan, "Bloody Sunday", Belfast: 13 civilians were shot in army/Catholic clashes spurring further antiBritish attacks throughout Ireland and in London. 30 Mar, end of 51 years' semi-autonomous rule in Ulster. Direct government from UK imposed ● 12 May: 1st treaty between E and W Germany	8 Mar: Referendum in N Ireland voted to remain part of UK. 21 Nov, compromise plan for coalition government of Protestants and Catholics ● 19 May: USSR and W Germany signed 10-year pact for economic, industrial and technical cooperation
● 28 Dec: Israelis took reprisals against Lebanese-based attacks: start of conflict throughout 1969	● 27 Jan: Mid-east crisis as Iraq executed 25 "spies" despite international criticism ● 17 Mar: Golda Meir became premier of Israel ● 1 Sep: Capt. Muammar el-Qadhafi proclaimed Socialist Libyan Arab Republic after military coup	● 28 Sep: Death of President Nasser (Egy); succeeded by Anwar Sadat	● 12 Mar: Bloodless military coup to resolve civil disorder (Tur) ● 1 Sep: New constitution for federal union of Egypt, Syria and Libya, supported in referendum, came into effect ● 6 Dec: India recognized rebel government of Bangladesh	● 6 Apr: Egypt cut ties with Jordan over plans for Israeli territory on West Bank ● 9 Apr: 15-year friendship pact signed (USSR, Irq) ● 22 May: Ceylon became independent Sri Lanka ● 3 Jul: Simla Pact: India and Pakistan renounced force in their dealings and resolved border conflict	● 1 Jun: Greece proclaimed a republic ● 6 Oct: Start of Yom Kippur war: largest Arab–Israeli conflict in 25 years ● 7 Nov: Resumption of diplomatic relations broken in 1967 between US and Egypt
● Aug: Nigeria rejected Red Cross plan to aid starving Biafrans ● Nov: Britain withdrew troops from Aden	● 30 Oct: Nigerian nationalist party banned by Jomo Kenyatta	● 12 Jan: End of Biafran secession from Nigeria on flight of leader	● 25 Jan: Idi Amin ousted Milton Obote in military coup (Uga)	● 27 Mar: End of 17-year state of emergency when treaty was signed ending civil war between Arab Moslem north and Black Christian and pagan south (Sud) ● 9 Aug: Asians expelled from Uganda by Idi Amin: many with British passports were accepted by UK ● 27 Apr: Death of Kwame Nkrumah, leading statesman of Ghana from 1957 to 1967	● Serious famine in Ethiopia with failure of annual rains, causing unprecedented distress
● 5–7 Feb: Revision of Canadian constitution: gave French and English official language status ● 4 Apr: Assassination of Martin Luther King at Memphis, Tennessee (US) ● 20 Apr: Pierre Trudeau voted prime minister (Can) ● 5 Jun: Assassination of Senator Robert F. Kennedy (US) ● 5 Nov: Richard M. Nixon elected US president	● 24 Jun: Undeclared war started between El Salvador and Honduras ● 15 Oct and 15 Nov: Mass national antiwar demonstrations (US)	● 6 Mar: Rise in terrorist bombings after explosion of Weather Underground bomb factory (US) ● 4 Jun: Demilitarized zone policed by OAS advisory force along agreed border between El Salvador and Honduras	● 21 Apr: Death of François (Papa Doc) Duvalier; replaced by son Claude (Hai) ● 8 Jun: President Allende imposed state of emergency following civilian unrest (Chi) ● 13 Jun: Top-secret Pentagon Papers, study of US involvement in Vietnam 1945–67, published in The New York Times	● 29 Sep: Accord signed ending technical state of war between China and Japan since 1937. Japan severed relations with Taiwan	● 11 Sep: Death of Allende and 2,700 others in bloody coup under military junta led by General Pinochet (Chi) ● 23 Sep: Perón elected president; wife, Isabel, vice-president (Arg) ● 10 Oct: US Vice- President Spiro Agnew sentenced on tax evasion charges
● Jan: Communist Tet Offensive gained much ground but was forced to retreat: the initial success further lessened US support for war (Vnm) ● 16 Mar: Massacre by US troops of hamlet of My Lai (S Vnm)	● Mar: Military clashes between Chinese and Soviet troops ● Jul: Start of "Vietnamization" with gradual withdrawal of American troops from Vietnam, handing combat role to S Vietnamese	● 9 Oct: Cambodia became Khmer Republic under Lon Nol. Supported by US troops, 30 Apr – 29 Jun	● 17 Jun: Return of Okinawa to Japan after treaty with US ● 18 Aug: Anzac troops to be withdrawn from Vietnam by Dec	● 25 Jan: US moved 8-point peace plan: US troops to be withdrawn in return for cease-fire and POW release. S Vietnam then to hold new elections: US to remain neutral. 30 Mar: US air force retaliated against strong N Vietnamese attack ● 2 Dec: 1st Labor Party election win in 23 years (Aus)	● 27 Jan: USA, N and S Vietnam and the Viet Cong signed agreement to end Vietnam war. 2-party version was signed by N Vietnam and US (28 Jan) as S Vietnam refused to recognize Provisional Revolutionary Government of Viet Cong. Last US troops left 29 Mar; 8,500 civilian technicians remained ● 27 Feb: Cease-fire between government and Pathet Lao announced ended 20 years' war (Laos)
● 20 Nov: Meeting of 10 leaders of noncommunist European nations regarding currency crisis	● 17 Nov: Start of US and USSR SALT talks, Helsinki. 24 Nov: Nuclear Nonproliferation Treaty signed pledging nonpromotion of nuclear technology to non-nuclear nations	● 13 Oct: Canada opened diplomatic links with China; broke those with Taiwan	● 11 Feb: Treaty signed by 63 nations banning nuclear weapon installations on seabed in international waters ● 21 Dec: Kurt Waldheim (Aut) appointed UN Secretary-general (to 1981)	● 5 Sep: Israeli Olympic team killed by Arab Black September terrorists, Munich ● 3 Oct: USSR and USA signed last papers implementing SALT accords limiting submarine-carried and land-based missiles	● 1 Jan: UK, Ireland and Denmark entered EEC ● 16–25 Jun: Antinuclear war accords (USSR, US) ● 19–21 Oct: Energy crisis and severe recession in US and Europe after Arab oil cuts and (from 2 Mar) European monetary crisis ● 25 Oct: US forces placed on alert for fear of USSR joining Middle East conflict

Datafile

In the early 1960s, the tension between the two superpowers mounted alarmingly in Europe and around Cuba. In Europe, problems centered on the divided nation of Germany. In Cuba, they were the product of Castro's successful Communist takeover and of subsequent US/USSR interference in domestic affairs. Expenditure on arms continued to increase, and the Western alliance prevailed simply because of its superior economic might.

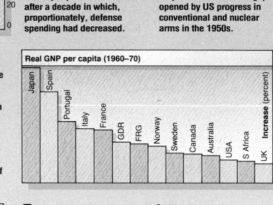

Defense spending in NATO

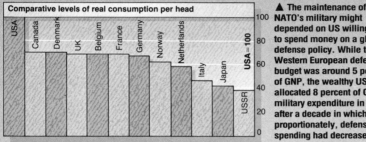

Comparative levels of real consumption per head

▲ Mid-1960s figures for comparative levels of real consumption highlight American, prosperity. Consumption even in advanced industrial nations like Canada, the UK and West Germany reached only 70 percent of US levels. With the USSR and Japan, the contrast was even sharper, neither nation reaching 50% of the US level.

▶ In the 1960s, the less developed industrial nations began to close the gap on the mature economics of the US and UK, where GNP per capita increased by less than 50 percent. The frontrunner was Japan, where rapid development of an export-driven manufacturing economy resulted in an increase in GNP per capita of almost 150 percent.

▲ The maintenance of NATO's military might depended on US willingness to spend money on a global defense policy. While the Western European defense budget was around 5 percent of GNP, the wealthy US still allocated 8 percent of GNP to military expenditure in 1970 after a decade in which, proportionately, defense spending had decreased.

▶ The defense expendure of the major Powers doubled in the 1960s as military technology became more complicated and costly. The USA and USSR continued to account for about 80 percent of the total, with Soviet expenditure rising steeply as they strove to close the gap opened by US progress in conventional and nuclear arms in the 1950s.

Real GNP per capita (1960–70)

Defense expenditure

US representation

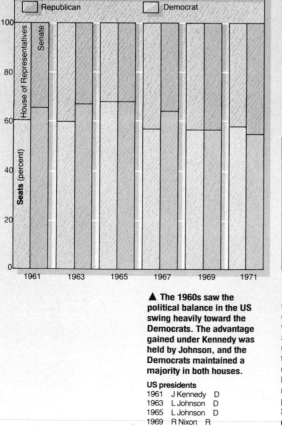

▲ The 1960s saw the political balance in the US swing heavily toward the Democrats. The advantage gained under Kennedy was held by Johnson, and the Democrats maintained a majority in both houses.

US presidents
1961	J Kennedy	D
1963	L Johnson	D
1965	L Johnson	D
1969	R Nixon	R

▼ In the early years of Castro's rule, Cuba lost large numbers of its best educated citizens in politically-motivated emigration to the USA. This phenomenon, damaging to both society and economy was, however, short-lived. But in 1962 and 1963, emigration fell by more than 75 percent and remained at a relatively low level.

▶ The US, while prosperous, remained an economically divided nation. Although family incomes rose steadily across the board, blacks continued to lag far behind whites and in many cases remained well below the poverty line – a major cause of the racial conflict which was to sweep the nation in the mid-1960s.

US income

Emigration from Cuba

Cuban imports

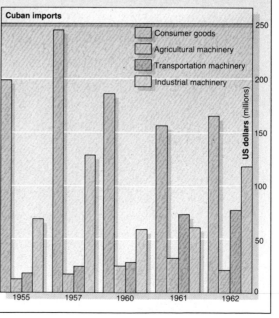

▶ The change in ideology in Cuba produced a dramatic change in trading partners, with the new regime looking abroad to Eastern bloc markets and suppliers, and trying to generate real domestic economic growth by centralizing and restructuring the production processes along established Soviet lines, concentrating on heavy industry.

POWERS IN CONFLICT

The United States and the Soviet Union, wartime allies, had become postwar rivals for the place in the global power structure once enjoyed by imperial Britain. In what became known as the Cold War, this rivalry threatened a conflict more terrible than any in human history, as both the superpowers built up arsenals of nuclear weapons capable of destroying the world several times over. Most attempts from either side to break the deadlock were received with distrust and suspicion.

Kennedy and Khrushchev

Soviet leader Nikita Khrushchev, believing that the Soviets' nuclear strike capability freed them from the danger of a US attack, advocated a new policy also aimed to win the support of the growing number of nonaligned countries and to woo the American public.

The election of John F. Kennedy to the US presidency in 1960 enhanced Khrushchev's hopes of achieving a superpower rapprochement. Kennedy presented an image of idealism and commitment to the betterment of all mankind, which augured well for international cooperation. In

1961, talks between the superpowers led to the McCloy–Zorin recommendations, laying down the ultimate goal of complete nuclear disarmament and the principles that would govern subsequent disarmament talks. Unfortunately, both sides lacked the political will to turn the recommendations into a binding agreement.

That same year, East–West tension rose again over the troubled city of Berlin. The East Germans were "voting with their feet" by crossing the still open frontier from Soviet-controlled East Berlin to West Berlin at the rate of several thousand a week. By July 1961 the figure had reached 1,000 a day, and on 12 August 4,000 crossed to West Berlin. On the next night, in the middle of the holiday season, the East German authorities erected a barrier, which became the Berlin Wall, permanently cutting off the east of the city from the west. The Western allies protested that the wall breached the agreement of 1945, under which all Berlin was to be governed as a single unit by the four Allied powers, but took no action for fear of escalating the crisis.

The Soviets and East Germans claimed that West Berlin was the center of a Western network

▼ **The ideological barrier assumes concrete form – Berliners watch the construction of the wall dividing their city. Berlin, divided between Allied and Soviet zones of occupation but located in the heart of East Germany, was the focal point of European confrontation. The construction of the wall was an attempt to block the easiest route to the West.**

◀ **Communism reaches the Americas** – Fidel Castro's successful Marxist revolution in Cuba threatened nervous US policy-makers. Castro's populist style made him appear all the more dangerous, persuading Kennedy to embark on the disastrous Bay of Pigs invasion in an attempt to overthrow him.

▼ ▼ **The Cuban missile crisis** brought the superpowers closer to war than any other event in the modern era. It was the result of the competitive buildup of arms over the previous decade, the failure of the superpowers to find effective diplomatic channels and, in the short term, of the fiasco at the Bay of Pigs and the emergence in both the US and the USSR of leaders intent on ending the Cold War. Kennedy and Khrushchev (see below) were the central players in the dangerous game of brinkmanship over Cuba. The crisis marked a turning-point in East–West relations, with both sides adopting more flexible attitudes to key issues and moving toward negotiation on nuclear arms reduction.

Revolution in Cuba

In 1959 the focus of East-West relations switched to the Caribbean island of Cuba. At the beginning of the year Fidel Castro had replaced the discredited dictator Fulgencio Batista as leader. At first, Castro did not claim to be a Marxist, or a Communist, perhaps because he feared that his country would share the fate of Guatemala, where a leftwing government had been overthrown by the United States in 1954 in the name of the Monroe Doctrine. In April 1959 Castro had visited the United States to give assurances that foreign investments in Cuba (mainly American) were in no danger. Shortly afterward, however, Cuba started to increase its trade with the Soviet Union, and in the course of 1960 nationalized all US property on the island. During the US presidential election campaigns of that year, both Kennedy and his Republican opponent Richard Nixon had promised to act against Cuba. In April 1961, President Kennedy, on the advice of the CIA (US Central Intelligence Agency) backed an invasion of Cuba by anti-Castro emigrés, at the Bay of Pigs. It failed miserably as the small emigré force was easily overpowered by Castro's troops. Kennedy admitted to a serious error of judgment, which admission was not lost on Khrushchev, and resolved to be less dependent on the CIA.

▶ **Che Guevara, guerrilla and student icon.**

of spies and saboteurs operating against East Germany: and the wall was designed to keep them out. While this was partly true, the main purpose of the wall was rather to keep the East German population in. The East German regime was losing too many of its citizens to the West – including highly skilled people – and needed to seal its frontiers to preserve its stability.

The Cuban missile crisis

During 1962 the Soviet leadership, perhaps encouraged by Kennedy's humiliation at the Bay of Pigs and by the West's refusal to respond to the Berlin Wall with force, began to build sites for nuclear missiles in Cuba. This action posed a direct challenge to the strategic supremacy of the United States in the Western Hemisphere. By mid-October the Kennedy administration, having rejected the options of a "surgical strike" against the Soviet bases, decided on a naval blockade to prevent further Soviet missiles reaching Cuba.

For a few days, an anxious world waited to see whether the Soviet missile-carrying ships would encounter the waiting ring of US warships. Kennedy insisted that no Soviet missiles would be tolerated in Cuba. Khrushchev demanded that, in return for withdrawing them, the United States remove its missiles from sites near the Soviet Union, particularly those in Turkey. On Sunday 28 October, after several critical incidents (including the boarding of a Soviet merchant ship by the US Navy, and the shooting down of an American U2 spy plane over Cuba), the superpowers reached a mutually face-saving compromise. Kennedy undertook not to invade Cuba, and Khrushchev withdrew his missiles from the island.

The Cuban crisis was a chastening experience for the Soviet Union, forcing it to back down before the eyes of European satellites and exposing its deteriorating relations with Communist China, who denounced Khrushchev's foolhardiness. Despite the illusion of Russian technological superiority over the Americans created by the successful firing of Russian intercontinental ballistic missiles (ICBMs) in August 1957 and launching of the *Sputnik* satellite three months later, the military balance between the superpowers clearly remained on the side of the United States. Following the Cuban missile crisis, the Soviet Union both resumed its diplomatic quest for peaceful coexistence, to avert the danger of

▼ ▼ Racial discrimination in the US had backed systematic government attention since the emancipation of slaves. The racist attitudes of many whites caused politicians to shy away from action and produced ugly incidents of harassment (such as that pictured below) when the first steps were taken toward desegregation. Civil rights campaigners like Dr Martin Luther King fought the existing situation to the attention of the nation in a series of rallies. Kennedy's Civil Rights Act of 1963 dismantled the formal framework of racial discrimination but tension remained high and often broke out into violence and riot.

nuclear war, and embarked on a long-term military armaments program designed to give parity with US nuclear and naval power by the early 1970s. Politicians in the Kremlin had concluded that arms control must be achieved by energetic participation in the arms race, and that meaningful superpower negotiations were possible only between equals.

By October 1964, when Leonid Brezhnev came to power, having ousted Khrushchev, the Russians were well advanced towards their goal of military parity. They had increased their strategic rocket forces and the number of submarine-launched and intercontinental ballistic missiles, and expanded the Soviet navy, previously confined to coastal defense duties, to project its power into the Mediterranean and the Pacific and Indian Oceans.

US Civil Rights movement

While abroad the United States' interests were threatened by the Soviet Union, at home civil unrest was beginning to take its toll. A century after President Lincoln's proclamation of 1862 freeing them from slavery, black Americans were still a long way from achieving their constitutional rights and equality of status with whites. Many lived in poverty and squalor, were poorly housed, fed and educated, and had a life expectancy barely two-thirds that of white Americans. By the early 1960s, black leaders had become impatient for change, and some, like Martin Luther King, organized nonviolent mass demonstrations and used civil disobedience tactics to instill a greater awareness in the whites. Sympathetic white Americans, especially the young, lent their support to the movement, which began to have an effect. Slowly, lunch counters, rest rooms and hotels were desegregated, and racial discrimination in employment was reduced.

President Kennedy's Civil Rights Bill, which became law the year after his death, represented a major breakthrough in establishing the principle of racial equality, though it did not go as far as many blacks would have liked. The Act empowered the attorney-general to prosecute those

employers who discriminated against blacks, and made segregation in hotels, restaurants and other public places illegal. It also forbade discrimination in any project or program receiving federal funds, and permitted the attorney-general to file desegregation suits on behalf of individuals or organizations who found it too risky or expensive to do so themselves.

Despite the Act, in the South many blacks were still prevented from registering as voters through delaying tactics and intimidation, so that President Lyndon Johnson was forced, in March 1965, to secure additional legislation authorizing federal officers to enter names on the voters' lists. Desegregation, too, was ignored as late as 1966, with many examples of blacks being deprived of state medical care because hospitals refused to comply with the law.

Yet even the modest laws passed provoked the Ku Klux Klan into launching a campaign of terror and murder against the black population. Young blacks retaliated by looting and burning property owned by whites. By the late 1960s, race riots had become commonplace in many American cities, especially those with large black populations such as Chicago, Miami and Los Angeles. As blacks and whites increasingly saw their interests as incompatible, and American society became engulfed in race war, the hopes of the moderate civil rights movement that the black population could be accommodated in mainstream American life looked less and less realistic.

Johnson's "Great Society"

Earlier, in 1964, in an effort to bridge the growing gap between "haves" and "have-nots", and avert its potentially explosive social consequences, Lyndon Johnson had produced the concept of a "Great Society" dedicated to the eradication of poverty, unemployment and racial conflict, and to the establishment of equal opportunity for all.

Aided by the mid-1960s economic boom, Johnson introduced new health provisions and sickness insurance for the elderly and increased social security payments. He set aside substantial sums for improving education, especially in the deprived inner-city areas, devoting extra funds to the recruitment and training of teachers, and established new scholarship schemes. He funded the building of new libraries and community centers and made available federal grants for the promotion of the arts. To combat inner-city decay, a federal agency for housing and urban development was set up, with an allocation of $7 billion for slum eradication and rehousing schemes.

Already by 1966, however, much of the impetus of the "Great Society" reform initiative had been lost. The United States had become deeply involved in the Vietnam War. Congress decided that US prestige in Southeast Asia was more important than the eradication of poverty at home, and so Johnson's reform program was scaled back, putting paid to his hopes of ending American poverty. Nevertheless, Johnson's initiative made subsequent administrations recognize the need to address the issues of poverty, inequality and injustice as a prerequisite to making progress on human rights issues.

The Assassination of Kennedy

The assassination of President Kennedy on 22 November 1963 was an event whose emotional reverberations were felt around the world. A widely popular leader, with the successful solution of the Cuban missile crisis and the passage of the Civil Rights Act behind him, Kennedy had become the symbol of America's emergence as a dynamic and liberal world power, and his violent death, in full view of a huge television audience, threw the entire nation into a state of post-traumatic shock. Driving in a highly publicized motorcade through the streets of Dallas, Texas, Kennedy was felled by bullets from an unseen sniper's rifle.

The authorities quickly discovered and arrested the supposed assassin, Lee Harvey Oswald, but Oswald was himself murdered, again in front of television cameras, by a local nightclub-owner before he could be fully questioned or put on trial. In the aftermath of the affair a host of unanswered questions, contradictory evidence and sinister rumors began to cast doubt on the officially accepted view that the president had been shot by a single assassin acting on personal motives. The possibilities – that more than one gunman had been involved, that Oswald was simply a pawn in a wider conspiracy who had been deliberately silenced before he could implicate others, and that the real agents of Kennedy's death had been either foreign Communists, the Mafia or members of his own government and the CIA, alarmed by the directions his foreign and domestic policies were taking – were all widely canvassed. Among the more lurid rumors, it was claimed that Kennedy's body was surreptitiously tampered with en route from Dallas to Washington, to disguise the evidence of the gunshot wounds.

President Johnson eventually commissioned a fullscale inquiry (the Warren Commission) in 1964. This inquiry collected a mass of evidence before concluding that the official "single assassin" hypothesis was correct. The Warren verdict went along way towards allaying public concern and brought the incident to an end as a political issue. A number of informed observers, however, have never been convinced by the report and have uncovered sufficient evidence of a possible cover-up and dubious official practice to cast a shadow over the accepted verdict. While it is most unlikely that any counter-hypothesis will ever be conclusively proven, questions remain about what actually happened, and the full story of how one of America's best-loved leaders was murdered will probably never be uncovered.

▲ President Kennedy tours the streets of Dallas on 22 November 1963 with his wife Jackie and the Governor of Texas, seconds before his assassination.

▼ One man's revenge or sinister cover-up when nightclub-owner Jack Ruby fatally shot Lee Harvey Oswald, President Kennedy's suspected assassin, as Oswald was being transferred from the Dallas city jail to a more secure prison. Ruby was arrested and shortly afterwards died in prison.

Datafile

Confrontation between the USA and USSR exercised a profound effect on Third World countries. Both superpowers had expansionist aspirations and were able to coerce the economically weak and politically unstable nations of the Third World by making strategic offers of aid and military assistance, often resulting in the creation of regimes which were little more than clients of superpowers. The presence of large, politically motivated armed forces wreaked havoc on fragile societies and undermined attempts to establish effective civilian rule. This form of war by proxy reached its most advanced form in Southeast Asia where the US actually committed its own troops in resisting a Soviet-backed North Vietnamese attempt to bring the entire area under Communist control. Meanwhile, other nations were emerging as major economic forces; the most obvious case being Japan, which within 25 years of near annihilation had become one of the major industrial powers of the world, with a booming economy which rivaled that of the USA.

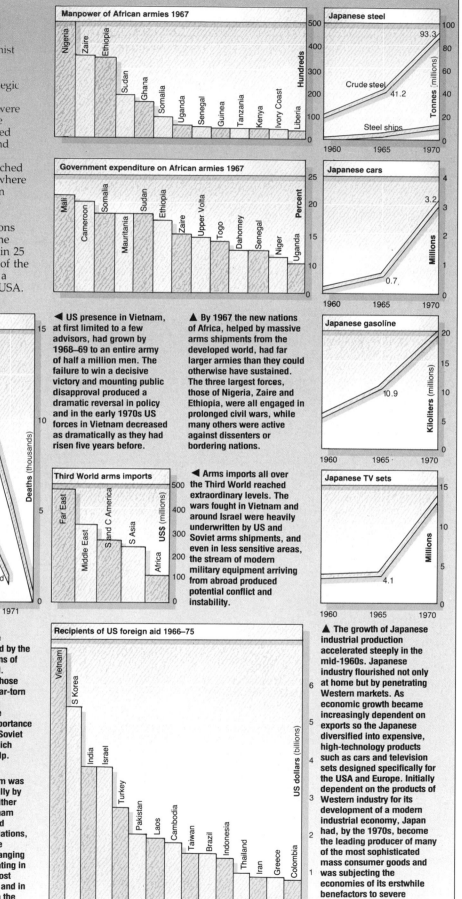

Manpower of African armies 1967

Nigeria, Zaire, Ethiopia, Sudan, Ghana, Somalia, Uganda, Senegal, Guinea, Tanzania, Kenya, Ivory Coast, Liberia — Hundreds

Government expenditure on African armies 1967

Mali, Cameroon, Somalia, Mauritania, Sudan, Ethiopia, Zaire, Upper Volta, Togo, Dahomey, Senegal, Niger, Uganda — Percent

Japanese steel

Crude steel 93.3, 41.2; Steel ships — Tonnes (millions)

Japanese cars 3.2, 0.7 — Millions

Japanese gasoline 10.9 — Kiloliters (millions)

Japanese TV sets 4.1 — Millions

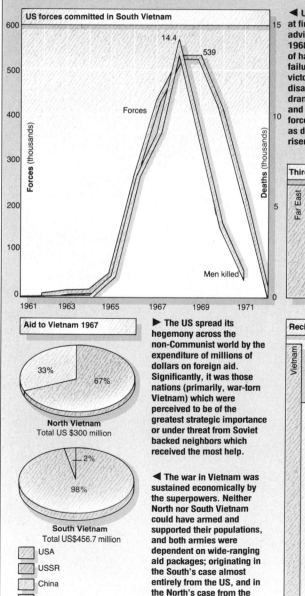

US forces committed in South Vietnam

14.4, 539, Forces, Men killed — Forces (thousands) / Deaths (thousands)

◀ US presence in Vietnam, at first limited to a few advisors, had grown by 1968–69 to an entire army of half a million men. The failure to win a decisive victory and mounting public disapproval produced a dramatic reversal in policy and in the early 1970s US forces in Vietnam decreased as dramatically as they had risen five years before.

▲ By 1967 the new nations of Africa, helped by massive arms shipments from the developed world, had far larger armies than they could otherwise have sustained. The three largest forces, those of Nigeria, Zaire and Ethiopia, were all engaged in prolonged civil wars, while many others were active against dissenters or bordering nations.

Third World arms imports

Far East, Middle East, S and C America, S Asia, Africa — US$ (millions)

◀ Arms imports all over the Third World reached extraordinary levels. The wars fought in Vietnam and around Israel were heavily underwritten by US and Soviet arms shipments, and even in less sensitive areas, the stream of modern military equipment arriving from abroad produced potential conflict and instability.

Aid to Vietnam 1967

33% / 67%
North Vietnam Total US $300 million

2% / 98%
South Vietnam Total US$456.7 million

- USA
- USSR
- China
- Others

▶ The US spread its hegemony across the non-Communist world by the expenditure of millions of dollars on foreign aid. Significantly, it was those nations (primarily, war-torn Vietnam) which were perceived to be of the greatest strategic importance or under threat from Soviet backed neighbors which received the most help.

◀ The war in Vietnam was sustained economically by the superpowers. Neither North nor South Vietnam could have armed and supported their populations, and both armies were dependent on wide-ranging aid packages; originating in the South's case almost entirely from the US, and in the North's case from the USSR and China.

Recipients of US foreign aid 1966–75

Vietnam, S Korea, India, Israel, Turkey, Pakistan, Laos, Cambodia, Taiwan, Brazil, Indonesia, Thailand, Iran, Greece, Colombia — US dollars (billions)

▲ The growth of Japanese industrial production accelerated steeply in the mid-1960s. Japanese industry flourished not only at home but by penetrating Western markets. As economic growth became increasingly dependent on exports so the Japanese diversified into expensive, high-technology products such as cars and television sets designed specifically for the USA and Europe. Initially dependent on the products of Western industry for its development of a modern industrial economy, Japan had, by the 1970s, become the leading producer of many of the most sophisticated mass consumer goods and was subjecting the economies of its erstwhile benefactors to severe competitive pressures.

CHALLENGE TO THE SUPERPOWERS

Sino-Soviet relations plummet

Mao Zedong's Cultural Revolution fails

Sino-Indian conflict

Indo-Pakistan war

The emergence of Bangladesh

War in Vietnam

Struggle in the Congo

Nigerian civil war

Arab-Israeli conflict

Differences between China and the Soviet Union dated back at least to 1935 when Mao Zedong broke with his Soviet advisors during the "Long March" and developed a version of Communist strategy and ideology more suited to China's needs. As long as Stalin remained alive, however, Mao paid lip service to the Soviet claim to leadership of the Communist bloc. But Mao despised Stalin's successor, Khrushchev, and disagreed with him profoundly over a whole range of issues, finding him too lenient.

Sino-Soviet differences became more critical in the early 1960s when Mao perceived that Soviet policies were actually detrimental to China's interests and even slighted its national honor. Moscow's refusal to share its nuclear secrets with China, its new policy of peaceful coexistence with the West, and its reluctance to give more than

verbal support to China's bid to regain the off-shore islands of Taiwan, Quemoy and Matsui convinced Beijing of the fickleness of China's former ally.

The rift between the two great Communist powers deepened after the Cuban missile crisis of 1962, when the Chinese publicly accused the Soviets of foolhardiness. During its border conflict with India in 1962, China was further angered by the Soviet Union's maintaining a strict neutrality and even condoning India's appeal for intervention by the United States. Furthermore, domestically Mao was now fighting for his political life and enmity with Moscow gave him a pretext for purging some of his major opponents.

Beijing publicly rejoiced at the fall of Khrushchev in 1964. In 1967, at the height of the Cultural

▼ Political radicalization in China – posters proclaiming Mao's Cultural Revolution cover the walls of Guanzhou.

▲ ▶ Two faces of ideological upheaval – (above) female Red Guards march through the streets of Beijing; and (right) a party militant forces commuters to read aloud from the famous "little red book". China's Cultural Revolution arose from diputes within the Communist party about the political future of the country. The aging Mao found his ideologically based leadership threatened by pragmatic modernizers drawing their inspiration from the Soviet Union. He responded with a drive for ideological purity, rejecting all forms of compromise with doctrinaire Communism, and utilizing discontented young workers and students, as Red Guards, to launch attacks on the existing bureaucracy at both national and local levels. For ten years China turned its back on modernization as ideological warfare burnt a violent path through the country.

Revolution, Red Guards sacked the Soviet embassy in Beijing, and in 1968 China condemned the Soviet invasion of Czechoslovakia. With relations between the countries at their lowest ebb, in 1969 a border dispute almost resulted in war, with the Soviets backing down at the last moment.

China's Cultural Revolution

By the early 1960s the fervor of the 1949 Chinese revolution had begun to wane. Mao Zedong feared the Chinese people's conversion to consumerism, which might lead to the reestablishment of capitalism in China. Opinion among China's leadership on how to cope with the country's problems was divided. Marshal Lin Biao, head of the influential Military Affairs Committee of the Chinese Communist party (CCP) Central Committee, emphasized morale and the need for recurring mass movements in order to prevent any dilution of revolutionary ideals. Liu Shao-chi, the president of the Republic, favored consolidation of the social and economic gains of the revolution by increasing reliance on bureaucratic and technocratic expertise. Beneath these ar-

guments was a power struggle between radicals and moderates.

In April 1966 Mao ended these debates by launching the Cultural Revolution. Its aim, as outlined in Mao's directive of May 1966, was to mobilize the masses and stimulate the growth of self-sufficient communes and rural industrialization. According to Mao, workers, peasants, students and artists were interchangeable. Urban professionals and students sent out to the communes to work under the direction of peasants would, he believed, develop a better understanding of the rural economy. He hoped to create a healthy and self-sufficient rural economy. The decentralization of economic control and the encouragement of mass participation was also intended to curb the spread of bureaucracy and check the trend towards capitalization of production and exchange.

As always, Mao tried to combine ideological aims with practical realities. By 1966, the Chinese higher education system was swamped by the huge rise in student numbers resulting from the post-1949 baby boom, so that all student entries

for that year had to be postponed. Mao decided to recruit these young people into the newly-established revolutionary Red Guards, the spearhead of the Cultural Revolution in the countryside. Mao also hoped that sending the Red Guards into the countryside would help to boost agricultural production.

From Beijing the Red Guards fanned out into the countryside, with an estimated twenty million having been mobilized at the height of the Cultural Revolution. They organized mass rallies, wrote wall posters attacking party officials, bourgeois intellectuals and "capitalist roaders", denounced their teachers and parents, and ransacked party offices. Many ordinary Chinese were killed or tortured by these young fanatics. Economically, culturally and socially, the years of the Cultural Revolution were a disaster for China. Agricultural production and industrial output actually fell, devastating the country.

With the fall of the ultraleftist faction in the Central Committee of the Chinese Communist party in September 1967, the Cultural Revolution began to ebb. Mao himself recognized the difficulties and grew increasingly disillusioned with faction fighting among the Red Guards and eventually ordered them to return to their studies. In October 1968, the party congress confirmed the swing away from revolutionary violence and the return to a semblance of normality.

The Sino-Indian conflict

In 1962 a longstanding border dispute between China and India erupted in conflict. Historically India had secured its northern frontiers by establishing its influence over a string of buffer states – Sikkim, Tibet, Bhutan and Nepal – situated high on the slopes of the Himalayas. However, when China invaded Tibet in 1950–51, Tibet's position as a buffer state was transformed, exposing India's northern frontiers to Chinese penetration. Initially India accepted the situation, but China's ruthless suppression of the uprising in the

Tibetan capital, Lhasa, in March 1959 and the later subjection of Tibet to direct Chinese rule alarmed the Indians, who now faced a massive Chinese military presence on their northern border.

When the Communists took power in China in 1949, they had inherited border problems with several of their neighbors dating back to the colonial period. However, by the early 1960s, Beijing had, by a process of negotiation, already resolved most of its outstanding boundary disputes with its South Asian neighbors. The boundary dispute with India was more difficult to settle and complicated by the Chinese occupation of Tibet. To secure their new territory, the Chinese had started to build a military road to link up with Sinkiang, but this passed through territory claimed by the Indians in the Aksai Chin area north of Kashmir. To make matters worse, on the Assam frontier in the east, the Chinese demanded a revision of the 1914 MacMahon line, which drew China's boundary along the spine of the Himalayas from Bhutan to Burma but had never been formally ratified by Beijing. They insisted that the line pass along the southern slopes of the Himalayas.

In 1962 China suggested to India that the *status quo* on the border be maintained while the two countries negotiated a settlement. However, Jawaharlal Nehru, the Indian prime minister, rejected the proposal and ordered the Indian army to expel the Chinese. The first skirmishes took place on 20 September 1962 and a month later the Chinese launched a decisive full-scale attack. On 21 November, the Chinese declared a unilateral ceasefire, by which time they had securely occupied almost all the territory they had claimed.

The defeat was a humiliation for India and a blow to the aspirations of the nonaligned movement, as Nehru, its chief spokesman, had been forced to appeal to the United States to consider direct military intervention. On the other side, the Soviet Union's neutrality in the face of an attack upon its Communist ally angered the Chinese and led to the Sino-Soviet split.

Indo-Pakistan conflict

At the time of the British departure from India, and its division into the sovereign states of India and Pakistan in 1947, the political status of the numerous states ruled by princes was left unresolved. It was hoped that they would seek accession to India or Pakistan in accordance with the broad principles of partition, the majority Muslim states acceding to Pakistan and the rest to India. In Kashmir, however, a state with a three-quarters Muslim population and sharing borders with both Pakistan and India, the local Hindu ruler demanded autonomy. The Muslim population rose in revolt, giving Pakistan the pretext to invade. Belatedly, the ruler opted for accession to India, and, against all the principles on which India was partitioned, the Delhi government accepted, dispatching troops to Kashmir to drive out the Pakistanis. Kashmir's incorporation into India, however, was never accepted by Pakistan.

Unable to deal with India on its own, Pakistan sought outside help and, in 1954, signed a mutual

defense agreement with the United States, which was looking for an ally to contain Communism in Asia. Early in 1965 rioting in Kashmir gave a newly fortified Pakistan the opportunity to reopen the Kashmir question by force. Politicians in Islamabad hoped that as the Pakistani armored columns punched deep into the Himalayan province, the Kashmiris would rise in support and drive the Indians out. The plan backfired, however, because India, believing Kashmir to be indefensible, launched a massive attack on Pakistan itself. Islamabad was forced to pull back its forces from Kashmir to protect its frontier with India and the war ended in stalemate on 17 September 1965. Under Soviet persuasion, both sides agreed to withdraw their troops and the *status quo ante bellum* was restored.

The emergence of Bangladesh

The Indo-Pakistan war of 1971, which led to the secession of East Pakistan as the new state of Bangladesh, was a sequel to the 1965 conflict. Many in the predominantly Bengali Muslim province of East Pakistan did not share the hostility toward India of the politicians in Islamabad. Before 1965 the two wings of Pakistan, East and West, had been held together by the threat of Indian expansion. Yet in 1947 and 1965 India had made no attempt to take advantage of East Pakistan's defenselessness.

Increasingly, after 1965, the Bengalis, convinced that India had no designs on them, began to demand greater autonomy in order to escape the economic exploitation of West Pakistan. Mass agitation eventually forced the military rulers in Islamabad to hold a general election in 1970, the first since Pakistan's formation in 1947. The result was a clearcut victory for the Awami League, the Bengali party, which had led the preelection agitation for autonomous status. The Pakistani junta, however, refused to hand over power to a civilian regime in East Pakistan, particularly one dominated by the despised Bengalis.

In March 1971, West Pakistan invaded, forcing millions of Bengalis to flee into neighboring India. At first, the Delhi government refrained from intervention, but provided weapons and supplies for the Bengalis to continue their fight for independence. However, on 3 December 1971, the Pakistani airforce rashly launched a preemptive strike on India, and the two countries found themselves at war for the third time. The outcome was never in doubt. East Pakistan, separated from West Pakistan by over 1,500 kilometers of hostile Indian territory, was virtually impossible to defend and Pakistan's international allies proved unreliable. On the Indian side, the Soviet Union, by contrast, used its veto in the UN Security Council to ensure that no hasty ceasefire would deprive Delhi of total victory. Unlike the previous wars, this conflict was decisive: Pakistan was truncated and Bangladesh emerged as an independent state.

The United States and the Vietnam War

At the Geneva conference of 1954 Vietnam, a former French colony, was handed over to the Vietnamese. The country was divided between

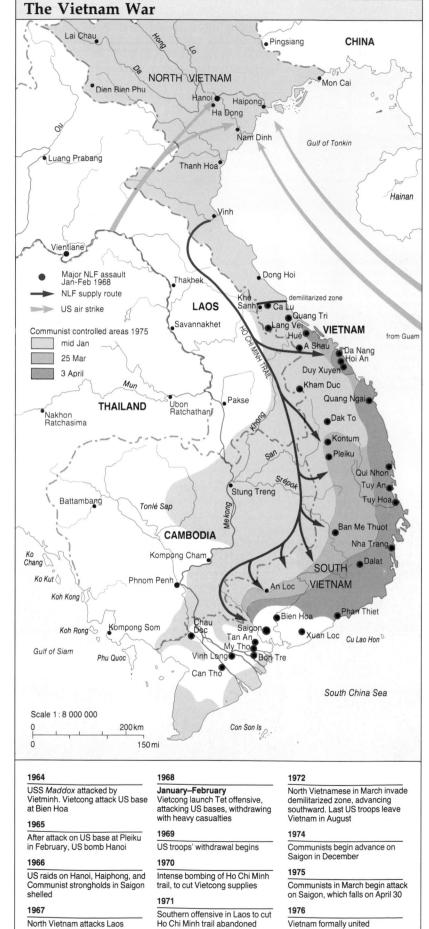

The Vietnam War

Major NLF assault Jan–Feb 1968
NLF supply route
US air strike

Communist controlled areas 1975
mid Jan
25 Mar
3 April

Scale 1 : 8 000 000

1964	1968	1972
USS *Maddox* attacked by Vietminh. Vietcong attack US base at Bien Hoa	**January–February** Vietcong launch Tet offensive, attacking US bases, withdrawing with heavy casualties	North Vietnamese in March invade demilitarized zone, advancing southward. Last US troops leave Vietnam in August
1965 After attack on US base at Pleiku in February, US bomb Hanoi	**1969** US troops' withdrawal begins	**1974** Communists begin advance on Saigon in December
1966 US raids on Hanoi, Haiphong, and Communist strongholds in Saigon shelled	**1970** Intense bombing of Ho Chi Minh trail, to cut Vietcong supplies	**1975** Communists in March begin attack on Saigon, which falls on April 30
1967 North Vietnam attacks Laos	**1971** Southern offensive in Laos to cut Ho Chi Minh trail abandoned	**1976** Vietnam formally united

▶ The real victims of the Vietnam War were the Vietnamese civilians. In the south, the situation was particularly severe, with people like mother and her mutilated child being caught between ruthless bids for political control by Communist guerrilla forces and clumsy US attempts at counterinsurgency in which devastating firepower was employed indiscriminately. These horrors were brought direct to the US public by newspaper and television, causing widespread revulsion against the war.

▼ The limits of air power – North Vietnamese peasants move past bomb craters left in their rice fields by US air attack. American air raids on the north were largely ineffectual, the predominantly rural economy of the country providing few obvious strategic objectives and little scope for serious damage or disruption by anything short of nuclear attack.

the Communist Democratic Republic of Vietnam in the North and the pro-Western South Vietnam. The terms of the Geneva agreement required that elections be held in 1956 to unify the country, but the South Vietnamese government, fearing a Communist victory, reneged on its Geneva pledge. Meanwhile the United States saw South Vietnam as a bastion against Communism in Asia and began to pour aid into the capital, Saigon, to build up South Vietnamese defenses against the North.

However, the South Vietnamese regime, under President Ngo Dinh Diem, was corrupt, and the Communist National Liberation Front (NLF), or Vietcong, a guerrilla force supported by North Vietnam and China, formed in December 1960, enjoyed widespread local support. To prevent a Communist takeover, President Kennedy massively increased US military assistance. In November 1963, Diem was killed in a US-backed coup and replaced by a military junta, who also proved powerless to halt the Vietcong insurgency.

The conflict intensified after the so-called Gulf of Tonkin incident in August 1964, when the US government accused North Vietnamese leaders of ordering the torpedoing of two US destroyers in North Vietnamese waters. Between 1963 and 1968, the number of US combat troops in Vietnam rose from 16,000 to over half a million. The

North Vietnamese responded by deploying regular forces in the South to aid the Vietcong. The United States launched massive bombing raids against the North and employed napalm and defoliants, but in vain. At last, in the face of mounting domestic opposition to the war, President Johnson made an offer of unconditional peace negotiations in April 1965. This was rejected, because both the North Vietnamese and the Vietcong were determined to secure a united Vietnam. The devastating Tet offensive of 1968 eventually forced the Americans to the conference table to sue for peace.

War in the Congo

After achieving independence from Belgium, the Congo, scene of some of the worst excesses in the history of European colonialism in Africa, remained a byword for political exploitation and brutality. Even as late as the mid-1950s, few in Belgium had given any serious thought to the transfer of power. This complacency was rudely shaken at the end of the 1950s when the Congo, like other African colonies, was caught up in a wave of anticolonial nationalist agitation. British withdrawal from the Gold Coast (renamed Ghana) in 1957 and the rapid devolution of power in Nigeria raised political expectations in equatorial Africa. In 1959 riots broke out in Léopoldville, and soon spread to other Congolese towns. A hastily convened decolonization conference, meeting in Brussels in January 1960, fixed the transfer of power for the following June after Belgian business interests had been secured.

However, the Congo was unprepared for independence. A huge territory, it contained numerous ethnic groups and tribes each with different political aspirations. Patrice Lumumba's Mouvement National Congolais tried to secure a national following by cutting across ethnic affiliations, but its main support derived from the Oriental and Kivu provinces. The other main party, Abako, led by Joseph Kasavubu, was a mouthpiece of the dominant Bakongo tribe from Léopoldville province.

Within hours of the independence celebrations on 4 July 1960, the Armée Nationale Congolaise revolted. Moise Tshombe, Prime Minister of the copper-rich Katanga province, declared Katangan independence and received the backing of Brussels and the main Belgian mining conglomerate, the Union Minière du Haut, as well as the influential Katangan elite, who opposed

sharing wealth with the rest of the country. Within weeks of their withdrawal, the Belgians had rushed paratroops back to the Congo, ostensibly to protect the lives of Belgian citizens, but in reality to support Tshombe and to protect Belgium's mineral interests in Kitona and Kanina. The Congolese president, Kasavubu, and his prime minister, Lumumba, appealed to the UN for assistance. The UN responded by dispatching a 20,000-strong force to the Congo. But it confined its activities to expelling the Belgians and gave no help to Lumumba's attempts to crush the Katangan rebellion. Following Lumumba's murder by Tshombe in February 1961, the Congo split into three parts, each with its own government: Tshombe in Katanga, Kasavubu in Léopoldville (now Kinshasa), and Antoine Gizenga, Lumumba's successor, in Stanleyville (now Kisangani). The civil war dragged on for nearly two years, with the UN forces rendered largely ineffective by the divided counsel of the major powers who were aligned on different sides of the conflict. Only after heavy fighting did Katanga finally fall to the UN forces, and on 16 January 1963 Tshombe agreed to end his secessionist movement.

The Nigerian civil war

Like the Congo, Nigeria was an artificial creation. Boundaries drawn for imperial convenience in the 19th century bore little relationship to cultural and tribal demarcations. The 1961 census estimated its population at 55 million and listed eight ethnic groups with populations of over a million, and a further twenty-seven smaller ones. Nigerian politics were dominated by three groups: the Muslim Hausa-Fulani in the north, who occupied nearly four-fifths of the entire country, the Yoruba kingdom in the west, with a mixed Muslim and Christian population, and the mainly Christian Ibo in the east.

The Nigerian constitution of 1960 retained the old colonial administrative units under a new federal system. The powers of the federal government in the capital, Lagos, were kept in check by

▲ UN forces arrive in Katanga at the height of the Congolese civil war. One of the most confused and bloody of Africa's decolonization conflicts, this war was complicated by Belgian interference and the use of white mercenaries by the rival Congolese factions. Its final resolution owed a great deal to one of the rare instances of effective UN intervention.

◄ Belgium, one of the smallest of the European colonial powers, was also one of the most tenacious in its attempts to maintain power in Africa. Cynical political maneuvering, and the use of military force to defend longstanding economic interests were in a large measure responsible for the bloody civil war which attended the Congo's passage from colonial rule to a precarious independence.

► Congolese soldiers torment prisoners prior to execution. The civil war in the Congo was notorious for the atrocities carried out by the rival forces. The causes of this barbarity were a complicated mixture of tribal rivalries, the disruption of normal patterns of life by colonial exploitation, the intrusion of white mercenaries and the widespread use of badly trained and undisciplined soldiers. Responsibility lay mostly with the departing colonial power – which behaved with cynical brutality throughout.

placing the government under the joint control of the three major ethnic groups. However, in the early 1960s, this delicate balance was upset when the numerically superior Hausa-Fulani attempted to gain control by manipulating electoral procedures, particularly in the Yoruba west, which soon became a client region of the north. Lagos's blantant interference in regional affairs provoked widespread popular unrest, which prompted the army to seize power in January 1966.

General Ironsi, the army strongman, had little understanding of the strength of interethnic feelings or the abhorrence of outside control among the minorities. When, in May 1966, he abolished the regional governments and placed them under direct central authority, the regions reacted violently. Ironsi himself was killed in July 1966 in a military coup which brought Colonel Yakubu Gowon to power.

The failure of the constitution invited calls for change. The Ibos, in particular, demanded greater federal autonomy and limitation of the powers of the center. However Gowon, like his predecessor Ironsi, was an advocate of centralization, and his attitude reflected the interests of the ethnic groups from the "Middle Belt". Moreover, a strong central government, which was-dominated by Gowon's fellow tribespeople, would be able to control the vital foreign exchange earnings from the Biafran oilfields in the east. In May 1967 Gowon divided Nigeria into 12 states answerable directly to a federal administration in Lagos.

On 30 May 1967 the Ibos revolted and Colonel Ojukwu proclaimed Biafra an independent state. In the ensuing civil war (1967–71), Gowon succeeded in preventing Biafran secession, but the costs in both economic and human terms were enormous.

The Arab–Israeli "Six-Day" war

The wars of 1948 and 1956 between Israel and its Arab neighbors had failed to resolve their differences. Israel, backed by her powerful Western allies, was able to defy the combined military strength of the Arabs and ignore international protests at the plight of Palestinian refugees. Tensions mounted in the early 1960s as the Palestinians began to launch guerrilla attacks on Israel from Arab sanctuaries. The immediate cause for renewed hostility, however, was Israel's irrigation and waterwork system, completed in 1964, which siphoned off scarce resources from the region between Lake Galilee and the Negev desert.

The crisis led to a rare moment of unity among the Arab states. In May 1967, the Egyptian president ordered the withdrawal of the UN emergency force which had policed Sinai since 1956 and threatened to close the vital straits of Sharm al-Sheikh at the head of the Red Sea, to Israeli vessels. In preparation for war, Egypt and Jordan placed their forces under joint command and were soon joined by Iraq. Israel, unnerved by the unprecedented Arab unity and chafing under the Al-Fatah guerrilla attacks, seized upon Nasser's threat to Sharm al-Sheikh as a pretext to strike. On 5 June 1967, Israel launched a devastating attack, destroying Egypt's air force on the ground. Deprived of air cover, the Egyptian armies were caught at the Gidi and Mitla passes in northern Sinai and annihilated. The war was over in six days. By the end, Israel had occupied Egyptian territory as far as the Suez Canal and the Straits of Tiran, had annexed all of Jordan west of the Jordan River, including Jerusalem, and had wrested control of the vital Golan Heights from Syria. These acquisitions made Israel far less vulnerable and far less amenable to a negotiated settlement on the Palestinian question.

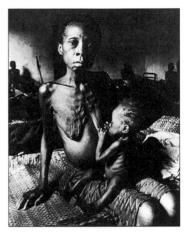

▼ Starvation in Biafra – a young Biafran mother, aged by malnutrition, tries to feed her baby from an empty breast. The Biafran war (1967–70) was a small-scale military conflict, prolonged by the low fighting capabilities of both sides, which turned into a human disaster of major proportions due to the collapse of the marginal economy of the breakaway Biafran state. A devastating famine ensued, whose effects were mitigated only slightly by the launching of a worldwide relief operation.

We have pretended for too long that there are no differences between the peoples of this country. The hard fact which we must honestly accept is that we are different peoples brought together by recent accidents of history. To pretend otherwise would be folly.

NORTHERN NIGERIAN 1966

Six-Day and Yom Kippur Wars

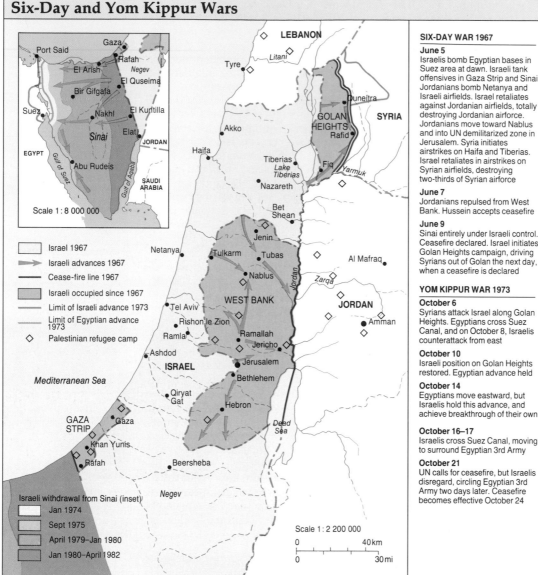

Israel 1967
Israeli advances 1967
Cease-fire line 1967
Israeli occupied since 1967
Limit of Israeli advance 1973
Limit of Egyptian advance 1973
◇ Palestinian refugee camp

Israeli withdrawal from Sinai (inset)
Jan 1974
Sept 1975
April 1979–Jan 1980
Jan 1980–April 1982

Scale 1 : 2 200 000
0   40km
0   30mi

SIX-DAY WAR 1967

June 5
Israelis bomb Egyptian bases in Suez area at dawn. Israeli tank offensives in Gaza Strip and Sinai. Jordanians bomb Netanya and Israeli airfields. Israel retaliates against Jordanian airfields, totally destroying Jordanian airforce. Jordanians move toward Nablus and into UN demilitarized zone in Jerusalem. Syria initiates airstrikes on Haifa and Tiberias. Israel retaliates in airstrikes on Syrian airfields, destroying two-thirds of Syrian airforce

June 7
Jordanians repulsed from West Bank. Hussein accepts ceasefire

June 9
Sinai entirely under Israeli control. Ceasefire declared. Israel initiates Golan Heights campaign, driving Syrians out of Golan the next day, when a ceasefire is declared

YOM KIPPUR WAR 1973

October 6
Syrians attack Israel along Golan Heights. Egyptians cross Suez Canal, and on October 8, Israelis counterattack from east

October 10
Israeli position on Golan Heights restored. Egyptian advance held

October 14
Egyptians move eastward, but Israelis hold this advance, and achieve breakthrough of their own

October 16–17
Israelis cross Suez Canal, moving to surround Egyptian 3rd Army

October 21
UN calls for ceasefire, but Israelis disregard, circling Egyptian 3rd Army two days later. Ceasefire becomes effective October 24

◀ In both 1967 and 1973 Israel successfully fought brief but decisive two-front wars against her Arab neighbors — in 1967 capturing the whole of Sinai, the West Bank and the Golan Heights in a daring pre-emptive attack, and in 1973 recovering from a surprise enemy offensive to cross the Suez Canal in the west and open the road to Damascus in the northeast.

▼ Jerusalem, August 1967: a young Israeli soldier makes his religious observances at the sacred "Wailing Wall", the Israeli capture of the city, had formed between the Israeli and another bloody episode in the bitter war with the Palestinians, for whom, also, this territory is home.

Kissinger and Shuttle Diplomacy

"Shuttle diplomacy" was the creation of Dr Henry Kissinger, US Secretary of State under President Nixon. His method was to travel to and fro between the capitals concerned, conveying the proposals and responses of each party to the other, but also injecting his own ideas and building up momentum in such a way as to give neither the chance to withdraw, until the point was reached where the parties were ready to sign an agreement which satisfied them both.

The first systematic use of this technique, and of the term "shuttle diplomacy" to describe it, can be dated to January 1974. In seven rounds of talks, four in Egypt and three in Israel, compressed into a single week, Dr Kissinger succeeded in drawing up an Egyptian-Israeli agreement for military disengagement in Sinai, which was signed on 18 January. In May of the same year, using the same method, he secured a parallel disengagement agreement between Israel and Syria on the Golan Heights: this time the shuttle lasted four weeks.

The Arab-Israeli "Yom Kippur" war

The death of the Egyptian leader Nasser in November 1970 led to a major shift in international alignments. Anwar Sadat, Egypt's pragmatic new President, responded to Washington's desire for improved relations by breaking with the Soviet Union. This new US-Egyptian rapprochement widened Washington's commitments in the Middle East beyond the preservation of Israel and enabled Sadat to forge a greater unity between Egypt, Saudi Arabia, Jordan and Syria in their opposition to Israel. Sadat also offered to negotiate bilaterally with the Israeli government.

The Palestinians were again central to the Arab-Israeli conflict. Following the Arab defeat of 1967, Palestinian guerrillas had decided that it was futile to depend on the Arab states for the recovery of their homeland. Instead, they determined to shock the world into an awareness of their plight by hijacking and blowing up passenger airplanes owned by Western countries, and by a spate of guerrilla attacks against Israel. But neither Sadat's sinuous diplomacy nor the terrorist tactics of the Palestinians could shake

▲ Israeli forces drive past Egyptian prisoners on their way to the Suez Canal during the Yom Kippur war of October 1973. The surprise Egyptian attack on the Israeli defensive line along the canal's west bank was a dramatic success, but failure to exploit the breakthrough and a rapid Israeli counteroffensive turned the situation into a disaster for the attackers. The Israelis threatened an advance on the Egyptian capital and a negotiated settlement was hurriedly reached under pressure from the USA and Soviet Union.

Israel's resolve. To break the deadlock, the Egyptian president, on 6 October 1973, ordered his forces to cross the Suez Canal, catching the Israelis unawares as they celebrated the Yom Kippur festival (day of atonement). The United States rushed to Israel's support, flying in massive military reinforcements, which helped Tel Aviv blunt the Egyptian attack, and soon put its own forces on the Cairo side of the canal.

The war ended in stalemate, exposing on the one hand Israel's vulnerability and on the other the continuing limitation of Arab arms. The conflict impressed on both sides the need for a political solution and gave the United States the opportunity to renew its role of mediator. The US Secretary of State, Henry Kissinger worked through shuttle diplomacy to bring about a reconciliation between Cairo and Tel Aviv. However, by concentrating on the Egyptian–Israeli border dispute, and failing to tackle the crucial Palestinian question, Kissinger and successive US administrations condemned the Middle East to continuing turmoil. Indeed, the unilateral peace between Egypt and Israel broke Arab unity, isolated Egypt and removed its moderating

influence in Arab affairs. The hope that similar agreements between Tel Aviv and other Arab states would follow was unfulfilleed.

The Yom Kippur War did nothing to resolve the Arab–Israeli conflict. However, the Arab states, in their newfound solidarity, emerged from it with a new economic weapon. Controlling the world's largest reserves of oil, they were in a position to disrupt supplies to the oil-dependent economies of the industrialized West. In December 1973, the Organization of Petroleum Exporting Countries (OPEC) announced a 70 percent increase in prices and threatened to lower production by five percent a month until Israel's Western backers forced them to evacuate the occupied territories. This did have some diplomatic impact. Britain stopped supplying arms to Israel, Japan reversed pro-Israeli policy, and the European Community (with the exception of the Netherlands) publicly censured Israel for obstructing the settlement of the Palestinian question. Even the United States was caught in the world recession touched off by the oil price increases. No longer could Israel's Western friends afford to ignore Arab demands.

PHOTOJOURNALISM

When American reporter John L. Spivak wrote an exposé of conditions in Florida chain gangs in 1931, he insisted on photographs to support his charges. Throughout the century photographs have been used as dramatic documents, not only illustrating historically significant events but influencing their reception.

In the 1930s the technology of small 35mm cameras and highspeed film made candid photography much easier, and created a new kind of news reporter, the photojournalist. Whether making single images for newspapers or for picture magazines such as *Life*, photojournalism was committed to the idea that the photograph was an impartial document.

And yet few forms of photography have shown themselves so open to distortion. Photographs rely on the words in their captions to supply and specify their meaning, a meaning which can be changed with the wording of the caption in perhaps the simplest and most obvious kind of manipulation. Among the most blatant instances of using photographs to reorder reality were Soviet pictures of the Politburo, in which discredited members had been removed by retouching. In the West the manipulation of the photographed image has more often been the result of a photographer's conflicting motivations. He or she has sought to present an "accurate record" of the event, yet also to provide a dramatic image.

After World War II the war photographer became an alternative hero to the soldier, shooting with a camera instead of a gun. In the wars since then, particularly in Vietnam, this heroic image was intensified by the unpopularity of the war. Every picture of the Vietnam war seemed to be an anti-war image, and photographers like Sean Flynn and Tim Page appeared as heroic figures who went into the hell of modern warfare.

But war photography required skills and a sense of detachment which seem frighteningly inhuman. On occasion, photojournalists become accomplices, however unwillingly, in the atrocities they photograph. The presence of news and television cameras guarantees publicity to those prepared to turn themselves or others into a spectacle for public consumption. Photographs of the atrocities of war or famine carry a powerful emotional charge for their viewers, but the effects of that charge may be questioned. British photographer Don McCullin's acutely painful images of the war in Cambodia appeared opposite advertisements for cars and perfume in the *Sunday Times Magazine*, and whatever their emotional effect upon the newspaper's readers, they did not lead its editors to change their policy of support for the American presence in Southeast Asia.

Many commentators, however, concluded that the cumulative press and media coverage of Vietnam had been an important factor in generating domestic opposition to the war, and military advisors voiced their reluctance to allows journalists free access to battlefields again.

▲ ▲ The Hungarian-born Robert Capa developed many of the techniques of modern photojournalism during the Spanish Civil War. His image of the decisive moment — such as this one of a Loyalist soldier being felled by a bullet in 1938, influenced much later photography.

▲ News photography of events such as famines in Africa in the late 1980s has proved a powerful means of turning the attention of the world to a crisis. Overfamiliarity with such images, however, may tend to soften the effect.

► The photograph of the naked girl in Vietnam, fleeing down the road and screaming from napalm burns, became world-famous as an indictment of the horrors of modern war. Yet other pictures taken at the same scene show the photographer as detached observer, seeking the most powerful image rather than helping the victims: journalists shot them with cameras while soldiers shot with rifles.

◀ When a Buddhist monk decided to burn himself to death in 1963 in protest at the Vietnam war, his sacrifice was consciously captured. His fellow monks recorded the event on film, ensuring that the protest would not be in vain, even if the world's press failed to arrive.

▼ While some photo-opportunities are carefully exploited, others are created. This image of the raising of the American flag on Iwo Jima in February 1945, was carefully posed and photographed by Joe Rosenthal hours after the actual event.

Datafile

The turmoil of the 1960s had far-reaching effects in the First World. Advances in levels of education had produced a large and politically radical student population. Demands for increased government spending on social services were leading to large increases in the public sector. Internationally, the antagonism between Israel and its Arab neighbors was reaching crisis point, exacerbated by increased superpower interest in the strategic assets of the Middle East.

▼ In addition to the rapid growth in overall student numbers in many countries, the proportion studying liberal subjects, sociology and politics also rose, contributing to student radicalism. Student unrest was felt all over Europe and Japan as well as in the USA.

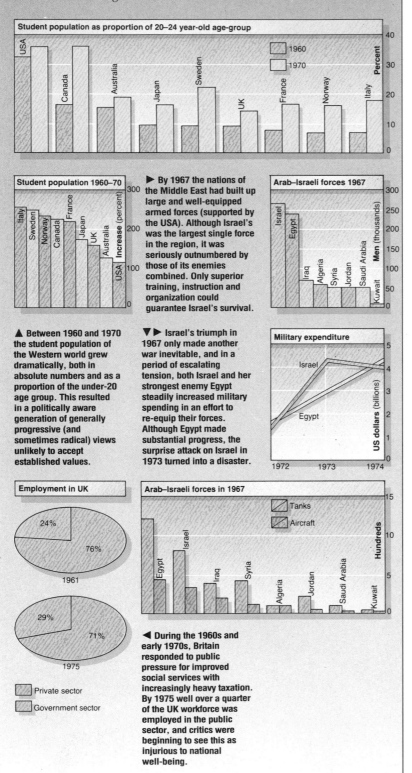

Student population as proportion of 20–24 year-old age-group

1960
1970

USA · Canada · Australia · Japan · Sweden · UK · France · Norway · Italy · Percent

Student population 1960–70

Italy · Sweden · Norway · Canada · France · Japan · UK · Australia · USA · Increase (percent)

▲ Between 1960 and 1970 the student population of the Western world grew dramatically, both in absolute numbers and as a proportion of the under-20 age group. This resulted in a politically aware generation of generally progressive (and sometimes radical) views unlikely to accept established values.

► By 1967 the nations of the Middle East had built up large and well-equipped armed forces (supported by the USA). Although Israel's was the largest single force in the region, it was seriously outnumbered by those of its enemies combined. Only superior training, instruction and organization could guarantee Israel's survival.

▼► Israel's triumph in 1967 only made another war inevitable, and in a period of escalating tension, both Israel and her strongest enemy Egypt steadily increased military spending in an effort to re-equip their forces. Although Egypt made substantial progress, the surprise attack on Israel in 1973 turned into a disaster.

Arab–Israeli forces 1967

Israel · Egypt · Iraq · Algeria · Syria · Jordan · Saudi Arabia · Kuwait · Men (thousands)

Military expenditure

Israel · Egypt · US dollars (billions)

1972 · 1973 · 1974

Employment in UK

24% / 76% — 1961
29% / 71% — 1975

Private sector
Government sector

Arab–Israeli forces in 1967

Tanks
Aircraft

Egypt · Israel · Iraq · Syria · Algeria · Jordan · Saudi Arabia · Kuwait · Hundreds

◄ During the 1960s and early 1970s, Britain responded to public pressure for improved social services with increasingly heavy taxation. By 1975 well over a quarter of the UK workforce was employed in the public sector, and critics were beginning to see this as injurious to national well-being.

Since World War II the Eastern bloc states, held together largely by Soviet military might, have harbored the desire for greater autonomy. Beneath the Cold War rhetoric and outward displays of Communist unity nationalist aspirations have continued to burn strong, often flaring up as in Czechoslovakia in 1968.

Until then Czechoslovakia had been a most docile satellite, primarily because of the repressiveness of the regimes of Klement Gottwald and Antonin Novotny. In the mid-1960s, however, the worsening economic situation there provoked a movement toward political liberalization. Czechoslovakia's industrial decline was partly due to the Cold War and the consequent erection of economic barriers between East and West. Trade restrictions hit Czechoslovakia particularly hard because earlier it had been economically more allied with Western Europe than had its neighbors.

The Novotny regime cautiously accepted the need to decentralize economic planning, but found it difficult to implement reforms in a society dominated by the Czech Politburo's rigid adherence to Soviet-style Communism. By the late 1960s, with the Communist world in ferment, Czechoslovakia was ripe for change.

In January 1968, First Secretary Novotny was stripped of power and replaced by the reform-minded Alexander Dubček. Five months later, General Ludvik Svoboda, a nationalist and war hero, became President of the Republic. Dubček immediately relaxed press censorship, removed a number of hard-liners from the government and initiated a debate on the democratization of the Czech Communist party (CCP). In April, the Presidium of the CCP drafted an Action Program. This Program marked the beginning of the short-lived "Prague Spring". Its demands included the rehabilitation of victims of the 1940 Stalinist purge, the freedom of minor parties within the Communist-controlled National Front government, the democratization of the social and political system, equal rights for minorities, and, above all, more open government.

Whereas Dubček ensured that his personal relations with the Soviets remained cordial, he could not hide the fact that the reforms in Czechoslovakia implied a criticism of Soviet policies. Most alarming from the Soviet point of view was that the Czech reform program implicitly called into question the role of the Communist party and its relationship to government. The Soviets had learned from past experience that demands for political change in one Eastern bloc state would inevitably spread to others. Dubček had not only drawn closer to Tito and Ceauşescu, but, the Soviets feared, was also seeking closer ties with West Germany.

1968 AND AFTER

Tensions mounted, and on 15 July the leaders of the USSR, East Germany, Hungary, Poland and Bulgaria met in Warsaw to send a joint communication to Dubček urging him to suppress his "antisocialist" program. Shortly afterwards, *Pravda* alleged that US arms had been discovered in Czechoslovakia, and a following Soviet note suggested that Soviet troops be posted on Czechoslovakia's western frontiers in order to guarantee its security. Dubček, sensing the danger of intervention, assured the Warsaw Pact allies at a meeting held on 3 August in Bratislava that Czechoslovakia would stand by its Warsaw Pact commitments.

On 10 August 1968, however, the CCP published new statutes aimed at ending "democratic centralism" (Communist orthodoxy) and granting substantial rights to the minor parties in the National Front. It seemed to the Soviets that Dubček could not, or would not, halt the reform movement and that their only option now was to remove him.

On 20 August Soviet troops, backed by other Warsaw Pact forces, crossed into Czechoslovakia.

They met with no resistance. The Soviet invasion met with worldwide condemnation, including criticism from many West European Communist parties. Moreover, as the Czechs remained firmly behind Dubček, the Soviets could not set up a collaborationist regime to replace him. Soon, he and other Czech leaders who had been arrested had to be reinstated.

However, this respite was only temporary, unlike the damage done to the Czech reform movement. In 1969, Dubček was dispatched to Turkey as Czechoslovakia's ambassador, before being recalled and expelled from the party. But the Czech people continued to see him as a hero. He was eventually replaced by Gustav Husak, a former member of Dubček's government.

The invasion of Czechoslovakia was one of several examples of the Soviet Union taking action against its allies; politicians in Moscow considered it their duty to prevent deviation. Under Leonid Brezhnev, this idea was developed into a doctrine named after him. This held that neither internal nor external forces would be permitted to change the socialist system into a capitalist one.

▼ **Men against tanks – Czech youths throw Molotov cocktails and stones in fruitless resistance as the Soviet army moves into Prague. Alarmed at the pace of liberalization under the new Dubček regime, the USSR sent in its army to reassert Communist orthodoxy and eliminate any chance of further reforms taking the country out of the Soviet bloc.**

LA POLICE VOUS PARLE
tous les soirs

ORTF

▲ ▶ **The state seen as the enemy of its people – this French portrayal of the police as armed, omnipresent (even on the radio) and unhuman typifies the attitudes of the student protestors of May 1968. In scenes reminiscent of the turbulent years of the previous century, barricades were thrown up, and cars and other property destroyed. Armed riot police were deployed, with tear gas and baton charges the order of the day. Eventually, the center and right rallied to the government and massive pro-government demonstrations (left) faced down the crisis. Although order was restored without revolution, new forms of government were clearly necessary.**

▼ **Make love not war – an anti-Vietnam War demonstrator confronts a nervous National Guardsman. In the US, opposition to the stalemated war in Southeast Asia and to the military draft escalated in the late 1960s. Media coverage of the conflict transformed protest into a broad-based rejection of war and the sinister role of the state.**

An extension of the "Brezhnev doctrine" was later invoked as justification for the Soviet invasion of Afghanistan in December 1979, and the threat of intervention hung over the Poles during the crisis with the Solidarity movement between 1980 and 1982.

Uprising in France

The Paris student uprising of May 1968, which was sparked off by problems within the French university system, formed part of a broader movement against governmental insensitivity, authoritarianism and patriarchalism everywhere. When, at the tailend of the "swinging sixties", inflation pushed up prices and wages could not keep pace, a niggling dissatisfaction peaked. To many of the young, in particular, modern society was cruel and unjust.

In the late 1960s student unrest was common, perhaps especially in France, where an inadequate system was strained to breaking point by an ever-increasing student influx. But, on 3 May 1968, a conflict that had started at Nanterre, an annex of Paris University, spread to the Sorbonne itself, and became a national movement. Moderate and radical students erected barricades on the left bank of the Seine. Police excesses were widely reported in the media, earning sympathy for the students from the French middle class. Workers in education and industry soon joined the students on the streets. By mid-May strikes in factories and mines resulted in some ten million workers being laid off.

President de Gaulle, encouraged by receiving pledges of support from the military, decided to see the crisis through and ignored calls on him to resign from members of his government.

By the end of May, the initial enthusiasm for the uprising had begun to wane, for although some students were political revolutionaries out to overthrow the state, most were concerned primarily with educational reforms. The French workers who had supported the movement were for the most part moderates whose grievances were economic.

De Gaulle's firm resolution and acute understanding of the crisis had enabled the government to weather the storm. When he sensed that the mood of the French people had become one of alarm, he called a snap general election. The result was a resounding victory for the Gaullists who mustered 291 seats, enough to form a government on their own for the first time.

With the elections over, the government began to address student grievances. Edgar Faure, the new Education Minister, drew up extensive reforms, whose effect, however, was limited. Paris continued to have the final say over the content of university curricula and examinations as well as the allocation of funds. Indeed, through lack of finance many reforms did not go beyond the planning stage. Instead, the government tried to reduce overcrowding by making university entry more selective – a risky policy which might have sparked off another revolt had it not been for the political caution exercised by the French government after May 1968 as well as the earnest desire of most middle-class French people to avoid further major upheavals.

The anti-Vietnam War movement

No conflict since the US Civil War (1861-65) has left deeper scars in the United States than Vietnam. The first war to receive extensive television coverage, it invaded the homes of millions of Americans, who nightly saw their young men dying in the jungles and on the battlefields. Many American liberals began to question the wisdom and morality of committing half a million GIs to the defense of a corrupt and incompetent regime in Saigon. Some even admired the courage and resourcefulness of the Vietcong, the liberation fighters in the South, and their North Vietnamese allies.

President Johnson saw his popularity plummet. Protesters who gathered in their thousands outside the White House taunted the President with their chants of "Hey! Hey! LBJ! How many kids did you kill today?", as mass antiwar demonstrations engulfed Washington. Across the country on university campuses students protested their opposition to the war and the drafting of young men to fight in it by actions of civil disobedience. Some of the demonstrations turned violent when police or National Guardsmen clashed with students, and thousands of arrests were made.

As the US casualty toll in the Vietnam War mounted, so the protests increased. By the end, the war had claimed some 44,000 American lives. The protests began overtly to flout the law, as many young Americans refused to be drafted and faced imprisonment. Some of the protesters were so appalled by the war, and by middle-class American values generally, that they simply "dropped out" of society or took to drugs. They included disillusioned Vietnam war veterans. The late 1960s were the high-water mark of the "counter-culture", represented by "hippy" communes, psychedelic drugs and free love.

With Johnson's dream of a "Great Society" shattered, and the morale of the US military devastated by the success of the North Vietnamese Tet offensive of January 1968, even members of Johnson's own party called for his removal.

Germany and *Ostpolitik*

For a long time, the question of Germany remained the main stumbling block to superpower détente. Despite the construction of the Berlin Wall, many of the older generation of Germans still clung to the hope that the country would be reunited. When Willy Brandt came to power in 1969, however, he announced that he would accept the political *status quo* in Europe and initiated a policy of détente between East and West. In August 1970, Brandt signed a nonaggression pact with the Soviet Union which recognized the existing frontiers in Eastern Europe. This move opened the way to the Soviet leader Brezhnev's agreement to a Mutual and Balanced Force Reduction (MBFR) conference, which met in Helsinki in January 1973.

Brandt's *Ostpolitik* (East European policy) also achieved some success in its own right. In 1971 East and West Germany signed an agreement which for the first time tacitly endorsed the separate status of the two states. The German settlement removed a vital impediment to the normalization of East-West relations.

Arms control talks

As the arms gap between the United States and the Soviet Union narrowed, it became clear that neither could hope to win a nuclear war. In these circumstances, the superpowers sought to resume the arms limitation talks that had stalled since 1963.

In 1969 President Nixon announced the start of a phased withdrawal of US troops from Vietnam. The West Europeans too looked for a new agreement on arms control to maintain the military balance between NATO and the forces of the Warsaw Pact.

Political Extremism in West Germany

Between 1966 and 1969, during the time of the so-called "big coalition", there was virtually no organized opposition in the West German federal parliament. The worldwide economic crisis increased the disillusion with government and once again facilitated the rise of rightwing extremism.

Founded in 1964, the rightwing National Democratic party (NPD) attracted considerable attention through its fierce antigovernment stance. It demanded the immediate expulsion of foreign workers and the end of war-crime trials for former Nazis. The party's call for the restoration of pride in the "Fatherland" also won the vote of sections of the German youth. By 1969, it had secured some 60 seats in seven state assemblies.

The successes of the NPD angered German students and leftwing groups. The student movement, at first focused on the reform of German universities, soon widened its demands to include social reform. On the far left, Rudi Dutschke's Socialist Students' Federation called for a revolution to overthrow liberal democracy in Germany. The protest movement soon spread to most German university campuses.

To the older generation these events awakened uneasy memories of the 1930s. The Soviet Union, fearing a revival of German fascism, even hinted at the possibility of military intervention to stamp it out. Such a threat coming so soon after the Soviet invasion of Czechoslovakia, the Germans decided, could not be taken lightly and so in the elections of September 1969 they voted heavily for the center-right and center-left parties. The NPD failed to capture even the 5 percent minimum vote needed for a seat. A subsequent upswing in the economy put paid to the resurgence of the right.

► In the Kurfürstendamm, West Berlin's main street, in April 1968, demonstrators are savagely assaulted by police as they make their way to a meeting in protest against the attempt on the life of Rudi Dutschke, a leading member of the Socialist Students' Union (SDS).

▼ The leftwing student movement gave rise to urban terrorist violence with the emergence of the Baader-Meinhof group, which was formed in 1968. After a campaign of violence against economic and political targets, most leading members were arrested in 1972.

Other factors also influenced superpower relations during these years. In 1964, the withdrawal of France – a nuclear power – from the NATO alliance and the economic success of the European Community had made Western Europe less dependent on the United States. The unity of the Soviet bloc was tested by the invasion of Czechoslovakia in 1968, while the improved relations between China and the United States aroused old fears in Moscow. Many newly independent states were nonaligned and their collective political weight represented a third major political force.

While there was little prospect of complete disarmament by the superpowers, the fear of nuclear weapons proliferating to other states eventually drove them toward serious arms limitation talks. When the superpowers' (and Britain's) nuclear monopoly was broken by France in 1964 and China in 1970, arms control suddenly became top of the agenda, with the superpowers united in their desire to prevent others developing a nuclear capability.

In July 1968 the United States, the Soviet Union and Britain signed a Nuclear Non-Proliferation Treaty (NPT), undertaking not to transfer nuclear technology or weapons to nonnuclear powers. The nonnuclear powers were invited to join the NPT by pledging never to develop or acquire nuclear weapons. By 1980, 114 countries had become signatories, although Israel, South Africa, India, Pakistan and Brazil, all of which had nuclear programs capable of weapon production, were significantly not among them.

First proposed by the Soviets, the Strategic Arms Limitation Talks (SALT) began in Geneva in 1969. The SALT I interim agreement, which was eventually ratified by Nixon and Brezhnev on 26 May 1972, stipulated that each side would have only two defensive systems, each with a maximum radius of 120 kilometers. One would protect the capital city and the other, at least 1200 kilometers away, would defend major provincial centers. The treaty was intended to last indefinitely, but was subject to review every five years.

◄Republican supporters celebrate Nixon's landslide victory in the presidential election of 1972. Defeated by Kennedy in his first bid for the presidency, Nixon had narrowly won the right to lead the nation in 1968. While benefiting from a relaxation of the domestic tension of the 1960s, he made his reputation in foreign affairs, successfully extracting the US from the Vietnam War and making milestone visits to the Soviet Union and the People's Republic of China which established him as the unlikely apostle of détente.

◄ US foreign policy continued to revolve around the maintenance of an overpowering nuclear deterrent – a policy which guaranteed US leaders domestic support from traditionalist voters but damaged America's reputation abroad. In both Europe and the Third World, the US came to be seen as the main stumbling-block to progress with arms control.

Although it was modest in scope and had little effect on offensive weapons, SALT I represented the first successful attempt by the superpowers to agree on arms limitations. SALT also provided the basis for future negotiations between Gerald Ford and Leonid Brezhnev, resulting on 24 November 1974 in an agreement on the guidelines for the SALT II treaty. This was eventually ratified by Jimmy Carter in 1978. Indeed, it was not until President Reagan's ambitious Strategic Defense Initiative (SDI) of the 1980s that the strategic parity principle, on which the SALT treaties had been based, was challenged.

US withdrawal from Vietnam

Following Johnson's withdrawal from the political scene, Republican candidate Richard Nixon, campaigning on the twin themes of Vietnam and national unification, defeated Hubert Humphrey in an election which many voters felt had denied them any real political choice. He immediately embarked cautiously on a policy of disengagement from Vietnam. When US forces intervened in Cambodia (Kampuchea) to support the new military government, more than a quarter of a million people marched on Washington and student strikes and sit-ins closed down university campuses right across the country.

US military involvement in Vietnam finally ended in January 1973 with the signing of the Paris Peace Accord. Both sides agreed to end their direct military intervention in the South. On 30 April 1975, North Vietnamese tanks entered Saigon, ending a war that had lasted for 15 years.

Sino-US relations

Ever since Mao Zedong's Communists came to power in 1949, China had been ostracized by the West. The government of the island of Taiwan – all that remained to the Guomindang nationalists after the Chinese civil war – was recognized by the United States and most of its allies as the only legitimate government of China, and accorded a permanent seat in the United Nations Security Council. However, once the Sino-Soviet split became public, Washington began to reassess its policy. A rapprochement with mainland China offered distinct advantages to the Americans. It would drive a deeper wedge into the Communist bloc, and at the same time enable the United States to force the pace in the arms negotiations with Moscow. There were other attractions, too. Despite Mao's quixotic leadership and the failure of the Great Leap Forward, and the Cultural Revolution, the billion-strong Chinese market offered a most tantalizing prospect for American

▲ ▼ **By the end of the 1960s, US disillusionment with military involvement in Vietnam was extreme. Frustration at the failure to make any impact on Communist fighting capability was heightened by the high casualties and additional psychological distress of many soldiers.**

businessmen. To the Chinese, the Americans offered an opportunity to escape from economic dependence on the Soviet Union.

In 1971, the United States revoked its trade embargo against China, and a visit in July by Henry Kissinger to Beijing paved the way for Nixon's historic tour of China in February 1972. Before his visit, Nixon jettisoned his "two Chinas" policy and did not exercise the US veto in the UN Security Council when China applied to replace Taiwan as a permanent member.

The improvement in Sino-US relations increased pressures on the Soviet Union to reach agreement with the United States on strategic arms limitation. However, speculation concerning the emergence of a tripolar international political system dominated by Beijing, Moscow and Washington was premature, as China, although a fully fledged nuclear power by 1970, remained technologically backward. Burdened by overpopulation and administrative inefficiency, China, even as late as 1960, experienced terrible famines. Internationally, China's alignment with the United States against the Soviet Union on a whole range of issues allayed Western fears of the solidarity within the Communist bloc.

The Watergate scandal

President Nixon's first term of office was marked by important achievements in foreign policy. When Nixon stood for reelection, a nation weary of the Vietnam War continued to see him as its best hope for peace and returned him to the White House for a second term with one of the largest majorities in American history. However, the administration was soon beset by a scandal which exposed corruption, deceit and perjury at the highest level, and led to the ignominious resignation of the president himself.

During the 1972 presidential election campaign, there had been a break-in and bungled attempt to bug the Democratic party offices in the Watergate Building in Washington D.C. Two investigative journalists of *The Washington Post* had reported a link between this burglary and the White House, but few had taken this seriously. The trial of the seven men charged with the Watergate break-in, including three connected with the White House and Nixon's re-election campaign, aroused no more than passing interest. But the presiding law officer decided to withhold judgment in the case pending further inquiries. On promise of a lighter sentence, James McCord, one of the Whitehouse aides, produced evidence which sparked off the Watergate scandal. McCord confirmed previous press speculation that attempts were being made by senior White House staff to block the investigation. The Senate decided to launch its own full-scale inquiry in February 1973.

It soon became clear that White House involvement was much greater than had been admitted. Until March 1973, President Nixon had maintained that he had no knowledge of any of his personal staff being implicated in the cover-up, but on 17 April he was forced to admit that they might have been and to agree to their testifying before the Senate Committee. By the end of the

▶ ▲ Fallen hero. Just as it was basking in the glory of international achievement, the Nixon regime was brought crashing down. The Watergate affair began as a bungled burglary but spread to entangle the entire Republican hierarchy in a sordid web of corruption. Nixon was forced to resign.

month, the Attorney-General, Richard Kleindienst, and two senior presidential aides, John Ehrlichman and Robert Haldeman, had resigned, while a third, John Dean, a White House counsel, had been dismissed. Not even these drastic measures, however, could divert the growing suspicion away from the President himself.

When the Senate hearings resumed on 17 May, John Dean claimed that Nixon had not only offered executive clemency to the Watergate defendants, but had also tried to buy their silence. It was then revealed that, since 1971, Nixon had recorded all his own conversations and telephone calls and that it would therefore be possible to confirm Dean's testimony.

The president, however, now refused to hand over the recordings. But the Federal Court of Appeal refused to be browbeaten and ordered him to deliver the tapes. In October, after a Supreme Court ruling, Nixon finally surrendered them, after the House of Representatives had initiated impeachment proceedings.

To the American public Nixon's guilt looked still more certain when it was revealed that two of the tapes were missing, which included the vital meeting with Dean. Moreover, part of a recording of a meeting between the president, Ehrlichman and Haldeman had been clumsily erased from another tape. Despite the evidence against him, Nixon hung on until February 1974, when he finally resigned and handed over power to Gerald Ford. Ford promised Nixon executive clemency so that he would escape trial for perjury.

The European Economic Community

When the European Community (EEC) came into existence in 1958, Britain refused to join it because of the difficulties of combining the EEC's common external tariff policy with its own existing trading obligations, the legacy of its imperial past, for Britain preserved its trade connections with the former colonies that made up the new Commonwealth.

To the countries engaged in building up the close-knit Community, Britain's attitude seemed inappropriate. So when in 1961 prime minister Macmillan, partly at the prompting of President Kennedy, began to explore the possibility of British membership, the French president de Gaulle gave a very cool response. At this time, Kennedy was urging Macmillan to seek a new role for Britain as part of the West European "pillar" of the Atlantic alliance.

President de Gaulle, however, was determined to develop the European Community as a "third force" independent of both the United States and the Soviet Union. He felt that admitting Britain would be letting in an undesirable bias toward US interests. During 1962 Edward Heath took part in intensive negotiations in Brussels covering all the technical details of Britain's application to join the EEC. By the end of the year, however, the application had fallen through, after a row over the politics of Western nuclear defense. Whereas the French nuclear force was being developed by and for France alone, Britain's had always been based on cooperation with the United States. In December 1962, President Kennedy met Macmillan in Nassau in the Bahamas and agreed to continue this arrangement. To de Gaulle this was further proof of Britain's non-European character and he used his veto to break off the EEC's entry negotiations with Britain.

By the mid-1960s Britain was regretting its isolation from Europe, for the importance of the European market had steadily grown. Encouraged by the other members of the EEC, apart from France, Harold Wilson's Labour government, in 1967, tried again to gain entry. De Gaulle still believed that Britain was too close to the United States, and too tied by obligations to the Commonwealth, but hoped for an Anglo-French alliance to balance West Germany's influence in the Community and help contain US dominance overseas. When the French president's motives were revealed by a British diplomatic leak, there was a public outcry in Europe and negotiations for Britain's entry once again collapsed.

In December 1969, after de Gaulle's resignation, the six heads of the member governments announced their willingness to let Britain join. On 1 January 1973, Britain was formally admitted to the EEC. However, public opinion in Britain was divided on whether to accept the new European commitments or pursue the older ties with the Commonwealth. The Labour leader Wilson, not wishing to jeopardize his party's electoral prospects, promised a national referendum, the first in modern British history. Wilson became prime minister in 1974 and held the referendum in 1975. The result was an overwhelming endorsement of Britain's EEC membership.

Northern Ireland

From the early 1920s the six counties of Northern Ireland have been a partially self-governing province within the United Kingdom. Throughout its existence the province has been dominated by what has been called a "double minority" problem. Within the island of Ireland the Protestant "unionist" population, who are opposed to the "nationalist" cause of independence and wish to remain a part of the United Kingdom, are in a minority position numbering about a quarter of the total. The Northern Ireland state was set up to protect their interests with its boundaries carefully drawn to ensure a unionist electoral majority. However, one effect was to create a disaffected nationalist minority of some 30 percent within the new state which was hostile to its very existence and sought unification with the "Free State" in the south.

◀▼ Ulster's political troubles are rooted in its religious past: evocations of the triumph of Protestant forces at the Battle of the Boyne in 1692 and the continuing strength of the Orange Order are products of the importation of a Protestant community into a traditionally Catholic society three centuries ago. The Catholic population justifiably claims that it has been discriminated against, while its Protestant counterpart defends rights which it fears would be swept away in a Catholic state.

The outbreak of civil strife in 1968 followed the demand by the nationalist minority, who felt themselves politically and economically discriminated against, for their full rights as United Kingdom citizens. This call for reform within Northern Ireland aroused the suspicion of many unionists who felt it was an attempt to undermine the very existence of that state and further the cause of a united Ireland. The failure of the regime to reform itself led to an escalation of the conflict and the decision in 1972 by the British government to suspend the northern parliament and rule directly from London.

Early attempts at a solution concentrated on tackling the minority's grievances and on efforts to promote some sort of power sharing between the nationalist and unionist communities within Northern Ireland. However, with the continued escalation of the conflict and the re-emergence of the Provisional Irish Republican Army (IRA), the military wing of radical nationalism, more fundamental questions about the constitutional status of Northern Ireland and the possibility of unification with the south forced themselves on to the agenda. These issues have provoked major disagreement between the southern Irish state, which claims *de jure* jurisdiction over the north, and the British government, which has pledged to maintain the constitutional position until a majority in the north demands change. In practice both sides made concessions. An agreement of 1985 indicated an unequivocal acceptance by both sides that the problem was a joint one: the southern state was given a consultative role regarding policy in Northern Ireland in return for which it recognized that Irish reunification could only follow from its acceptance by the majority in the north.

▼ Violence in an urban wasteland. While Ulster has always been troubled by politico-religious tensions, the upswing in violence and discontent after 1968 was strongly connected with the stagnation of the regional economy. Unemployment, poverty and urban decay produced a discontented young generation susceptible to the sectarian message and willing to look for escape either in the turmoil of riot and destruction of property, or, more dangerously, in enlistment in armed terrorist groups.

YOUTH POWER

A striking feature of the 20th century has been the major role played by youth in the many violent upheavals and revolutionary movements which have so dramatically affected traditional political structures all over the world. It was among the young that Lenin recruited the most enthusiastic supporters of his vanguard strategy for engineering the Marxist overthrow of czarist Russia and who went on to supply the new cadres of the Soviet state. It was squads of ex-combatants, many of them still in their teens, who made up the rank-and-file of Mussolini's infant *Fascismo* in 1919, and their ruthless use of terror tactics against the "reds" which culminated in the March on Rome in 1922. In Germany the Hitler Youth coordinated the disparate youth movements which had sprung up at the turn of the century into a highly politicized section of the NSDAP (Nazi party), while the membership not only of the paramilitary SA and the SS, but the entire Nazi movement, was predominantly under 30. In the 1960s the radical disaffection with consensus values experienced by the postwar generation erupted, and within a few years militant students were throwing down the gauntlet to governments in both East and West, accusing them of collusion with imperialist aggression or with suppressing "true" democracy.

The emergence of the young as a new constituency of political activism can be traced to the break-up of traditional power structures and the rise of populist and activistic politics. In the 19th century the most important ideologue of democratic nationalism, Mazzini, declared war against the old order in the name of a Young Italy, and the success of the *risorgimento* to unite Italy inspired "young" liberation movements in a number of European countries still under foreign domination.

But it was particularly in the wake of World War I that a small but vociferous section of the young became convinced that they had both the mission and the power to eradicate the evils of "old" Europe, whether absolutist or liberal, so as to create a new society. For a time the clashes between the ultra-left and the ultra-right which ensued threatened to eclipse liberalism for good. Though the defeat of fascism reestablished liberal norms in Europe and with them the rule of the older generation, the radicalism of youth continued to be the dynamo of political violence and mass militancy.

Since 1960 the fanaticism of youth has been the major component of the politics of violence which has erupted throughout the world. In China's Cultural Revolution and in many struggles against foreign domination or fight for a higher ideal of ethnic or human solidarity, young people have provided the bulk of the freedom fighters and terrorists. And in many instances, following the lead of the student radicals of the 1960s, their fight has been seen as a crusade against the "gerontocracies" (hierarchies dominated by the old) which seem to have lost sight of the true needs of society.

► In May 1968 a wave of hostility to proposals for changes in higher education in France quickly developed into a fullscale attack on the authority of the government. Its political and ideological foundations were questioned, and the students sought to combine their opposition movement with that of the leftwing trade unions. For several days the country approached civil war, as barricades were thrown up in the center of Paris and the riot police sought to re-establish government authority.

► A boy in Belfast, armed with petrol bomb and gas mask in the early 1970s, exemplified the trend towards the involvement of extreme youth in some of the world's most intractable political trouble-spots, such as Belfast and Beirut.

▼ The Khmer Rouge, who took over the government of Cambodia in 1975 and were responsible for the persecution of anyone with even the slightest contact with Western society or ideas, relied heavily on often undisciplined teenagers. Their fanatical xenophobia was inspired by a form of nationalist vision.

▲ The Hitler Youth movement combined a wholesome image with a paramilitary training that did much to make the rise of the Nazis acceptable to many Germans.

▲ Protests against US involvement in Vietnam resulted in the killing by the National Guard of four students at Kent State University, Ohio, in May 1970.

▶▼ Students protesting against corruption and the rule of old men in China in 1989 were seen as such a threat that the government killed more than a thousand.

THE
CONSUMER
BOOM

Time Chart

	1961	1962	1963	1964	1965	1966
Industry	• Jan: 60 million rouble credit for Poland to aid the construction of the Comecon pipeline (USSR) • Jun–Aug: Rural protest over the failure of the government to equalize living standards between industry and agriculture (Fr)	• Mar: Central committee and ministerial department of the Politburo decide to improve material incentives in agriculture (USSR) • Nov: US minister of agriculture criticizes agricultural policy of EEC • Agricultural crisis in the Soviet Union	• Mar: Five year supply contract signed between the US Standard Oil Company and the Italian enterprise ENI • May: Krupp manager B. Beitz begins trade negotiations in the Soviet Union (FRG) • Oct: Contract between the Phillips Petroleum Company, the Pan-American Oil Company and Egypt (USA/Egy)	• Jun: Soviet–Polish contract regarding Soviet aid for the Polish petroleum, natural gas and copper industry • Oct: US president Johnson signs the "Food for Freedom" program • Nov: Indonesia places British firms under Indonesian control to prevent the alleged British support for Malaysia	• Feb: West German company, Krupp, and Poland agree on industrial cooperation and on construction of manufacturing plants in Poland • Dec: East German leader Ulbricht announces the establishment of industrial ministries • Plans for land reform in Chile	• Aug: Contract between the Soviet Union and the Italian company Fiat regarding the construction of a motor plant on the Volga (USSR) • Sep: French automobile company Renault builds motor plants in Romania and Bulgaria
Technology	• 12 Apr: Soviet space station Vostok 1 begins operation, manned by the first cosmonaut Yuri Gagarin • W. Haack develops electronic flight security (FRG)	• The satellite Telstar allows TV transmission between Europe and USA • General Motors install the first industrial robots (USA)	• NASA news satellite Relay 1 transmits news exchanges between newspaper offices in UK, USA and Brazil	• Satellite Ranger 7 delivers pictures of the Moon surface at close range (USA) • Development of CT scanning by A.M. Cormack and G.N. Hounsfield (USA)	• First commercial satellite Early Bird begins transmitting TV programmes between USA and Europe	• First Moon satellite Luna 10 begins operation (USSR) • Development of laser radar (Jap)
Finance	• Oct: Gold pool established in London	• 5 Jan: General Arrangements to Borrow (GAB) among the ten major industrial countries decided by the IMF • Mar: First swap agreement between the Federal Reserve Board of the USA and the Bank of France, later also with the Bundesbank • May: Agreement between US Treasury and Swiss National Bank on long term monetary cooperation • New Industrial Development Bank established by the IFC	• May: Special credit of $250 million to support the pound (USA/UK) • Beginning of cooperation between the Deutsche Bank, the Midland Bank, the Banque de la Société Générale and the Amsterdam Bank • The first large loan of the World Bank (in 1947, of $250 million) repaid by the Credit National de France	• Dec: Prolongation of the European Monetary Agreement agreed until 1965 • IMF and central banks of Western Europe, USA and Canada support the British pound and the Italian lira with credits • Interest Equalization Tax in the USA aggravates the issue of foreign loans and shares	• Sep: Suspension of the 25% covering by gold for the minimum reserves (USA) • Currency reforms and the introduction of new currencies in Brazil, Argentina and Albania • Establishment of the African Development Bank • Merger of the Société Générale, Banque d'Anvers and Société Belge de Banque to form the Société Générale de Banque (Bel)	• Jun: Basle Agreement between UK and several European central banks to finance the short term deficit in the British balance of payments • Aug: The Development Bank of Asia established • Aug: Establishment of the Woschod Commercial Bank in Zürich by the Soviet government (Switz) • Formation of the Banque Nationale de Paris as a result of mergers (Fr)
Economic Policy	• Apr: Reorganization of the economic administrative structure agreed (USSR) • Jul: The committee for the United States of Europe demands a common fund of European currency reserves • Sep: Publication of the Jacobson plan to reform the world monetary system, involving the establishment of a fund of $5 billion.	• Mar: Constitution of the National Economic Development Council (UK) • Jul: Fourth economic and social plan enforced (Fr) • Oct: Trade Expansion Act initiated by US president Kennedy • Nov: Khrushchev demands a basic reorganization of the economic structure. Establishment of vertically structured organizations for the control of industry and agriculture (USSR)	• Jan: US president Kennedy publishes a program reducing taxes • Mar: Establishment of the Labor and Economy Council. Suspension of the seven-year plans (USSR) • Jun: EEC commission decides to intensify the common European monetary policy, but postpones monetary integration • Sep: French prime minister Pompidou publishes an economic stability program. End of the price spiral and a tax reform planned	• Mar: Economic Opportunity Act: the establishment of a corporation to counter poverty (USA) • May: Establishment of a committee of experts – the Segre commission – to survey the European capital market • Oct: Labour government imposes 15% import tax to improve the balance of payments (UK)	• Jan: Consumer goods enterprises freed from the constraints of the planned economy (USSR) • Feb: French president de Gaulle and the financial expert J. Rueff demand a return to the gold standard (Fr) • Jun: British prime minister publishes a ten-point economic program for modernizing industry by promoting investment, research and export (UK) • Reform of the world monetary system discussed	• Feb: Establishment of the Ministry of Technology for the modernization of British industry • Feb: New five-year plan in the Soviet Union. Transformation of the first 36 plants into a new centrally guided economic system • Apr: Agreement on economic cooperation between West Germany and Israel
International	• Mar: European Council demands increased cooperation with the OECD • Jun: Legislation regarding the establishment of the Latin American Free Trade Association (LAFTA) comes into force • Jul: 18th session of GATT requests negotiations on tariffs with the EEC, EFTA and LAFTA	• Jun: Council of the EEC decides to carry through the second step to a common market. Twelve decrees are issued regarding the creation of a common agricultural market • Jul: End of the fifth tariff conference of GATT with agreement on the reduction of tariffs	• Apr: Establishment of the Comecon Bank by the Comecon countries • Dec: First Comecon plan for common scientific and technological development enforced • Dec: EFTA countries agree with the demand for a 50% tariff reduction for the coming round of GATT talks • France opposes British application to join the EEC	• Mar: Opening of the UN conference on trade and development (UNCTAD) • May: Opening of the Kennedy round of the GATT talks. 50% tariff reduction demanded • Jun: Romania opposes establishment of a Soviet, Bulgarian and Romanian economic complex in the Danube area • Sep: EEC commission demands the suspension of all internal tariffs	• Jan: US government encourages trade with Eastern Europe • Mar: Decision on the combination of the three European communities, the EEC, ECSC and Euratom • Mar: 22nd GATT discusses the compatibility of regional tariff communities with the aims of GATT as a whole • Nov: An amalgamation of the EEC and EFTA discussed, to avoid the division of Western Europe into two economic communities	• Apr: 23rd session of GATT discusses trade with developing countries and free trade movements • Jun: Establishment of the Asian and Pacific Council (ASPAC) by Asian and Pacidic countries for economic and political cooperation • Jun: The EEC countries agree on a common agricultural market • Dec: EFTA discusses the possibility of joining the EEC
Misc.	• 13 Aug: Construction of the first stage of the Berlin Wall (GDR)	• Oct: US blockade of Cuba after the installation there of Soviet nuclear missiles	• 22 Nov: Assassination of US president Kennedy in Dallas, Texas. Mass demonstrations of the civil rights movement led by Martin Luther King (USA)	• Oct: Soviet leader Khrushchev is ousted by L. Brezhnev (USSR)	• USA officially takes part in the Vietnam War • West Germany and Israel take up diplomatic relations	• Jan: I. Gandhi becomes prime minister of India • Sep: Beginning of the Cultural Revolution in China

1967	1968	1969	1970	1971	1972	1973
• Apr: National aid for the French computer industry • May: US House of Representatives authorizes the building of the largest desalination plant in the world • Dec: Transformation of the first Soviet Kolchoses into a new centrally guided economic system (USSR)	• 27 Feb: Food and Agriculture Act passed to stabilize the US home market. "Food for Freedom" plan initiated to build up a national food reserve (USA) • 21 Mar: Merger of three British computer firms with government support to form International Computers Limited (ICL)	• Sep: Measures taken to protect agriculture after decontrol of the exchange markets (USA) • Dec: Renault shares distributed among employees (Fr)	• Feb: 20 year contract signed between USSR and West German company Mannesmann regarding the supply of Soviet natural gas to West Germany • Jun: Discovery of rich oilfields in the North Sea • 4 Jul: Libya nationalizes all its oil companies	• 4 Feb: Bankruptcy of the British Rolls Royce company. Government announces a partial takeover (UK) • Feb: US aircraft manufacturer Lockheed in financial difficulties (USA) • Libya nationalizes British Petroleum (BP)	• May: Decision to build a petroleum pipeline from Alaska into the USA	• Jan: Merger of the two British airlines BEA and BOAC to form British Airways (BA) (UK) • Oct: Iraq nationalizes US oil companies Exxon and Mobil Oil • Dec: Peru nationalizes largest US mining concern Cerro de Pasco Corporation
• 30 Apr: Opening of the 577 m high Moscow TV and telephone aerial mast	• Negative effects of thalidomide drug on children discovered • 31 Dec: First commercial flight of a supersonic passenger aircraft (USSR)	• E. Hoff constructs the first silicon microprocessor (USA)	• 12 Jan: First flight of a Boeing 747 • Supersonic passenger aircraft Concorde reaches Mach 2 (twice the speed of sound) (Fr/UK)	• 18 Dec: Completion of the world's largest hydroelectric power station in Krasnoyarsk (USSR)	• 17 Feb: The Volkswagen overtakes the sales record of the Model T (FRG) • Prohibition of DDT in the USA because of environmental damage	• 1 Oct: Opening of a natural gas pipeline from the Ukraine to West Germany
• 18 Nov: Devaluation of the pound. UK receives a large international credit of $3 billion to support the pound • Nov: Devaluation of currencies in Israel, New Zealand, Spain and Denmark • Nov: Introduction of minimum reserves for banks (Fr) • Establishment of the International Commercial Bank and the Société Financière Européenne	• Mar: Suspension of the 25% covering of banknotes by gold (USA) • Mar: Dissolution of the gold pool as a result of international speculation in gold • 17 Mar: Monetary conference held in Washington to organize the international gold market. A gold price of $35 per ounce agreed for transactions among central banks • Nov: French franc under pressure	• Aug: Devaluation of the franc. Credits from the IMF and some central banks made to support it (Fr) • West Germany becomes the greatest exporter of capital in the world with an amount of DM 23 billion per annum • Apr: Poland demands the transferability of the currencies of the Comecon countries	• Sep: Conference of the IMF in Copenhagen. Three alternatives proposed to reorganize the international monetary relations: freeing of the exchange rates, alteration of the exchange rates step by step, extension of the margins of fluctuations of the exchange rates • Banque Européenne de Credit à Moyen Terme established by several European private banks	• 16 Aug: US balance of trade shows a deficit for the first time since 1894. Suspension of the convertiblity of the dollar into gold • Dec: declaration of 77 developing countries, demanding participation in decisions on a new world monetary system	• 24 Apr: Currency agreement of the EEC countries enforced. The margin of fluctuation between currencies not to exceed 2.1/4% • Temporary flotation of the pound (UK)	• 12 Feb: Devaluation and flotation of the dollar • 9 Mar: EEC countries decide to introduce a joint float against the dollar • Mar: Temporary closing of exchange markets around the world. End of the Bretton Woods monetary system, and a new system of floating exchange rates comes into being • Nov: Agreement signed allowing central banks to sell gold at market places
• May: legislation enforced enabling the French government to execute economic and social measures by decree • Jul: Nationalization of the British steel industry • Jul: Transformation of the first Sovkhozes and railways into a new economic system (USSR)	• Jan: Minister president Werner of Luxembourg demands a common European monetary policy • Dec: Publication of Barre plan for the introduction of a European Monetary Union (Fr)	• Jan: Report on the economic situation by the US government. Balance of trade positive for the first time since 1957 • Jan: Nationalization of the British steel industry completed • May: Appeal of 99 European scholars to reform the international monetary system. Free exchange rates demanded • Dec: Conference of the EEC countries in The Hague. Gradual introduction of European economic and monetary union discussed	• Consultations among the EEC countries regarding the introduction of a European Monetary Union (Barre plan) • Jan: National Council for prices and income replaced by the Commission for Industry and Labor force (UK) • Mar: Iceland becomes a member of EFTA • Oct: Werner plan for the introduction of European Monetary Union published • Oct: Council of EEC countries criticizes protectionism in US trade legislature	• Jun: Conference of the EEC countries to discuss a reorganization of the European monetary system and closer economic cooperation • 29 Jul: Comecon enforces a 20-year plan toward socialist economic integration • 16 Aug: US government declares introduction of a 10% tax and a wage freeze for 90 days due to national emergency. Consultations between US monetary experts and EEC commission to discuss the international monetary and exchange crisis	• Feb: UK Miners' strike. Increase in the rate of unemployment • Apr: Inaugural meeting of a commission for economic and scientific cooperation between the USSR and West Germany • May: West German finance minister Schiller demands a drastic reduction of public deficit spending (FRG) • Oct: Negotiations between the USSR and USA to set up trade relations	• Jan: British prime minster Heath publishes the second phase of his anti-inflation program • 9 Mar: Meeting of the finance ministers and the central bank governors of the "Group of Ten" countries in Paris to discuss the exchange crisis • Apr: The ministers of finance of the EC countries decide to establish a European fund for monetary cooperation • Oct–Dec: OPEC raises the oil price from $3.01 to $11 per barrel. Shock for the Western industrial nations
• Jan: Complete tariff freedom among the EFTA countries comes into force • May: Conclusion of the Kennedy round of the GATT talks. Reduction of tariffs demanded • Jun: Monnet commission of the EEC proposes economic cooperation between the EEC, Comecon and the USA • Aug: Plan published for a second world trade conference and a common international trade center	• Feb: UN conference on trade and development opened. Discussion on development assistance and East–West trade • Aug: Romania rejects the proposal to transform Comecon into a supranational organization with a supranational plan • 25 Nov: GATT session agrees on enlargement of trade • Dec: EEC countries agree upon cooperation in scientific research	• Apr: Romania demands the opening of Comecon to non-Communist countries • Jun: Association agreement between the EEC and 18 African countries • Sep: Meeting of the council of EFTA attempts to overcome the economic division of Europe • Oct: East German government demands a greater integration of the economies within Comecon	• Feb: 26th GATT session discusses the problem of enlarging trade in industrial and agricultural products • Jul: Establishment of an International Investment Bank by Commonwealth countries • Jul: CECLA countries formulate their intentions regarding economic relations with the EEC • Oct: UNCTAD conference agrees on a program in favor of developing countries	• Jun: Australia gains membership of the OECD • Jun: First special conference of UN Industrial Development Organization (UNIDO). Developing countries demand that this organization be more independent from the industrial countries • Nov: 26th GATT session defines special rights for developing countries • Austria, Sweden and Norway seek entry to the EEC	• Mar: US finance minister Conally proposes the enlargement of the "Group of Ten" in the IMF • Apr: Comecon bank issues a loan of $60 million to the Eurodollar market • Jul: Interim agreement between the EEC countries and Austria comes into force • Jul: Free trade agreement between the EEC and EFTA countries signed	• Jan: UK, Denmark and Ireland join the EEC • Jun: 27th session of Comecon discusses closer cooperation between its member countries and the machine-building industry • Sep: Conference in Tokyo discusses the necessity of new negotiations in connection with GATT
• 5-10 Jun: Six-Day War, the third Arab–Israeli conflict	• 20-21 Aug: Dubček's "Prague Spring" reform movement suppressed by the Red Army (Czech)	• Aug: Riots in Belfast and Londonderry lead to British military intervention (Irl) • Sep: Military revolt in Libya led by Colonel Muammar Qadhafi	• Salvador Allende becomes president of Chile	• 25 Apr: Establishment of Bangladesh	• 30 Jan: Escalation of the civil war in Northern Ireland leads to "Bloody Sunday"	• Oct: Yom Kippur war, the fourth Arab–Israeli conflict, leads to a worldwide oil crisis

Datafile

The outstanding features of this period for the advanced Western nations were steady prosperity and economic growth. Never before had the world known so high a rate of economic expansion so free of major disturbances. In consequence, for the first time in history the large mass of the population was lifted out of the realm of the elementary curses of humanity, hunger, cold and preventable disease. An expanding net of social services allowed even the weaker members of the community to share in some of the economic goods now available. The population settled down to low rates of increase, so that high overall economic growth was translated into high growth per head.

The main structural changes associated with this expansion were the move out of agriculture and the rise in services and in goods formerly considered luxuries. After traditional needs such as housing and clothing had been met, consumers turned to products made available by new technologies such as electronics, and to leisure pursuits, above all travel.

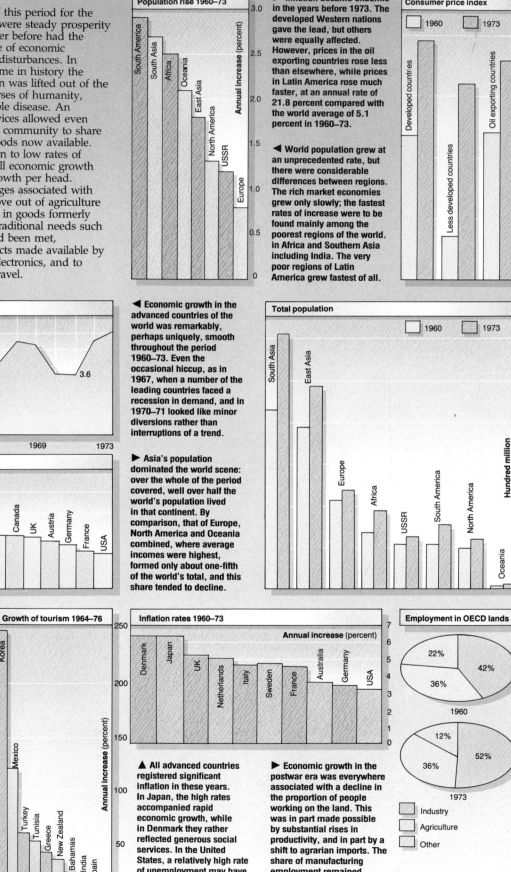

Population rise 1960–73

► Inflation became endemic in the years before 1973. The developed Western nations gave the lead, but others were equally affected. However, prices in the oil exporting countries rose less than elsewhere, while prices in Latin America rose much faster, at an annual rate of 21.8 percent compared with the world average of 5.1 percent in 1960–73.

◄ World population grew at an unprecedented rate, but there were considerable differences between regions. The rich market economies grew only slowly; the fastest rates of increase were to be found mainly among the poorest regions of the world. In Africa and Southern Asia including India. The very poor regions of Latin America grew fastest of all.

Consumer price index

Western GDP growth rate

◄ Economic growth in the advanced countries of the world was remarkably, perhaps uniquely, smooth throughout the period 1960–73. Even the occasional hiccup, as in 1967, when a number of the leading countries faced a recession in demand, and in 1970–71 looked like minor diversions rather than interruptions of a trend.

Total population

► Asia's population dominated the world scene: over the whole of the period covered, well over half the world's population lived in that continent. By comparison, that of Europe, North America and Oceania combined, where average incomes were highest, formed only about one-fifth of the world's total, and this share tended to decline.

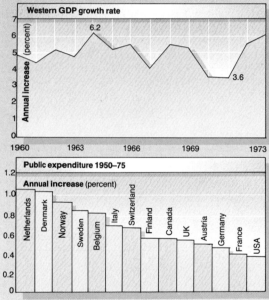

Public expenditure 1950–75

Annual increase (percent)

▲ Public expenditure is made up of several different items, including the costs of government and defense, social welfare costs including education, and transfer payments, such as pensions, among others. It is noticeable that the smaller democracies of northern Europe had the highest rates of public expenditure as a share of national income.

► Tourism is a fickle industry, and popular preferences may change rapidly. Korea's rise in popularity started from very low figures, whereas the poor showing of Italy, Spain and Greece relates to their high starting position. Ever more exotic countries were being developed for well-heeled Western and Japanese tourist.

Growth of tourism 1964–76

Inflation rates 1960–73

Annual increase (percent)

▲ All advanced countries registered significant inflation in these years. In Japan, the high rates accompanied rapid economic growth, while in Denmark they rather reflected generous social services. In the United States, a relatively high rate of unemployment may have helped to keep cost increases down.

► Economic growth in the postwar era was everywhere associated with a decline in the proportion of people working on the land. This was in part made possible by substantial rises in productivity, and in part by a shift to agrarian imports. The share of manufacturing employment remained virtually constant; service industries grew.

Employment in OECD lands

1960: 42%, 36%, 22%
1973: 52%, 36%, 12%

Industry
Agriculture
Other

PROSPERITY AND OPTIMISM

High employment and
increasing affluence

A new lifestyle

Transport and tourism

The education explosion

Social and welfare
provisions

Inflation, tariffs and
trade

Exchange rates and
currency systems

In view of the immense physical and economic damage suffered by the belligerent countries in the course of World War II, it was not surprising that in the immediate postwar years plenty of work was available for all who wanted it. Towns and cities needed rebuilding, and capital equipment had to be brought up to prewar levels. In the early 1950s, the needs of the Korean war kept up the level of demand in Western countries and in Japan. After that, however, it was widely thought that a slump would set in, following a pattern seen at similar times in the past. But that slump never came. Instead, in the years to 1973, the world enjoyed boom conditions and rapidly rising incomes for longer and at a higher level than ever before.

This great boom was worldwide, affecting the Western capitalist countries, the Eastern planned economies and even the poorer and developing nations of what came to be known as the "Third World". As far as the market economies were concerned, it had its origin in the advanced countries of the West – in effect, Western Europe, the United States and Canada, Australia and New Zealand, and Japan – and from there it spread by means of international trade, international capital transfers in the form of loans and investments, and the consequent opportunities to catch up on the latest technological advances. The growth

▼ The Easter holiday crowds
on the beach at Ostend,
Belgium, in 1964 show how
increased prosperity has
brought more leisure as well
as the means to travel. In the
postwar years, the working
population in most Western
countries has achieved a
higher income and more free
time.

path was not entirely smooth, and there were years of slower growth, like 1967 and again 1970–71, but these were minor disturbances only, and the faster upward movement was soon resumed. Not all countries advanced at the same speed, as measured by the annual increases in gross national product (GNP) or gross domestic product (GDP), which are taken as representing the sum total of all economic goods and services created. Japan's high growth rate, for instance, was in a class of its own. But even the laggards, like the United Kingdom, year after year achieved rates of growth without parallel in their history.

There is no agreement about the causes of this long period of high employment and fast growth in the West. Certainly, most governments set out to achieve one or both of these aims, and many took as their guide the ideas of the British economist John Maynard Keynes (1883–1946), who believed that the level of employment could be influenced by government action. The apparent success of the boom years even led to the widespread belief that the means of preventing unemployment and stagnation were now known and that national economies could in future be steered at will. Unfortunately, this proved to be wrong, and the causes of the end of the boom have turned out to be as controversial as the causes of its long duration.

▼ Carnaby Street, London, became a symbol for one area of development in the consumer society. Its fashion goods were not necessarily cheap, but they could be afforded by the young wage and salary earners. The emphasis was not merely on brightness and color, but on unconventionality and irreverence. What was new was the independence and spending power of that age group. Whole new industries and distribution agencies were called into being to cater for this new market selling pop records, clothing and holidays abroad. Fashion remained, as ever, at the center of this new lifestyle.

Growth in output and productivity was, as always, not merely the result of technical improvements. It was also accompanied by structural changes, some of which had already been going on for a long time, and continued, or accelerated, in this period. Among the most important of these was the reduction in the share of agriculture, and the rise in the share of services, within the totals of employment and output of each country. This was a pattern to be found in all economies, poor ones as well as advanced ones. There was also a shift out of less productive industries such as textiles into more productive ones such as motor manufacturing, and a relative expansion of industries using newer technologies, including electrical and electronic equipment, chemicals and machine tools. This reflected partly the new technical possibilities, partly the changes in consumer demand. For as incomes rose, the consumption of food in the richer countries increased only slightly, though its composition changed, and the demand for clothing also rose relatively little. Against this, however, expenditure on consumer durables,

luxury goods and relatively fast leisure pursuits rose. The mass consumption of goods formerly available only to the rich, or to the richest countries, was a major feature of this long boom. The rise in ownership of private motor cars is typical of this development. Its widespread use brought about alterations in the location of housing, workplaces and shops; and such increased mobility in turn required more roads, more garages and more filling stations.

Leisure and travel

In all countries, people tended to claim some of the increase in productivity not in the form of more goods, but of more leisure. In all advanced countries in the West total annual hours worked were reduced, on an average by one-ninth, in the period 1960–73. In their free time, people were able to seek new forms of cultural activities, of sports and entertainment. Above all, they took the opportunity to travel farther for their holidays. Increasingly this meant travel abroad, and in Europe and North America, especially to the sun. Every summer, a wave of tourists now descended on the Mediterranean from northern Europe, and on Central America and the Caribbean from North America, arriving by boat, by rail, by car and bus, and increasingly by air.

Mobility and migration

Centers of employment themselves now enjoyed greater freedom of choice of location, now that the source of power was no longer the nearby coalmine or the local waterfall. Instead, the electricity grid now supplied power equally to all parts of most advanced countries. As a result, the new factories were found increasingly in the most pleasant parts of their countries, such as the Mediterranean coast in France, the south coast in Britain, the southern Länder in Germany, and California in the United States. A gap began to open up in some countries, such as Britain and Italy, between the prosperous regions of the country, with their new industries and modern cities, and the older industrial areas, with their grimy towns and declining industries.

People moved to the new jobs within their countries, but there was also a high rate of migration across the borders, from the poorer, less developed countries of Europe to the industrial

▲ With rising standards, consumers began to demand fashion and design. Some retailers profited by offering to a wide public the kind of up-market design in goods for the home that had previously been the preserve of a small privileged class. Some most interesting developments in retain distribution have taken place among those catering for upwardly mobile newly prosperous consumers.

► The every-increasing streams of summer tourists led to new developments in the areas they visited. The poorer countries around the Mediterranean gained particularly, partly because their prices were still low, from the new opportunities opened up for holidaymakers from the industrial countries of Europe and their families. In many favoured spots tourism brought much-needed capital investment and employment, and raised incomes. Hotels and apartment blocks began a new era of development. Spain was one of the first countries in southern Europe to benefit from this new influx of tourism. Cadaqués in Spain was once an exclusive resourt for artists; by the 1970s it had begun to cater for a much wider clientele.

The Tourist Industry

Tourism was one of the fastest growing industries worldwide. In the ten years from 1962 to 1972 tourist expenditure probably trebled. In some cases, the very high annual increase in tourist receipts reflected a low starting point, in others they continued to rise from a level that was initially high. Spain, for example, which had received 200,000 foreign tourists in 1930 and 6 million in 1960, welcomed 33 million in 1973. The other "cheaper" Mediterranean countries, including Greece, Turkey, Malta, Israel, Cyprus and Portugal as well as North Africa, also registered large increases. Mexico and the Bahamas had the same experience in the Western Hemisphere. Growth rates were lower in some of the more traditional holiday areas, such as Austria, Switzerland, France and Italy. But in these countries winter tourism was expanding fast. In West Germany, for example, where 565,000 took a winter holiday in 1960–61, this figure reached 3,157,000 in 1975–76. However, even in 1976 the developed countries still took 83 percent of tourist receipts, the developing world only 17 percent. It was a form of expenditure which, on a mass basis, was confined to the richer countries; for some of the poorer it was becoming a vital source of income.

◀ In Europe skiing, once an exclusive sport of the very rich and highly privileged and of a small number of fanatical sportsmen, became a mass sport, as more and more people were able to take a second holiday in the winter, and travel abroad to enjoy it. But the conditions under which skiing took place changed as it attracted more and more people. The journey to the resorts became increasingly overcrowded and uncomfortable, and formerly quiet Alpine villages were turned into busy townships as huge concrete hotels were built to accommodate the tourists.

regions, from the French and British colonies to the mother country and from Latin America to the United States, as well as, in more traditional paths, from Europe to Canada, the United States and Australia. Between 1960 and 1974, Belgium, France, West Germany, Luxembourg, Sweden, The Netherlands, and Switzerland accepted between them a net total of 1,655,000 immigrants. Altogether, the nine countries of the EEC had 10.4 million immigrants inside their borders at the beginning of 1973, more than four percent of the population. In the United States, despite immigration controls imposed in the 1950s, migration represented almost 16 percent of the population increase in the 1960s, and in Canada it was 21.9 percent, not counting the illegal immigrants. Welcoming the immigrants in the period of labor shortage, most Western countries began to introduce restrictions on further immigration in 1973–74, when the boom appeared to be over and rising unemployment raised the specter of anti-foreigner sentiments.

▼ The consumer boom also spread to other continents. São Paulo, the industrial capital of Brazil, with a population of some eight million people at the time, was forced to separate cars and pedestrians to allow the rush-hour traffic to proceed. The cars on the streets were mainly Americna imports, but Volkswagens were also prominent; increasingly, large multinational companies were building factories in developing countries to produce vehicles on the spot.

The education explosion
It is possible to see the rising provision of education as yet another way in which people made use of the increasing flow of goods and services now available to them. Education may be viewed as being valuable in itself, as well as a way of increasing the productivity of the labor force in the long term. In the postwar boom, there was a veritable explosion in the numbers going to universities or other institutes of higher education.

The United States led in this respect, spending a higher proportion of national income per head than other countries on education, yet keeping its lead even as the rest of the Western world also advanced. This emphasis on education has been seen as an alternative to the provision of other social services, in which the United States was lagging behind, perhaps reflecting the American preference for individual self-help as against social care. In 1960, the United States spent 5.3 percent of its national income on education, compared with 5 percent in Sweden and 4.7 percent in The Netherlands; most of the rest of Europe, as well as Japan, spent between 4.5 and 3.5 percent. In the following years the proportion of secondary scholars among the 10- to 19-year-olds in the 13 developed countries of Western and Northern Europe rose dramatically and the proportion of university–level students among the 20- to 24-year-olds almost doubled.

The expansion of welfare provisions
General social and welfare provisions by the state were also everywhere on the increase. Formerly separate provisions were being consolidated into single, unified schemes, as in Italy in 1965, The Netherlands in 1966, Norway in 1970, Belgium in 1970 and West Germany in 1972.

A specific development which caused much controversy was the support given to regions and to economic sectors suffering from longterm industrial decline. There was widespread consent for sharing out, in the form of aid, some of the benefits of progress among less fortunate groups, such as Belgian coalminers, the inhabitants of the old industrial areas of Britain and of the impoverished South in Italy. There was less agreement on the Common Agricultural Policy (CAP) the European Community's scheme to encourage and enlarge production by offering subsidies to farmers. By the later 1960s it had led to massive overproduction of food and other agrarian products to the point of endangering the finances of the community by its high cost, while it also blocked the export chances of poorer nations into the rich EEC market. Ironically, farming incomes still remained well below national average incomes everywhere, and the subsidies helped rich farmers more than poor ones.

The rise in social provisions was not unexpected, since there is always a tendency for government expenditure to rise disproportionately in booms, only to be cut back again in periods of stagnation. What was unusual was the continuing rise of wages as part of the national income. Normally their share falls in booms and rises in slumps, thus remaining more stable than

*The driver is not a
member of a class; by the
progress of motorization
he already represents the
mass of the population.
... The car is symbol and
instrument of the striving
of humanity for new
aims which can be
achieved only by
building good roads.*

GERMAN AUTOMOBILE
CLUB, 1965

the overall national income, while profits, the
other main component, take the brunt of the fluctuations. The reason why wages now continued
to rise has probably to be looked for in the longer-
term trend of income redistribution in the direction of greater equality. The strengthened social
security net, which set a floor to wages, may have
played a major part, together with the voting
power of wage earners at national elections.

These increases in government expenditure as
a share of total national outlay affected all Western
countries. By the mid-1970s, it was exceeding the
40 percent mark in most countries. Its momentum
was also kept up by the general wish to maintain
a high level of employment. This generally meant
that any perceived shortfall in overall demand
was met by increased government expenditure.
Such "Keynesian" methods did indeed lead to
high levels of employment throughout the
Western world, but they also led to a persistent
tendency to rising prices. It seemed that rising incomes and full employment were not to be enjoyed without a measure of inflation.

Inflation, tariffs and trade
Inflation became endemic in the Western world
in these years. However, inflation advanced at
different rates in different countries, and this was
bound to lead to problems in the trading and
payments balances between countries. In the

postwar years, statesmen had attempted by international agreements to remove many of the
causes of international imbalance which had
disrupted the world economy in the 1930s. The
International Monetary Fund (IMF) had been
designed to make it possible to hold to stable exchange rates between the different currencies,
and the General Agreement on Tariffs and Trade
(GATT) had tried to remove trade barriers by encouraging and spreading tariff concessions, while
inhibiting tariff rises or other obstructions to
trade. Both had had some effect, though possibly
less than their sponsors had hoped.

Many tariff rates were pushed down in the first
flush of enthusiasm, but thereafter they tended to
stick. The European Common Market and Free
Trade Area were matched by regional free trade
agreements in Latin America, the Caribbean,
Central Africa, East Africa and Southeast Asia,
though several of these had only modest significance.

The liberalization of world trade helped trade
to grow faster than production, so that international interdependence increased. But it increased much faster among the industrial nations,
in the form of the exchange of manufactures, than
between these nations and the developing world,
let alone between the developing countries themselves. Capital exports also expanded fast, and
a highly significant feature was the growth of

"multinational" concerns. About one-sixth of the world's total output of goods and services was at that time produced by the multinationals.

The American balance of payments crisis

Much of the undeniable success of liberalization in the postwar world rested on an unique configuration of the international economy. It depended, in fact, on the huge balance of payments surplus of the United States, which in turn rested on that country's overwhelming superiority in production and productivity. This surplus enabled the United States to finance the operations of the IMF, to provide loans and Marshall aid, to organize development aid in various forms, to make large capital inverstments abroad and still to conduct widespread military operations in many parts of the world as well. Backed by this surplus, the American dollar remained a desirable, "hard" currency throughout those years.

In the course of the 1960s the United States' lead in production fell rapidly as other countries began to catch up on American technology. In those years the growth in GNP and in manufacturing production was consistently lower in the United States than in any other advanced country except Britain. As a result, GDP per man hour fell heavily between 1960 and 1970: a lead of 90 percent over other advanced countries shrank to under 49 percent, and it continued to fall rapidly. Similarly, as a proportion of the total output of the world's market economies, measured as GDP, the figure for the United States fell from 45 percent in 1960 to 34 percent in 1973.

In the early postwar years, the strength of the dollar had made other countries willing to hold it as their national reserve currency, and this in turn confirmed it as a "hard" currency. As the American payments surpluses turned into deficits, the world found itself in the unaccustomed position of having to deal with a weakening dollar. Many transactions were adversely affected. Sterling was devalued in 1967 and the London gold pool, symbol of a common policy on gold, was suspended; the French franc was devalued in 1969 and general monetary uncertainty spread across the world. It was clear that the dollar had become overvalued, and in August 1971 US president Richard Nixon announced that the convertibility of the dollar (into gold) was suspended. Further, a temporary import tax of ten percent was introduced in the United States, and the IMF was asked to consider a new international monetary system.

This unilateral action taken in the interests of the United States while bypassing accepted international channels of consultation marked the end of a major phase of world monetary history, that of the gold–dollar standard. In an effort to prevent monetary chaos, representatives of the ten leading nations met at the Smithsonian Institution in December 1971 and agreed to a devaluation of the dollar against gold by 7.9 percent to $38 per ounce, without restoring the former obligation on the American monetary authorities to sell gold at that rate on demand. They also agreed on a widespread realignment of currency parities

or rates of exchange. Henceforth currencies should be allowed to diverge from those parities by a maximum of ±2.25 percent only, thus providing a new form of stability. At the same time, the US ten percent surcharge was scrapped.

This left the European countries dissatisfied. In March 1972, as the first stage towards a planned single European monetary system, they agreed to keep the permitted deviations from the official exchange rates to half the width of the band allowed under the Smithsonian agreement. However, by June the pound sterling was allowed to "float" free, and several other countries also left the monetary "snake". Others joined, and a bewildering series of changes ensued before the group emerged essentially as a cluster around the Deutschmark. Early in 1973 the dollar was devalued once more, by ten percent, making a total of 23 percent against OECD currencies (except Canada). In March of that year the European Community decided to float as a bloc against the dollar and against other currencies, and in April it agreed to start the Fund for Monetary Cooperation. The dollar itself was now floating and the brief phase of the dollar standard had, in effect, changed into a system of mutual "managed floating", with no firm anchor point for the system as a whole. It was not long before the system was put to the test: in October of the same year the first massive OPEC price rise for oil was announced. A major new source of world instability had emerged.

▲ Multinational companies were increasingly moving their production units into developing countries. Hundred of girls worked in serried ranks for the Philips electronics firm in a factory near São Paulo in Brazil. In the first phases of this transfer across cultures, the multinationals were making use of cheap, willing labor in order to lower their own costs, and were contributing to the movement of population into overcrowded Third World cities marked by poverty, pollution, exploitation and violence. However, in several cases it was just such foreign initiatives which provided the capital, and the knowhow as well as the training, both for workers and managers, on the basis of which native entrepreneurs were gradually able to develop their own economies and to strike out on the path of industrialization and modernization themselves.

The Multinationals

The period saw a sharp rise in the power of multinational corporations, based in one country but with branches in others. They were particularly strong in the extractive industries (notably oil), in manufacturing, and also in the service industries such as banking, retail distribution and hotels. In part, they represented the strength of American production after the war, carried beyond the borders of the home country into an economically weakened world; and American companies furnished by far the largest proportion of the multinationals. However, companies with headquarters in other countries also operated in the same manner. In the early postwar years, Britain was the second most important headquarters country after the United States, but more recently Japan-based companies have expanded fast in all continents. By 1978 the top 20 Japanese multinationals employed a total of 140,000 persons overseas. In the case of some European companies, so many changes have taken place that it is difficult to be certain where the centre of gravity lies or in whose interests the companies are administered. By the 1980s several of the largest multinationals had turnovers equivalent to the GNP of a moderate-sized industrial country.

The objects of expanding abroad were mixed. They included the wish to get inside a tariff barrier, to use cheap labor or cheap raw materials available abroad. There were also potential gains to be had from setting up subsidiaries outside one's own borders by the use of available capital, managerial and technical know-how, or the market created by advertising at home. A growing part of international trade went on within the multinational companies themselves,

supplying member units with raw materials, components and semi-manufactures for which prices could be artificial and unrealistic for the companies' own strategic reasons. There was growing fear in the receiving countries that significant parts of their economies would be controlled from abroad, and might be managed in the interests of foreign shareholders with no commitments to the communities in which the branches were established.

Concerned by these issues, the OECD in June 1976 produced a series of guidelines to member countries, which were intended to ensure that they should "refrain from actions which would adversely affect competition in the relevant market by abusing a dominant position of market power".

▲ Neon lights in Times Square, New York City, in the 1970s advertised brands of multinational products known practically all over the world. Goods were becoming increasingly standardized in more and more countries.

▼ Rio Tinto Zinc (RTZ) is a typical multinational. As it spread from its early mining interests in Spain, Latin America and Africa, it expanded from mining into smelting, making engineering products, construction materials and services, chemicals, oil and gas.

Rio Tinto Zinc: Portrait of a Multinational c.1973

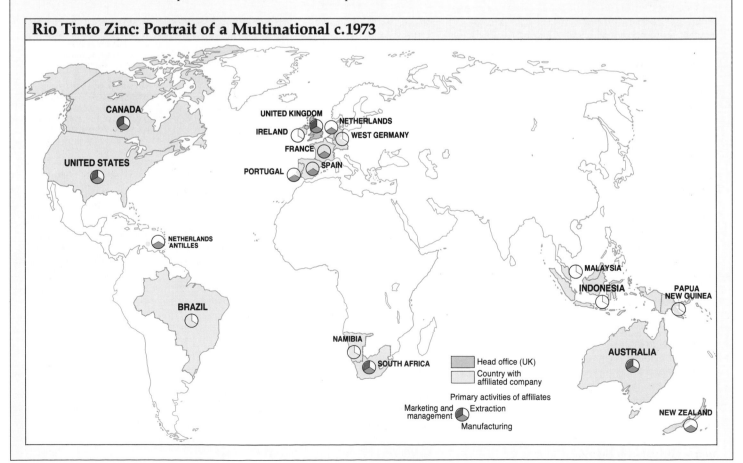

THE CONSUMER SOCIETY

As the basic necessities of life were increasingly well covered by the productive apparatus of the advanced industrial societies, the economic problem shifted from production to the sale of goods and services that can be considered luxuries rather than necessities. There had always been luxuries for a privileged section of the population, and their market had always been uncertain, but bulk products had varied only little. From the early 20th century, even the mass market for the population at large had become uncertain, while producers needed quantity orders to keep down costs of production. One method of bridging this contradiction between a fickle market and high fixed cost was advertising. This began to take up more and more resources, while making itself indispensable to the manufacturers. At the same time, it also began to affect the moral climate: the greed for possessions, the desire to outdo one's neighbor, the quest for luxury were made into acceptable virtues. Purchasing could turn into an end in itself – by the late 20th century the consumer society came into its prime.

Given that there were numerous people with spare income looking for something to spend it on, one method adopted by the advertisers was to create, in the interests of the producers, needs that had not existed before. In some cases, desires were nurtured for entirely new products or services. At other times, they were roused for the latest model, encouraged by built-in obsolescence. The discarded goods, such as second-hand cars, were then disposed of among ever-lower income strata until they landed on enormous scrap heaps, matching the waste of resources at one end with the disfigurement of the landscape at the other.

Moralists and those hostile to capitalism found much to criticize. Yet it could also plausibly be argued that an element of waste was a necessary price to pay for the undoubted drive to progress in the industrialized market economies. Certainly, no alternative proved equally effective, least of all the economies governed by planners with more puritan attitudes as to what constituted the necessities of life. Indeed, there were some indications that those brought up on limited goods without frills, for example in the Soviet Union, were even more easily swayed by glamor than those in daily contact with it.

The emphasis on female consumers, found in the advertising of the 1960s, has given way to a rather more balanced appeal in the 1980s, though the pretty girls were often meant to appeal to male, rather than female, buyers just as the handsome men were to catch the eyes of women. Many of the products and services pushed by the advertisers have lightened the burdens of women as housewives and as producers in the West. By contrast, the women in the East carried many of the burdens of the planning failures on their backs, as they spent their time in queues, struggled with inferior materials, and were expected to engage in full time work outside the home.

► Most Third-World large cities contain abject poverty as well as wealth and luxury. The people picking over a rubbish dump in Manila hope to live on the detritus of a consumer society, and their continuous daily activity proves that there is indeed sufficient among what has been discarded by others for families to live on, no matter how offensive and unhygienic the circumstances.

► Hairdressing salons were typical of the service element within the consumer economy, requiring frequent repeat visits and emphasizing a certain luxury by the rather lush image and the foreign name (French in English-speaking countries, English in France), which they sported. Curiously, in the inter-war years, most hairdressers cut men's hair, not women's. Women, except for the very rich, had their hair cared for at home.

►► Supermarkets not only lowered the costs of distribution compared with the small corner shop; they also developed new techniques of encouraging purchases, by making it easy to see the whole range available and help oneself to desirable goods.

▼ Naked girls as sales gimmicks for motor cars represent an attempt to make the particular model desirable by the association of ideas, and the abuse of women. By the 1980s, such exploitation of sex was frequently criticized though still used, even if more subtly.

▼ These 1960s women in a Moscow street, looking at high-fashion fur coats in a shop window, were probably not able to afford them. Yet there is clearly an appeal, even in a poor, planned economy, in luxury goods beyond immediate needs; the consumer society reached even the Soviet Union, if only in a limited form.

▲ This advertisement in a Bangladesh street for a Western-style bedroom furniture, expresses the drive to create consumer needs in any circumstances.

Datafile

During this period several countries in the Far East achieved economic growth rates unmatched anywhere else. In the early stages, economic growth at 9 percent or 10 percent a year might be explained by the low starting position, but such an explanation cannot hold once a substantial degree of industrialization has been reached. Undoubtedly one cause of success lay in intensive labor effort, long hours and relatively low wages, which kept costs down and thus allowed the prices of foreign competitors to be undercut. But there were also more positive causes – an eagerness to save, to invest and to innovate; a remarkable adaptability both of managers and workers, together with a willingness to learn new techniques; and the ability to create and maintain a political-legal framework to make modernization and industrialization possible. Japan stands out among the rest of the economies of the Far East, being a larger economy and much earlier in the field. By the 1970s it was a world leader in many product areas.

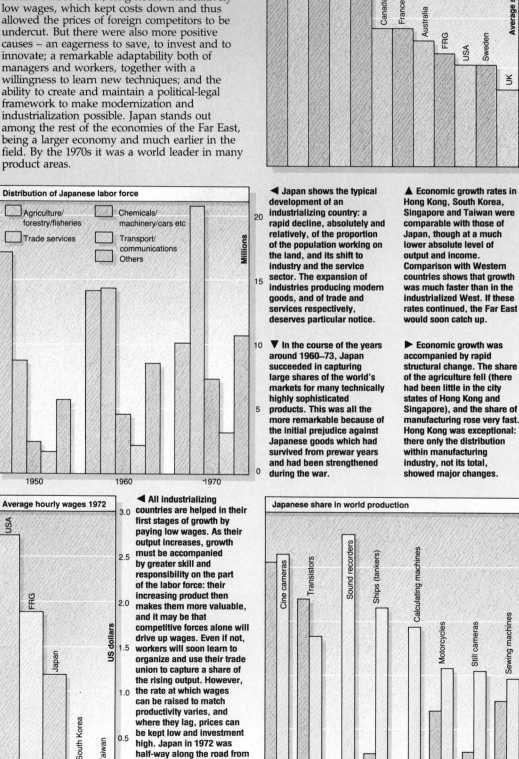

GDP growth 1960–73

Japan, Singapore, Taiwan, South Korea, Hong Kong, Canada, France, Australia, FRG, USA, Sweden, UK

Average annual increase (percent)

Distribution of GDP

- Commerce, transport/communications
- Construction
- Transport/communications
- Agriculture
- Commerce
- Industry
- Others

Percent

Japan 1960, Hong Kong 1960, South Korea 1960, Singapore 1960, Taiwan 1958–60, USA 1960

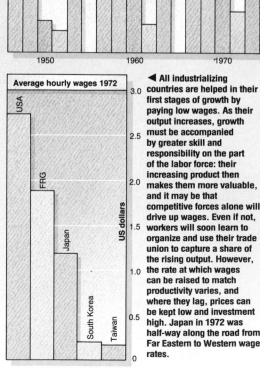

Distribution of Japanese labor force

- Agriculture/forestry/fisheries
- Trade services
- Chemicals/machinery/cars etc
- Transport/communications
- Others

Millions

1950, 1960, 1970

◀ Japan shows the typical development of an industrializing country: a rapid decline, absolutely and relatively, of the proportion of the population working on the land, and its shift to industry and the service sector. The expansion of industries producing modern goods, and of trade and services respectively, deserves particular notice.

▼ In the course of the years around 1960–73, Japan succeeded in capturing large shares of the world's markets for many technically highly sophisticated products. This was all the more remarkable because of the initial prejudice against Japanese goods which had survived from prewar years and had been strengthened during the war.

▲ Economic growth rates in Hong Kong, South Korea, Singapore and Taiwan were comparable with those of Japan, though at a much lower absolute level of output and income. Comparison with Western countries shows that growth was much faster than in the industrialized West. If these rates continued, the Far East would soon catch up.

▶ Economic growth was accompanied by rapid structural change. The share of the agriculture fell (there had been little in the city states of Hong Kong and Singapore), and the share of manufacturing rose very fast. Hong Kong was exceptional: there only the distribution within manufacturing industry, not its total, showed major changes.

Average hourly wages 1972

USA, FRG, Japan, South Korea, Taiwan

US dollars

◀ All industrializing countries are helped in their first stages of growth by paying low wages. As their output increases, growth must be accompanied by greater skill and responsibility on the part of the labor force: their increasing product then makes them more valuable, and it may be that competitive forces alone will drive up wages. Even if not, workers will soon learn to organize and use their trade union to capture a share of the rising output. However, the rate at which wages can be raised to match productivity varies, and where they lag, prices can be kept low and investment high. Japan in 1972 was half-way along the road from Far Eastern to Western wage rates.

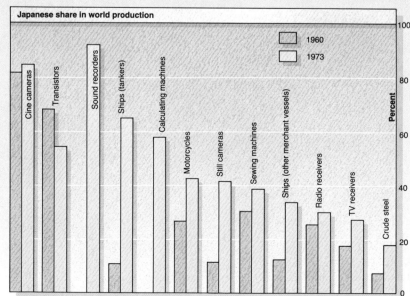

Japanese share in world production

Cine cameras, Transistors, Sound recorders, Ships (tankers), Calculating machines, Motorcycles, Still cameras, Sewing machines, Ships (other merchant vessels), Radio receivers, TV receivers, Crude steel

1960, 1973

Percent

THE RISE OF THE FAR EAST

The successful economies

Japanese expansion

Tradition and innovation

Education and organization

The breakthrough to modernity

Economic growth and general prosperity were found in these years not merely in Europe and North America, but in a modified form all over the world. In one area it was more spectacular still than in the West: a group of Far Eastern countries – South Korea, Hong Kong, Taiwan, Singapore and Japan – succeeded in breaking through to modern forms of industry from low beginnings by an exceptionally steep growth path. The earliest of these, and much the most important, was Japan.

Japanese expansion

The rise of Japan from defeat and devastation at the end of World War II to become the second industrial power among the market economies was remarkable enough. It is even more astonishing when the country's limited natural resources are remembered. Overcrowded, with a cultivable area per head one-fortieth of that of the United States, Japan is also poor in mineral deposits, and was forced to export to pay for necessary imports of raw materials and food. Yet exports were made difficult by anti-Japanese feeling and political changes among its Asian neighbors, its most natural markets, and by over-concentration on cotton textiles, which had little growth potential; the prewar reputation of Japanese goods as being shoddy and imitative did not help, either. Nevertheless, after the immediate tasks of postwar reconstruction were completed, Japan's course towards economic modernization and the economic "miracle" was well and truly set by the mid-1950s. In the period 1960–73 Japan's rates of growth of output and exports were leaving all other advanced countries behind and were in a class of their own. Moreover, while exports had gone at first largely to neighboring countries, before long they also achieved great success in the United States and in Europe, the most sophisticated markets. Similarly, the goods in which Japan scored her greatest successes – ships, cars, motor cycles, cameras, television sets, calculators and electronic equipment – were technically among the most complex products of their day.

Japanese economic prowess was based at first on imitation, but before long Japanese industries proved capable of striking out on their own and getting ahead of the West in certain fields. The causes of this astonishing success have been frequently studied as providing a possible model for others.

One evident cause was the low starting point, which lay well below the technical levels that Japan had reached in the 1930s and 1940s. To regain those levels was not too hard. Moreover, the large agricultural sector – in the later 1940s about half the population worked on the land – provided a useful population reservoir. Agrarian

reform was enforced by the Allied occupation authorities, and agriculture itself became highly efficient. Structural changes, including the relative decline of agriculture as well as of other low-productivity industries like textiles and food processing, gave a further impetus toward a high rate of growth.

The new workforce

An easy labor supply was a striking feature of the Japanese experience. Fed by the massive influx of labor from the land into the cities, it was further helped by the peculiar structure of Japanese industry, frequently referred to as industrial "dualism". A large part of the labor force – some two-thirds in 1962 in all occupations, 62 percent in manufacturing alone – worked in small firms, employing 300 or fewer; indeed, 15 percent of

▼ Fierce competition helped Hong Kong to become one of the most successful economies in the Far East.

▲ Japanese children are introduced early to the intensive study of science. Schools are demanding and highly competitive, and a rich and varied system of further and tertiary education is used by a large proportion of the adult population to acquire additional skills and advance their knowledge of the latest discoveries of science and technology. More than in most other countries, educational achievement in Japan tends to determine occupation and status in later life.

▼ It is common in Japanese offices and factories to engage in communal keep-fit exercises during the working day. Apart from their beneficial effects on health and efficiency, such activities are expected also to foster a corporate spirit and a sense of loyalty towards one's firm and one's superiors. In the larger firms, jobs are regarded as being for life and mobility of labor is low. Promotion and pay increments based on length of service tend to strengthen that attitude. In turn, firms are expected to keep their workers on even in difficult times.

workers in manufacturing were in plants employing nine or less, compared with four percent in the United States. These small firms used little capital and applied older techniques, but survived by paying low wages. The smallest of them paid only 33 percent of the wage rates of the large firms (compared with 67 percent for equivalent businesses in the United States). The differences in productivity were equally striking. Yet the small firms were extremely useful. They acted as subcontractors for the giant corporations who were the real carriers of Japanese economic expansion. They also provided a recruiting ground for newly arrived rural workers, who might, if they were lucky, ultimately join the permanent workforce of the large firm. Meanwhile, this large labor pool helped to keep wages down.

Even in a large company, the workforce for various reasons exercised far less pressure for wage increases than their counterparts in the West. For one thing, trade unions were weak and tended to work within the firms. Perhaps more important were the Japanese tradition of lifetime employment with job security and mutual loyalty, and the widespread *nenko* system of seniority-based wages. It is notable that several of the Japanese export successes, for example electronic goods, were produced with cheap, barely skilled labor.

These exceptionally low wages at any given level of productivity not only kept Japanese exports up, they also helped toward a high rate of saving which, allied to negligible expenditure on defense, gave Japan what was possibly its most distinctive characteristic: much the highest rate of investment in the developed world. Moreover, a smaller share of investment was put into housing in Japan than elsewhere, and there was less older capital stock to be renewed, so that about twice as much – measured as a proportion of GNP – was invested in new productive equipment in Japan as elsewhere. In absolute terms, the input of the new capital in Japan had by 1963 easily surpassed

▲ ▶ The assembly line in this washing machine plant and the steelworks control room are ample evidence that Japan has long ceased to rely merely on cheap labor for being competitive in world markets. Productivity nowadays is based on high investment in modern equipment and the most up-to-date technology. In many areas Japan has become a model for others.

The post-war period has ended; growth as reconstruction is over. Our foremost task is to start building a new Japan, eagerly importing the West's technical innovations.

JAPANESE ECONOMIC WHITE PAPER, 1954

that in France and Britain. Japan also began to make heavy investments abroad. Its direct investment in foreign subsidiaries rose from $1.5 billion in 1967 to $15.9 billion in 1975 (from 1.4 percent to over 6 percent of the world total), and continued to rise fast thereafter.

One particular form of investment which is thought to have contributed very largely to the Japanese success story lay in the field of education. Respect for learning was traditional and the skill of copying from the advanced economies had been practiced since the Meiji era. (Emperor Meiji reigned from 1868 until his death in 1912.) The level of Japanese educational provision and its expansion was among the highest in the world. The high educational standards achieved, together with the success of the larger industrial companies in attracting some of the best graduates, may have contributed to the highly positive attitude to innovation found in Japan.

The government's role

The Japanese government, too, is generally considered to have played a positive role. Among its achievements were the ending of the postwar runaway inflation and the stabilization of the economy thereafter; the provision of much capital (about one-quarter of the total), above all for the larger companies but also for some medium-sized firms; its support for cartels; and the skill with which it kept out foreign manufactured imports while nominally adhering to the GATT rules. Protectionist measures included differential tariff and excise tax rates favoring home producers; restriction of imports by foreign exchange rationing; control of foreign investments; and administrative chicaneries such as frequent changes in obscure technical details demanded of imported automobiles. The government's identification of the major growth industries, beginning with the courageous decision early on to back the heavy industries, was also important. These planning decisions were enforced by favorable conditions for imports of technology and components, by cheap capital, by subsidies and the provision of the necessary infrastructure, and by "administrative guidance" on the part of the responsible ministry, MITI (Ministry for International Trade and Industry).

Traditional and innovation

Beside these general factors, some specific Japanese features have often been noted which might have had positive effects on growth. Among these were the traditional loyalty and lifelong attachment to one's firm and the "family" attitude to one's superiors. Further, although the old *zaibatsu* industrial combines were broken up, new associational groupings, not very dissimilar in structure, known as *keiretsu*, were formed, with one or more banks at the center, much common selling, planning, and again a certain group loyalty as important features. Around 1971, the six leading groupings (Mitsubishi, Sumitomo, Fuji, Mitsui, Dai Ichi and Sanwa) had 387 associated companies between them. Since the banks and the associated companies provided most of the capital, and shareholders only a small fraction, the managers as a group had a free hand. These groupings drove Japanese growth.

Another factor was the dismissal of the old owner class of the major firms in the course of postwar democratization, and its replacement by able and ambitious professionals unafraid of innovation. Lastly, there was the modesty of the demands made by the employees. The low level of wages has already been mentioned; in addition, Japanese workers worked on average some four hundred hours a year longer than those in other industrial countries. Social expenditure by the state was very low, and the Japanese were slow to take to "luxury" goods like cars. In fact, there seems to have been a cultural lag in the demand by the population for the rising standard of living commensurate with their productivity.

The breakthrough to modernity
Yet the fact that the example of Japan's rapid industrialization was followed very soon after by a number of other countries makes it unlikely that specific Japanese cultural traditions played a major part – unless it can be claimed that a similar role was performed by Chinese and Korean traditions in South Korea, Taiwan, Hong Kong and Singapore. For these countries all showed annual growth rates of GNP of around ten percent a year, and of real GNP per head of around seven percent a year. From almost total postwar dereliction and abject poverty in 1960, incomes caught up rapidly by 1973, South Korea lagging slightly behind, and were to approach those of European states in the next decade. Productivity rises took place in all sectors, but in each case it was manufacturing production which was in the lead. Typically, the greatest successes were achieved with labor-intensive products like electrical goods, plastics and textiles, though shipbuilding was important in Singapore and South Korea, and motor cars soon became a major industry in South Korea.

There were no clear, and possibly no common, causes for this breakthrough into modernity. Apart from South Korea, these countries were very poor in raw materials and energy sources. By their character, they fell clearly into two groups. Hong Kong and Singapore were busy trading ports without hinterland. In the case of Singapore, some 75 percent of GNP and in the case of Hong Kong, some 60 percent was generated within the tertiary sector. In the 1970s Singapore became in the fourth largest port in the world, possessing five kilometers (three miles) of landing shores and, in addition, engaged in commercial activities such as insurance, communication, finance and science consulting. Hong Kong also derived income from tourism.

Taiwan and South Korea had large agricultural sectors with rapidly rising efficiency in this period, growing at well over three percent a year in output while still being able to shed substantial numbers of workers to boost manufacturing employment. In the early stages, the processing of agricultural products and the textile industries were important for both. All had reasonably stable governments, low taxation, and fairly free trade, deeping the prices of imported goods low. Hong Kong received no foreign aid; that received

◄ Mass-produced electrical goods were among the most significant of Hong Kong's export industries. Women workers in this transistor plant, which employed 3500 people in the mid-1970s, were willing to accept low pay, and without protection by trade unions or social legislation they helped the city's exporters to undercut the prices of products of European and American factories. Low wages, however, are not enough by themselves to found modern industries, or the rest of the world would also be industrialized.

"Made in Hong Kong"

The manufacture of articles made of plastics was among the first to be established in Hong Kong after the war – the earliest factory dating from 1947 – and among these toys play a prominent part. Over ninety percent of the output goes abroad, and among the world's toy exporters, Hong Kong occupies first place. Though representing only 0.1 of the world's population, the crown colony was in 1986 responsible for 22 percent of the world's toy exports. An early reputation for shoddy, even dangerous, products has given way to admiration for the ingenuity of design at low prices. Hong Kong toys are geared to a world market, and there is rarely anything to indicate their Chinese origin.

▲ Toys, produced by cheap labor in small firms using relatively little capital, played an important part in Hong Kong's export drive. This Christmas collection at the Trade Development Council's Display Center underlines the fact that much of the city's production has no real base in the home market, as would be normal for industrial countries, but was intended mainly for overseas buyers and consumers.

by the other three petered out in the 1960s. They were all able to attract foreign capital, and showed strong signs of a dual economy, with large, modern factories usually financed from abroad, and a mass of small workshops. They all had, by Third World standards, a well-educated working population, though few craft or industrial traditions; and they all had low, if rising, wages.

Two different explanations have been offered for these success stories. The first is largely economic. According to this view these countries, possessing a cheap labor force in elastic supply, together with weak or docile trade unions, could undercut prices in world markets for goods requiring much unskilled labor but little capital. Input prices were kept low, while high interest rates encouraged saving and led to "correct" decisions, free of the dogmatic government "planning" characterizing the less successful developing countries. Governments further encouraged industry by subsidies and tax concessions. It may not be without significance that the three independent countries in this group had undemocratic dictatorial governments, while in the crown colony some key powers were still reserved for the governor, so that state power could be used to make the way clear for the single-minded pursuit of profitable investment without significant concessions to either public

◄ After Japan, South Korea: motor car production on a large scale, using up-to-date technology, expanded almost tenfold between 1976 and 1986. Much of this was destined for the overseas market, but home sales also rose with rising incomes. By the late 1980s, traffic jams in downtown Seoul began to resemble those of the capital cities of older industrial economies.

opinion or the interests of the poor. The other explanation runs in terms of cultural tradition. According to this, Chinese and Korean culture (three-quarters of Singapore's population is Chinese) favours industriousness, self-discipline and thrift in the general population (though, curiously, only Taiwan had a low consumption ratio), and active enterprise among capital owners. This cultural tradition would also embrace Japan. It may be that the functioning infrastructure and the efficient administration left by the colonial powers, Britain and Japan respectively, also contributed to the "economic miracle".

▼ Hong Kong's modern skyscraper building line provides an appropriate background to the container berths at Kway Chung, which at the time of their opening in 1975 formed the largest and most modern cargo-handling complex in Asia. Hong Kong is a trading as well as an industrial center, with a flourishing service sector contributing a high proportion of GDP.

Datafile

The countries of Eastern Europe, as well as China after the Communist revolution, started out with concepts very different from those of the Western market economies. Nevertheless, there were some remarkable similarities between Eastern and Western Europe, and between China and India. The outstanding difference was the much stronger emphasis on the building up of capital goods industries in the East. Whatever was produced for consumers was quickly sold, since incomes were greater than the output of consumer goods, so that there were shortages everywhere. However, the control that Eastern planners were able to maintain over their economy allowed them to keep prices of necessities, such as bread and housing, low and below cost. By fixing prices they also avoided the inflation current in the West. China, a much poorer country, was able to take only the first steps on the road to modernization. Planning may have made these faster, but subject to more violent swings, than was the case in the comparable economy of India.

▼ In the planned economies of Europe foreign trade played a subordinate role. In this period, these countries became increasingly unable to pay for the needed products of the superior Western technology, possibly a sign of an underlying flaw in their planned growth. The situation parallels the rising debt mountain of the Third World.

► In this period, the economies of Eastern Europe grew about as fast as comparable countries in the West and in the Far East, if official statistics are to be believed. It should be noted that the measure used, the "net material product", NMP, is different from the measure favored in the West and tends to exaggerate Eastern European success.

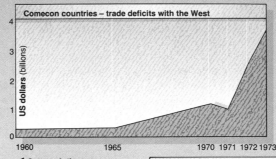
Eastern bloc growth

Comecon countries – trade deficits with the West

▼ Steel, cement, and chemical fertilizer are often taken as indicators of economic maturity that are comparable between countries of different traditions and different economic systems. In this respect China and India belonged together, as did the Soviet Union and Japan, both still well below the United States.

▼ China's economic data are extremely difficult to establish and to compare with those of other countries. In broad outline, however, the irregular growth path shown here, the direct result of violent swings in government policy, may be taken as reasonably correct. The figures do, however, hide enormous regional differences.

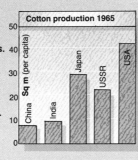
Cotton production 1965

◄ Cotton cloth was a consumer good of major importance in many countries. The gap in production between China and India, and the United States as the most advanced industrialized country, was far narrower than in the case of capital goods. Even here, however, output per head was around five times as high in the United States.

Industrial production 1965
- Cement
- Steel
- Chemicals

China: phases of growth

Gross industrial output

Gross agricultural output

▼ National income in the Comecon countries tended to fluctuate more than in the West, though the method of calculation may tend to exaggerate the changes in direction. The tendency for the poorest of these countries to grow fastest may be connected with the gains that can be achieved by moving workers away from agriculture.

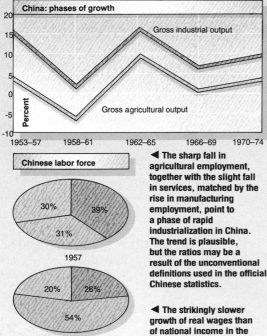
Chinese labor force

1957

1974

- Agriculture
- Industry
- Services

◄ The sharp fall in agricultural employment, together with the slight fall in services, matched by the rise in manufacturing employment, point to a phase of rapid industrialization in China. The trend is plausible, but the ratios may be a result of the unconventional definitions used in the official Chinese statistics.

◄ The strikingly slower growth of real wages than of national income in the Comecon countries is explained by the very large share of national output converted to investment. As in the Soviet Union under Stalin, the generation of workers who lived through the early years of planning were obliged to make sacrifices for a better future.

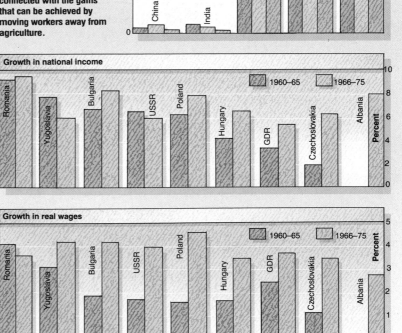
Growth in national income
1960–65   1966–75

Growth in real wages
1960–65   1966–75

THE PLANNED ECONOMIES

Similarities with the West

Experiments and reforms

Technological development

Comecon and mutual cooperation

The Chinese experience

Those countries which had "socialist" planned economic systems – Bulgaria, Czechoslovakia, the German Democratic Republic, Hungary, Poland, Romania, the Soviet Union and Yugoslavia – showed economic growth rates that were not dissimilar to those of the market economies of the West and Far East. By the standard of the "net material product" (NMP) which was applied in Eastern Europe, annual growth rates for the years between 1960 and 1974 varied from 4.6 percent for the technically most advanced (the German Democratic Republic, GDR) to 9.4 percent for the most backward (Romania).

The measure of NMP tends to exaggerate the rate of growth compared with the GDP measure current in Western calculations, but there is no easy way of comparing the two accurately. The United Nations Economic Commission for Europe translated the data for 1965 into absolute figures of GNP per head, and concluded plausibly that the eight Eastern European countries achieved levels of output ranging from 48 percent to 98 percent of the average of all Western and Southern European market economies. The com-

parable figures for consumption were, however, much lower. Moreover, the quality of the goods of the centrally planned economies was low, choice was restricted, supplies were unreliable, service (including that in shops) was poor, transport was overcrowded and housing greatly inferior. These items, which do not enter the official comparisons, make it likely that real income and the standard of living it could buy in the East were considerably lower in relation to the West than the official statistics imply.

In comparison with the West, the planned economies continued to devote more resources to the heavy and investment goods industries. Consequently, the immediate interests of the consumers were neglected in favor of faster future growth, and real wages rose much more slowly than output. Growth was aided by a large exodus from the land. More than a quarter of the total workforce left the land for other occupations between 1950 and 1973, and in Bulgaria this figure was nearly 50 percent. This movement was brought about by a number of factors – by a technological catching-up process, by improvement

▼ **Consumer goods took second place in the planned economies, the emphasis throughout being on heavy industry and capital goods. As a result, the quality of goods in the shops was poor, service minimal, choice very restricted and queueing common. This Moscow queue waits patiently for ice-cream.**

in the quality of labor through education, and by a dramatic rise in the number of women in employment.

Experiments and reforms

In the 1960s the supply of free resources was reduced and it became necessary to change from extensive to intensive progress, that is to say from continually increasing inputs to using the given inputs in a better way. This is clearly demonstrable in agriculture. The ploughing up of "virgin" land, initiated in the Soviet Union in 1954, was the last of the extensive campaigns. By 1960 some sixty million hectares (148 million acres) had been sown, and the newly won land carried over 40 percent of the country's grain. But soil erosion and a vast dustbowl effect followed, and the experiment was halted with Nikita Khrushchev's fall in 1964. Instead, more capital had to be applied to the available soil, both to replace labor and to achieve the necessary increases. The number of tractors, for example, more than doubled between 1960 and 1973. Yet despite increased output, the Soviet Union had to import grain in large quantities by the late 1960s.

Faced with the task of dealing with an ever more complex economy, the rigid Soviet planning system, adopted also by the other "socialist" economies, began to show weaknesses. While quite capable of following a set path, such as reaching certain output targets with a given technology, industrial management by bureaucrats reacted poorly to change and to innovation.

A series of reforms initiated by Khrushchev in 1957, which shifted the centers of control from specialist ministries to regional authorities, was reversed by Alexey Kosygin in 1965, but some decentralization was encouraged. Enterprises were permitted to form "associations" with others, as an intermediate layer of authority between the center and the factory. By 1973, there were over eleven hundred of these. Further, the number of planning targets for industrial managers was reduced from 20–30 to only eight. Instead, monetary incentives were introduced, in the form of bonuses to employees, of social expenditure (especially on housing) and of development funds for the works. Cost reductions were also encouraged and a rate of interest, generally of six percent, was charged. By 1970, more than 41,000 enterprises had been converted to the "new system", accounting for about 92 percent of the output and of the workforce.

These reforms found an echo in the other countries of the Eastern bloc. There were formal decisions to steer a new course in East Germany and in Czechoslovakia in 1963, in Poland in 1964, in Bulgaria in 1965, Albania in 1966, Romania in 1967 and Hungary (the "New Economic Mechanism") in 1968. However, little seemed to change as a result, except in Hungary and temporarily in Czechoslovakia, for purely economic rationality could not easily be reconciled with a command economy in which economic targets and methods were fundamentally the subject of political decisions.

Technological development

The failure to come to grips with the latest technology, which was reflected in the waves of reforms and their lack of success, is all the more remarkable since the ruling philosophy placed a

The Space Race

◀▲ **Yuri Gagarin, much-decorated hero of the Soviet Union, was the first man in space. The success of the Soviet program of space exploration shocked the West, which had underestimated Soviet technological capability, but it may be that too much of the best Soviet top scientific manpower went into this prestige project.**

The development of military rocketry in World War II made it clear that rockets might be developed powerful enough to propel payloads into orbit round the earth and even into outer space. The practical problems were formidable, but in the years after the war both the United States and Soviet Union devoted considerable financial and technological resources to developing programs to overcome them. The Soviet Union succeeded first, and Sputnik I was launched into orbit on 4 October 1957. Sputnik II followed a month later. After sending Luna II to land on the Moon in 1959, the Soviet Union launched Sputnik IV in May 1960. Finally, on 1 April 1961, Vostok I returned after circling the Earth once: in it was the cosmonaut Yuri Gagarin, the first man in space.

These successes caused consternation among American scientists and apprehension among the American public. It became a political necessity to show that American technology could match the Soviet Union's achievements in this field. The space program was stepped up, and in 1962 the first American manned flight took place. In the years to come, both superpowers continued to devote a large proportion of their resources to space technology. Many argued that this was money that could barely be afforded, especially in the Soviet Union; and after the success of the Apollo moon program, both countries cut back on their space exploration programs.

▲ The annual parades in Red Square in Moscow have always included a mighty array of military hardware. The technical equipment of the Red Army is undoubtedly impressive, but it reduced production and productivity available for civilian use far more than comparable expenditure in Western countries. Apart from the use of scarce technical resources, the general burden of the large standing army has also been high, though no exact figures are available, since military expenditure is hidden in many different items in the budget.

high premium on scientific and technical progress. Certainly, the Eastern European countries made great efforts in the educational field, including the universities, and in research and development. The proportions of the total workforce with higher education in the Soviet Union doubled between 1960 and 1973; it more than trebled in East Germany and rose substantially in the rest of the planned economies too. Yet technology remained behind that of the West, and in fact much of the rising import bill which the Eastern bloc countries had to meet in the early 1970s arose from their need for advanced machinery, sophisticated control mechanisms and other "high-tech" goods from the industrialized "capitalist" states. Part of the reason for this may be that a large amount of their research effort was devoted to armaments and to prestige objectives like space travel: some 12 percent of the Soviet national income was spent on defense, compared with nine percent in the United States and six percent or less in Western Europe.

The Eastern investment ratio remained high,

well above that of the West, and investments continued to grow faster than national income. What was unusual among these economies was the very high incremental capital output ratio – that is, the amount of additional capital required to generate a given additional output.

Comecon and economic cooperation

The Council for Mutual Economic Assistance (CMEA, also called Comecon), which had had a rather inauspicious start in 1949, began to be revitalized in the late 1950s and early 1960s. Partly this reflected the need to catch up technically with the West, to switch to producing more consumer goods, and to move away from the Stalinist aim of autarky – independence of the need for foreign commodities. The first international agreement made by the CMEA as an entity was with Finland in 1973.

In 1963 the International Bank for Economic Cooperation was founded to facilitate mutual clearing, using the jointly agreed "transfer rouble", though its effect was limited since trade

◄ **The Soviet Union is rich in natural resources, though many of them are in areas difficult of access and far from the European centres of population.** Costly investment has been needed to develop them, as in this gas main station in Bukhara, not far from the border with Afghanistan. Transport to major centers of population proved similarly expensive.

► **As a major industrial power, the Soviet Union exported manufactured goods, mainly to the less industrialized parts of the world.** Heavy goods vehicles like these being loaded at the port of Odessa for the United Arab Republic were typical of this trade. The Soviet Union also supplied technical know-how, helping to build industrial structures such as steelworks in Third World countries.

▼ **The natural resources of the Soviet Union were not only developed for domestic use.** Oil and gas pipelines were built to convey Soviet products to Eastern bloc countries and to Western European countries as far apart as Finland and Italy. They were among the Soviet Union's main exports and significant earners of much-needed hard currency.

between the member states continued to be conducted by bilateral agreement and in terms of actual goods. Other common institutions were also gradually built up. A rail wagon pool was formed in 1964, followed by coordination or indeed joint enterprises in a number of industries, including the building of rolling mills, iron and steel, chemicals, measuring instruments and space research. From 1973, there was growing collaboration in shipping services on the Danube and in the Baltic. Oil and gas pipelines were built to link Soviet sources with the markets of Russia's Western neighbors. In 1971, the International Investment Bank was set up with a nominal capital of 1000 million transfer roubles: by the end of 1973 it had provided part credit for 33 ventures, at a cost of 588 million transfer roubles. Possibly of greater importance was its ability to take up credits in the West.

Yet the main apparent object of the CMEA, the coordination of economic plans and the expansion of an international division of labor, was not realized, let alone the aim of freer trade between the member countries. On the contrary, in their search for vital machinery imports from the Western countries on credit in the early 1970s, there was a clear tendency for each of the Eastern bloc countries to try and gain some advantage by going it alone. The result was a weakening of CMEA links, and a certain amount of reintegration of the European economy across the East–West divide.

China and modernization

During the 1950s, the industrialization of the People's Republic of China had proceeded at breakneck speed on the Russian model. In 1958, encouraged by this, Chairman Mao Zedong planned to bypass conventional methods by taking what he regarded as a "Great Leap Forward". This was launched with high expectations, but the failure of China's newly established heavy industries, which were carried out with small-scale methods in the villages, combined with a series of bad harvests and the withdrawal of Soviet experts following the political break in 1960, turned it into an economic catastrophe. Agricultural output fell by a quarter to its lowest point in 1960, and industrial output may have fallen even more to its 1962 trough.

As a result, the "Leap" was abandoned and a high rate of growth resumed by traditional methods. Both agriculture and industry made good their losses and by 1965–66 reached their previous peak again, though the population had meanwhile also increased. Much attention was now paid to monetary incentives, to demand and to the market, as well as to economical, efficient production, rather than aiming to maximize output at all costs. But the pattern of growth was interrupted once again by the "Cultural Revolution" of 1966–69, which involved the transfer of production decisions from ministries and experts to groups of revolutionary guards. The Marxist ethos of Mao's revolution contained a strong element of seeing in the peasantry an exploited class that embodied values that were of great significance for the new China. Consequently, millions of skilled workers and specialists were sent to do unskilled work on the farms for the benefit of their ideological education. Agricultural output fell less drastically this time, but manufacturing, transport and foreign trade suffered severely. Finally, about 1970, the "Revolution" was reversed and economic growth resumed once more.

This seesaw between ideology and prosperity in China's progress in the 1950s and 1960s reflects a central dilemma or contradiction in Communist

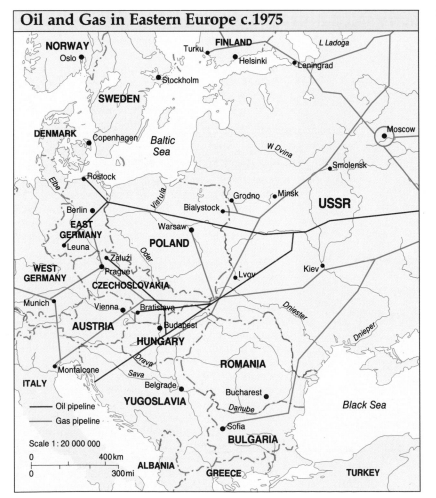

Oil and Gas in Eastern Europe c.1975

NORWAY
Oslo
Turku
FINLAND
L Ladoga
Helsinki
Leningrad
Stockholm
SWEDEN
DENMARK
Copenhagen
Baltic Sea
Moscow
W Dvina
Rostock
Smolensk
Elbe
Berlin
Grodno
Minsk
EAST GERMANY
Bialystock
USSR
Leuna
Warsaw
Záluží
POLAND
Oder
Prague
WEST GERMANY
CZECHOSLOVAKIA
Lvov
Kiev
Munich
Vienna
Bratislava
Dniester
AUSTRIA
Budapest
Dnieper
HUNGARY
Drava
ROMANIA
Monfalcone
Sava
ITALY
Belgrade
Bucharest
YUGOSLAVIA
Danube
Black Sea
Sofia
—— Oil pipeline
—— Gas pipeline
BULGARIA
Scale 1 : 20 000 000
0   400km
0   300mi
ALBANIA
GREECE
TURKEY

▼▶ The Chinese economy was still largely agricultural; even in 1975 around three-quarters of the population were still working in the villages. But Mao's revolution was essentially a peasant revolution, and from time to time city intellectuals, like these young graduates, were sent to work in the fields.

economic management which also affected Eastern Europe, especially in agriculture. It was possible to have ideological purity, by collectivization, communes in the villages and other cooperative measures, or to have efficiency and economic growth, but did not prove possible to have both at the same time, once a certain primitive stage was passed. It is noticeable that it was precisely the periods of ideological enthusiasm that showed the worst economic results. Thus GNP in the first five-year plan of 1953–57 rose by 7 percent a year (5 percent per capita), only to fall in the Great Leap Forward of 1958–61 by −3 percent (−5 percent). In the following period of consolidation it rose by no less than 13 percent (11 percent), but during the years of the Cultural Revolution of 1966–69 it dropped again. As soon as that phase was over, growth accelerated once more during 1970–74.

In view of the zigzag course of Chinese economic development, overall growth rates are difficult to establish. Reasonable estimates show that the rates of annual growth of GDP, agriculture and industrial products were all around four percent.

Chinese agriculture remained highly intensive, switching in some areas from one crop a year to two, elsewhere from two to three and in other respects undergoing its "green revolution". In much of the country, rice is the staple food, and it was possible sufficiently to increase output of that crop by better techniques and new varieties, together with using the immensely important enlarged supply of chemical fertilizer, for China to remain essentially self-sufficient in food for her growing population. Thus it was able to maintain a quarter of the world's population on seven percent of the world's cultivable surface. Methods, however, remained primitive, and agriculture had to suffer numerous upheavals on ideological grounds. Equipment belonged to the 19th century rather than the 20th, even though the workers were members of a "brigade" rather than individual peasants.

Some industrial sectors increased rapidly, in the 1960s especially the production of fertilizer, of machinery and of vehicles, as well as of oil and (rather more slowly) of electric power. Others, including textiles and food processing, but also the steel industry, grew slowly. Growth was helped by a massive transfer of population from the land, amounting, according to different estimates, to between 15 and 19 percent of the total working population. For a country as poor as China, the proportions employed in industry were exceptionally high. This can be explained, in part, by the strongly "dual" nature of industry, in which modern large works existed side by side with much, partly rural, small-scale and handicraft production.

The proportion of national income represented by foreign trade remained small, at about four percent of GNP, but it was crucial in bringing in advanced machinery from Japan and from the West. By about 1966 it had made up the losses sustained in the "Great Leap" and it then rose rapidly. Industrial and mineral products rose from about 30 percent of total exports in 1960 to 39 percent in 1975, while "means of production" accounted for between 80 and 90 percent of imports. The "socialist" countries' share in China's trade fell from 64 percent in 1958–61 to a mere 19 percent in 1970–4, while Japan's share correspondingly rose from 3.5 to over 21 percent. Trade connections also expanded with Hong Kong, Western Europe and the United States.

By the standards and from the point of view of

▲ The "Cultural Revolution" involved much enthusiasm among young people and party activists, as well as a very pronounced personality cult. In part a simple struggle for power, it also represented the genuine fear that privileged intellectuals and bureaucrats were drifting into middle-class attitudes of mind, and had to be reeducated by being forced to do hard manual work.

much of the Third World, Chinese economic progress, seen as a whole, had to be accounted a success, in spite of temporary setbacks. The curtailment of freedom for individual peasants, traders and professionals, and the relatively brutal directives, especially during the "Great Leap" and the Cultural Revolution, seemed less abhorrent to people who enjoyed few privileges themselves. The reiteration of the popular, if not populist, character of the Chinese experiment and the repeated, much publicized, attempts to "mobilize" or activate the masses, seemed to be in stark contrast to the procedures of the generally corrupt, selfish and incompetent ruling elites which lorded it over much of the Third World. Against this, the expansion of production capacity in the Chinese industrial sector, especially in the more advanced industries, down to the dispatch of China's own rocket into space in 1971, made a considerable impression. For a number of industries, the technological gap between Japan and China has been estimated at only 15 years in 1966.

The encouragement of partly rural small-scale industry which was a particular feature of the Chinese way to socialism was something which could well appear to be within reach of other less advanced economies. At the other extreme, it was not unreasonable to suppose that it would require a centralized planning machinery, such as the Communist government advocated, before the more impressive large-scale engineering schemes of those years could be carried out. Thus there were large-scale irrigation developments in

Hunan and Fujian provinces; large-scale reafforestation projects in Hunan, Guangdong, Anhui, Henan and Jiangxi provinces; the completion of water conservancy work on the Grand Canal in Hubei province; electrification schemes, and other ventures. Large canal schemes had, however, been a feature of China's history and China – unlike many other poor countries – possessed a long tradition of literacy and learning, of technical competence and administrative experience, on which the Communist planners could build. Moreover, even a tiny proportion of resources devoted to an advanced sector in a vast country can produce a concentration of impressive achievements.

▶ Industrial growth was slow in the People's Republic of China, and suffered several setbacks. Nevertheless, China also possessed some advanced technology: this worker was employed in a plant making modern electrical generating equipment.

FEEDING THE WORLD

Technical and scientfic progress benefited agriculture as well as industry and the services, but in the less developed parts of the world, the gains were largely swallowed by the rapidly increasing populations. Thus between the early 1960s and 1973, world agricultural output rose by 29 percent, and most major regions were near that average, only Africa lagging with about 20 percent; but output per head actually fell in Africa, Latin America and the Middle East; only the industrialized economies kept well ahead of their population growth. Taking them as a whole, the developing countries, which still had an export surplus of grain in 1954, began to be net importers in 1955, and by 1965 their total imports amounted to 16.5 million tonnes; India's imports alone in 1966 were equivalent to one quarter of the whole American crop. The costs of these growing food imports from the developed world became an impossible burdens for poor nations to bear.

Increases in their own agrarian output could be dramatic, with the appropriation of Western technology, best exemplified by the "Green Revolution" – a term which found ready acceptance at the time. In its narrow meaning, it referred to the development of high-yielding, fast-growing and adaptable strains of wheat, maize, rice and other food grains, but it could also be taken to refer to every aspect of improved agrarian technology and structure. The first high-yield varieties (HYV) of maize were created in Mexico in a Rockefeller-Foundation-financed research center. By the mid-1960s, maize yield per hectare in Mexico had been doubled, total output trebled. Some new wheat and rice varieties improved yields by up to 350 percent. By 1970 the highest acreages under HYV of rice were Taiwan (74 percent ot total production), the Philippines (50 percent), Pakistan (42 percent) and South Korea (40 percent), and for wheat in Mexico (90 percent), Nepal (50 percent), Pakistan (49 percent) and India (33 percent). Proportions elsewhere were much lower, and the new varieties were not without their problems. They needed careful water allocation, weeding, protection from diseases, more mechanization (as the times of ripening were much shorter) and good merchandizing organization, for seeds had to be bought in instead of holding back part of the crop for seed grain as had been traditional. Improved infrastructures, such as roads and irrigation, and structural change, such as larger farms with more resources, were frequently required. All this meant that improved yields tended to benefit the better-off farmers, not the poorest. Also, the poorest countries could not benefit.

The term "Green Revolution" may also have failed to do justice to the steady improvements, including seed experimentation, that had gone on before. Perhaps it comes closest to the truth to say that the "Green Revolution" played its part in the long-term increase of some of the poorer countries' agricultural output, desperately needed to keep pace with their growing populations.

▶ Sacks of grain, supplied by West Germany, being unloaded in a deficit area in Africa. Such aid is often of the most immediate benefit to a population near starvation, and can easily be spared from European farming surpluses. In the long run, however, the deficit countries can only be helped by providing means for them to feed themselves.

▶ Vast mountains of grain and full silos mark the capacity of the United States not only to produce enough for their own population, but have enormous reserves of capacity, artificially kept down by legislation passed in the interest of farmers, which could satisfy the deficit areas of the world. The main problem, however, is that most of the poorest areas cannot afford to buy from North America since they have little or nothing to sell to the outside world.

◀ Large and well-endowed research institutes test different varieties of wheat, many for application in the climatic and soil conditions of the less developed countries. This is one of the most effective ways in which Western science helps the Third World.

▶ New seedlings are being planted in a co-operative farm in Africa. Women in the fields are burdened by their children as they always were, and the watering equipment is elementary. Sometimes new methods have to work within a traditional structure to become socially acceptable.

▲ A well being dug in north-east Mali. Frequently small scale technical improvements, provided by traditional means within the capability of local communities, will be as effective as grandiose schemes drawn up on a national level.

◀ The tin of skimmed milk was no doubt sent to hungry villages as food aid with the best of intentions, but may turn out to be inappropriate and a source of danger. It may give a false impression of nutritional value, while there is a danger of water-borne diseases when the milk is reconstituted from the powder.

Datafile

Poverty still characterized the countries of the "Third World", that is, the countries other than the advanced Western nations, the planned economies and the rapidly expanding economies of the Far East. Extremely rich individuals and groups, as well some as well-to-do cities and regions, could indeed be found in the Third World, but these made the poverty of the rest of the population all the harder to bear.

Rising prosperity in the advanced nations produced two reactions in the poorer countries. One was to make great efforts to break through into modernization, in many cases by economic planning and by other ambitious programs. The other was to apply for aid and loans from the richer economies. By these and other means, the incomes of the less developed world were raised quite substantially. However, in many cases much of the increased output was swallowed up by rising populations. Moreover, the loans they took up required servicing and this caused difficulties where they had not been invested productively.

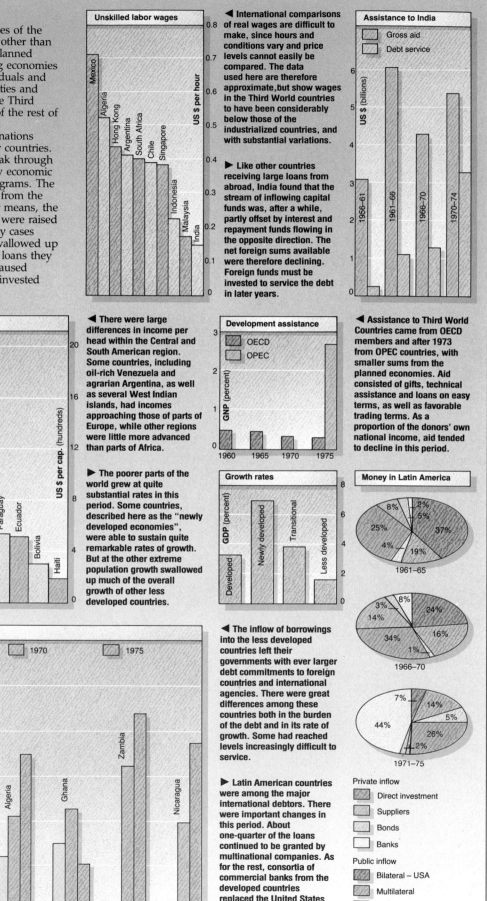

Unskilled labor wages

◀ International comparisons of real wages are difficult to make, since hours and conditions vary and price levels cannot easily be compared. The data used here are therefore approximate, but show wages in the Third World countries to have been considerably below those of the industrialized countries, and with substantial variations.

▶ Like other countries receiving large loans from abroad, India found that the stream of inflowing capital funds was, after a while, partly offset by interest and repayment funds flowing in the opposite direction. The net foreign sums available were therefore declining. Foreign funds must be invested to service the debt in later years.

Assistance to India

- Gross aid
- Debt service

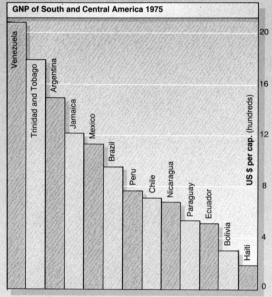

GNP of South and Central America 1975

◀ There were large differences in income per head within the Central and South American region. Some countries, including oil-rich Venezuela and agrarian Argentina, as well as several West Indian islands, had incomes approaching those of parts of Europe, while other regions were little more advanced than parts of Africa.

▶ The poorer parts of the world grew at quite substantial rates in this period. Some countries, described here as the "newly developed economies", were able to sustain quite remarkable rates of growth. But at the other extreme population growth swallowed up much of the overall growth of other less developed countries.

Development assistance

- OECD
- OPEC

Growth rates

◀ Assistance to Third World Countries came from OECD members and after 1973 from OPEC countries, with smaller sums from the planned economies. Aid consisted of gifts, technical assistance and loans on easy terms, as well as favorable trading terms. As a proportion of the donors' own national income, aid tended to decline in this period.

Money in Latin America

1961–65

8% 2% 5% 25% 37% 4% 19%

1966–70

3% 8% 14% 24% 34% 16% 1%

1971–75

7% 14% 44% 5% 26% 2%

◀ The inflow of borrowings into the less developed countries left their governments with ever larger debt commitments to foreign countries and international agencies. There were great differences among these countries both in the burden of the debt and in its rate of growth. Some had reached levels increasingly difficult to service.

▶ Latin American countries were among the major international debtors. There were important changes in this period. About one-quarter of the loans continued to be granted by multinational companies. As for the rest, consortia of commercial banks from the developed countries replaced the United States government.

Private inflow
- Direct investment
- Suppliers
- Bonds
- Banks

Public inflow
- Bilateral – USA
- Multilateral
- Bilateral (others)

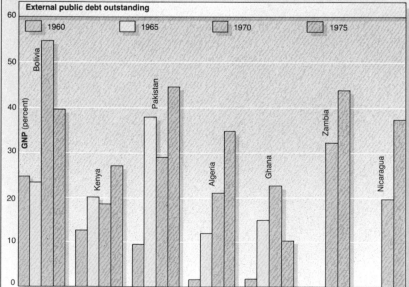

External public debt outstanding

- 1960
- 1965
- 1970
- 1975

THE THIRD WORLD

Latin American
inequalities
The oil-rich states
India and Southeast Asia
African experiences
Aid and exploitation

The term "Third World" came into increasing use in this period to describe the countries neither in the Soviet bloc nor among the advanced industrial nations. There were considerable differences in per capita incomes among them. Even leaving out the oil-rich states, the richest had incomes per head more than thirty times as high as those of the poorest, and the gap was widening. However, given their low starting point and their primitive economies, statistics of GNP drawn up for poor countries on Western patterns have little meaning. Altogether, despite the convenience of the expression "Third World", there is little to be gained by regarding these nations as a single category.

Latin American inequalities

The countries of Latin America, together with the Caribbean islands, were among the better off, though there were wide differences even between them; several, indeed, approached European levels of income. But expectations in this period that they might break through into advanced levels were disappointed: their growth rates per head were low, and their economies frequently lacked a solid base.

One cause of this relative failure was an extremely high rate of population increase, averaging 2.9 percent a year with a rising tendency, among the highest in the world. Only Argentina and Uruguay were much below that, at 1.5 percent a year or less. Inevitably, this swallowed up much of the quite respectable annual growth rate. Moreover, the economic structure seemed remarkably resistant to change. Emigration from the poorest agrarian regions, which had the highest birth rates, reduced agricultural employment slightly, from 48 to 45 percent of total employment in 1960–73, but industrial employment hardly rose; in some countries it even declined. Instead, the migrants sought to scratch a living from providing unskilled "services", settling in ill-provided shacks on the outskirts of the large cities. Several of these doubled in size in a decade: the population of Mexico City grew from 3 million to 15 million between 1950 and 1980. Official statistics showed unemployment figures of around 6–8 percent; Bolivia had 15–16 percent unemployment in the early 1970s and Colombia 10 percent. In addition, underemployment was widespread in Latin America. In urban areas alone, it stood at 23 percent, and meanwhile agricultural output per head stagnated.

To create modern industries while absorbing all the additional labor would have required large investments, but Latin American savings remained low. Capital imports were needed, and Latin America seemed an attractive place for foreign investors, who were further encouraged by the

"Alliance for Progress" concept launched by the United States in 1961. Investments averaging $1.6 billion a year flowed into Latin America in 1961–65, rising to $2.6 billion in 1966–70 and $7.6 billion in 1971–75.

The sources of this capital changed significantly in the early 1960s from public authorities, mainly from the United States, to private investors, above all to international bank consortia. And in this lay the roots of one of the major problems of the following era, not only for Latin America; for by the mid-1960s the outflow required for dividends and repayments was beginning to exceed the new borrowings, and the countries concerned were set to slide into a large-scale foreign debt crisis. In fact, neither the political structure of Latin America, nor the attitude and technical competence of the business elite, nor yet that of the workforce, were favorable to modern industrial growth, as the low rate of savings demonstrated.

Yet another difficulty experienced by several of the largest countries in the area lay in their reliance on one, or at most two, major export commodities such as sugar from the Caribbean islands, or coffee from Brazil: as the prices of some to them fell in this period, expansion plans

▼ The stunning contrast betwen the luxury apartments of the Brazilian rich and the hovels of the poor could be found in every major South American city, where shanty towns have grown up alongside the city proper. Such contrasts are alsc typical of the large cities, particularly the capitals, of the other poor continents, Africa and Asia. The Third World now enjoys a high degree of mobility, but there is still no escape from mass poverty.

► It is evident that rich and poor countries are not scattered randomly around the globe, but cluster in certain very significant ways. Thus richer countries will be found in the temperate zones, while the poor are mainly, if not solely, in a broad belt north and south of the Equator. Some exceptions (oil in hot countries, deserts in others) do not alter the picture fundamentally. Poverty is therefore not simply the result of wrong policies, but is something that is exceptionally hard to combat in certain geographic areas.

It is machinery that has impoverished India. Machinery is the chief symbol of modern civilization. It represents a great sin. I am not fighting machinery as such, but the madness of thinking that machinery saves labor ... The spinning wheel is also a machine.

MAHATMA GANDHI

▼ India is dependent on the prosperity of its agriculture. Much of the agriculture on the subcontinent is conducted on traditional lines, the labor of the peasants being the main input, and most peasants remain poor and unable to afford modern equipment. Many parts of the country are subject to extreme changes in the weather, excessive rains or drought endangering a rural economy none too well prepared to withstand them. Such improvements as have been possible have ensured merely that output has kept pace with population growth.

had to be cut back. Since the regional economies were largely competitive with each other, there was little to hope for from the expansion of intra-regional trade. The Latin American Free Trade Association (1960) and the Caribbean Free Trade Area (1965) therefore had very little effect, though rather more was achieved by cooperation among the Andean Group (1969) of six countries – Bolivia, Chile, Colombia, Ecuador, Peru and Venezuela.

The oil-rich states
Other groups of countries well above the poverty level but associated with the Third World were the Arab states of North Africa and the Middle East, several countries in Southeast Asia, and the Philippines. The oil-rich countries were in a class of their own. Even in 1973, before the great oil price rise, their GDP per head was approaching – and some cases, notably Kuwait and Saudi Arabia, even exceeding – that of the richest developed economies.

At the other end of the scale, there was poverty-stricken tropical Africa, and there were countries in Southern Asia, such as India, Pakistan and Bangladesh, which the world's development almost seemed to have passed by. Moreover, their low average income figures hid enormous inequalities within their societies. India, which was much the most important country in this group, containing 15 percent of the world's population in 1973, may be taken as an example.

The Indian economy
India began its independence in 1947 with the advantages of a long experience of settled government and a highly educated elite, though their skills tended to be legal and administrative rather than technical. The country set out to develop by means of five-year plans, of which the first ran from 1951 to 1956, in the framework of a "mixed economy" in which some of the basic and heavy industries were to be nationalized.

The momentum of the first two five-year plans was carried over into the third (1961–66), but much of the growth was swallowed up by the

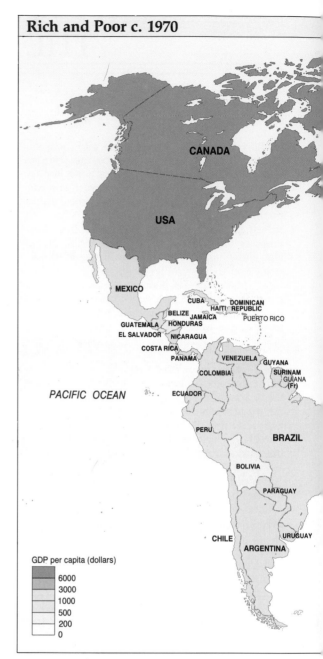

Rich and Poor c. 1970

GDP per capita (dollars)
6000
3000
1000
500
200
0

rapidly rising population. A poor harvest in 1966 helped to weaken the economy to a point where existing plans had to be suspended and the rupee devalued. There followed three years of no-plan fast growth, and a fourth plan period, which once more reduced growth; in 1972–73 growth stopped altogether.

Both agriculture and industry expanded faster than the population, but the fate of the economy was determined by its agricultural sector. Well over 70 percent of the occupied population, with the figures rising, worked in agriculture, producing 52 percent of the national income in 1960–61 and still as much as 43 percent in 1973–74. Its fluctuations and changing fortunes were largely responsible for the fluctuations in the economy as a whole.

From 1965 to 1966 agrarian growth was given a new lease of life by the "high yield varieties" of key crops. This "Green Revolution" was driven forward in India by the Intensive Agricultural

ALB   ALBANIA
AUST   AUSTRIA
BELG   BELGIUM
BULG   BULGARIA
CZECH   CZECHOSLOVAKIA
DEN   DENMARK
E GER   EAST GERMANY
EQ GUINEA EQUATORIAL GUINEA
LUX   LUXEMBOURG
NETH   NETHERLANDS
SWITZ   SWITZERLAND
UAE   UNITED ARAB EMIRATES
UK   UNITED KINGDOM
W GER   WEST GERMANY
YUG   YUGOSLAVIA

Areas Program (IAAP) of 1965. The program was not an unqualified success, since some of the necessary inputs for the high-yield, short-gestation crop varieties, such as fertilizer and water, were not always available, and it benefited large farmers much more than smaller. Nevertheless, while rice crops were little affected, the productivity of wheat went up by over one-half. The Green Revolution certainly helped to preserve India from starvation.

With regard to industry, the plan allowed for rather more labor-intensive, small-scale, traditional "Gandhian" industry than was the case in most other developing countries. But here also, as in agriculture, results were uneven: expansion was fastest in energy, heavy industry, engineering and chemicals, and slowest in textiles and food processing. Much of the heavy industry remained high-cost, delivering goods at prices above those at which India might have bought in world markets, yet still making huge losses for the state. Other industrial firms, which were run by foreign owners, were accused of taking too much out of the country in dividends.

Domestic savings were bound to be low in a country as poor as India. They ran at some 8–10 percent of NDP. They were helped out by foreign aid and foreign investment, but servicing the debt soon began to eat into the benefits. Because of this, net gains of foreign exchange from capital imports – that is, capital imports less repayments and interest payments – fell from 2.8 percent of national income in 1966–9 to 0.8 percent in the following period, and were bound to fall farther, finally to become losses.

There were, as always happens, some particular causes for India's poor results: poor planning, occasional bad harvests, high military expenditure. But, given the extreme poverty and the high rate of population increase, it is difficult to imagine how much more could possibly have been achieved.

▲ Planting rice by hand, in this case in Sri Lanka, is an example of the primitive form of agriculture still practiced in many poor countries. They lack the capital and the educational facilities for the peasants to use new techniques.

Nkrumah's plans for Ghana

A rather different pattern can be seen in Ghana, which in 1957 had been the first African colony to achieve independence. At the time it was the richest and best-educated of the black African territories, and it set out to industrialize with the advice of some of the best development economists in the Western world. Further advantages were an active population, which proved it could react fast to market changes, and a large foreign exchange reserve.

Under its charismatic leader Kwame Nkrumah, Ghana had extravagant plans for a big push of "unbalanced growth" in 1961–65, which was intended to build up a large enough industrial base to supply much of Africa. In 1959 work started on the Volta River project, which was a huge regional scheme involving the construction of a dam to be used for irrigation and for the provision of hydroelectric power. But despite heavy investment in industry on a socialist pattern, the plans failed dismally. Vast foreign deficits were incurred, and by 1966 the country was bankrupt and Nkrumah ousted. His successors had less grandiose concepts, but did not fundamentally change direction, nor did devaluations in 1967 and 1971 and revaluation in 1973 help much. Until 1965, output kept pace with the rise in population; after that output rose more slowly, and in the 1970s it stagnated in absolute terms, so that real income per head fell quite substantially, and Ghana became one of the poorer countries on the African continent. The collapse in the 1960s of the price of cocoa, the country's main export product, contributed to the failure. But among the more fundamental causes were unrealistic, high-prestige planning, inadequate finance, overmanning, technical incompetence and corruption in enterprises that were supposed to be run on socialist principles, and lack of foreign exchange despite aid and the rescheduling of debt.

A variety of experience

Ghana was not the only country in Africa to experience an actual decline in incomes per head, though in the case of Ghana the decline was one of the most spectacular. These were problems that could be found all over black Africa as the newly independent states tried to overcome their economic weaknesses. There was a great variety of experience to be found among Third World

▼ The granting of independence to former African colonies was a political necessity, but it is not clear that it brought much economic benefit. African aspirations, as well as the new architecture exemplified by this Ghanaian independence monument built in 1957, had often little relevance to the most urgent needs. Ghana's undoubted enthusiasm was soon dampened by over-ambitious plans and the almost inevitable rising debt mountain; optimism ended in stagnation and bankruptcy.

countries. Their overall rates of growth of output, as well as those in agriculture and manufacturing, were in most cases higher than anything they had previously known, but so were the growth rates of their populations. In some of the middle-income countries, output exceeded population growth to such an extent that the economies were rapidly catching up on those of the advanced industrial nations. Others, especially those among the poorest, fell farther behind, at least in per capita terms, though even they registered substantial improvements on traditional standards during this period.

The poorer countries in particular were also marked by striking inequalities of income. Nevertheless, growth was followed everywhere by a rise in real wages, and wages correlated quite well with national income, even where growth largely depended on cheap labor.

Aid and exploitation

The technical advances to make possible this sustained rise in output came almost exclusively from the advanced countries, as did the improvements in health, in education and in administrative methods. From them also came investment funds as well as aid in the form of technical assistance. There were widespread demands that direct aid to foreign countries should be given at the rate of three-quarters or even one percent of the donor countries' national income, but these rates were not often reached; one-third to one-half percent was more common. Even so, together with the special, one-sided trading concessions to some former colonial countries that were granted at conventions in Yaoundé (1964, 1970) and Lomé (1976), and to all under the Generalized System of Preference (GSP, 1968), this aid constituted a form of generosity on an international basis for which there is no historical parallel. However, assistance in the form of loans placed burdens on the poorer economies which they would soon prove unable to bear; and it is also arguable that the longer life that Western medicine was able to bring them led to population increases that overstrained their resources, as birth rates grew and death rates fell.

Doctrines which alleged that it was the advanced countries which caused the poverty of the poor by exploiting them found widespread support in those years, particularly among critics of "capitalism" in the West, and among the elites of the poorest and worst-governed countries in the Third World. Their views were aired at international meetings in which they often had a numerical majority. The high point of their attacks may well have been reached in 1974, at the United Nations meeting in April and at meetings on population in Bucharest, on food in Rome, and on the law of the sea at Caracas. However, the allegations that the rich countries had become rich by exploiting the others, founder on the fact that their trading connections with the Third World countries were much too small to have such an effect. This view also ignores the organized price rises of Third World goods such as tin and oil, as well as the aid flowing into these countries.

Whether Third World poverty was actually caused by the rich countries is, however, a much more complex issue. Some regions were doubtless induced to specialize in commodities which were later subject to strong price fluctuations. Many were inspired by the example of the West to try crash development programs, with disastrous results. In the unstable political conditions prevailing in many countries after independence, others still were persuaded to buy expensive arms – spending an average of some four percent of their national income on them – which helped to keep them poor. Yet all achieved high growth rates, and several of them managed without much difficulty to break through to advanced modernity, quite apart from those fortunate enough to find oil within their borders. The alternative concept of a stable peasantry and a traditional artisan population, untainted by contact with the West, working to supply their own needs and kept down in numbers by high death rates unaffected by Western medicine, can be made to appear attractive. Given the international contacts of the past few centuries and the new patterns of world history, it was, in the 1960s, scarcely a realistic alternative.

▲ The leaders of the newly independent countries, like Kwame Nkrumah at this conference in Casablanca, tended to adopt a lifestyle not entirely suited to the needs of their economies. Such conferences publicized the case for economic assistance.

▼ Western medical aid must rank among the finest examples of practical humanity in the modern world. Yet the result has not necessarily been a good one. In many areas, the population increase has outrun the technical means of feeding it.

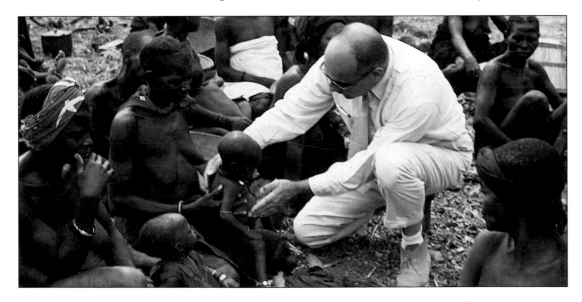

THE
RESTLESS
DECADE

Time Chart

	1961	1962	1963	1964	1965	1966	1967
Rural life	• Californian farmers plant a tougher-skinned tomato which can be picked mechanically, thereby cutting rising labor costs, and is used in processed tomato products • Crops fail again in China	• 14 Jan: EEC nations agree to formulating a Common Agricultural Policy (CAP) • Eight million Florida citrus trees are killed by 24 degrees F temperature (USA)	• In the aftermath of disastrous crop failures Khrushchev declares the Kazakhstan land experiment a failure, and seeks to buy two million tonnes of US wheat • 50% of Japan's crops destroyed by a typhoon	• New strain of high-yield rice introduced by the International Rice Research Institute for cultivation	• Starvation appears in India and Pakistan after the failure of the monsoon rains • USSR forced to purchase grain from Canada and Australia after another crop failure	• Food crisis becomes more acute as production falls by 2%; output in Latin America and Africa dips to prewar levels • US Department of the Interior publishes its first endangered species list	• China's Cultural Revolution reaches agriculture but peasants abandon collective farms in favor of private gardens • Fruit and vegetable surpluses destroyed in Europe to maintain price levels
Industry and labor	• 3 Jan: One millionth Morris Minor is produced (UK) • US president John F Kennedy announces Alliance for Progress to spur economic and social change in countries which cooperate with the USA	• 13 Feb: General strike declared in Paris (Fr) • 29 Nov: Britain and France agree to construct the Concorde airplane • First industrial robots installed by General Motors (USA)	• 17 Jan: Industrial action by electric workers causes blackouts in London • 27 Mar: British Railway Board announces huge cutbacks including closing 2,128 stations and cutting 67,700 jobs (UK) • Phillips Petroleum Co and Pan American Oil Co sign a contract with the Egyptian government	• 24 Mar: Egyptian leader Nasser orders the nationalization of the Shell and Anglo-Egyptian oil companies • Jimmy Hoffa unifies all US truckers under the Teamsters Union banner	• Feb: Agreement between Krupp (FRG) and the Polish government over the construction of manufacturing plants in Poland • British MPs approve a corporation tax on profits gained by companies (UK) • Wages for US workers in building, trucking and transit have doubled since 1949	• Feb: New Five Year Plan begins in the USSR • Aug: Fiat agrees to build a $1 billion auto plant on the Volga (USSR) • 27 Sep–Nov: British Motor Co lays off 13,000 workers • Shell Oil announces oil finds in Muscat and Oman	• 22 Apr: United Autoworkers union, with 1.6 million members, disaffiliates itself from the AFL-CIO in protest against undemocratic leadership • 28 Jul: UK government nationalizes steel as British Steel Corp • Soviet engineers complete the world's largest hydroelectric power project in Siberia • Fiat (It) automobile production is now greater than that of Volkswagen
Government and people	• 13 Apr: South African apartheid policies condemned by the UN General Assembly • 1 May: Cuba proclaimed socialist by Fidel Castro and elections are suspended • 13–20 Aug: East Germany closes the Berlin border and constructs a wall along its length	• 7 Aug: Plans announced in the USSR to eliminate single family houses in urban areas • 7 Nov: Nelson Mandela imprisoned for five years (SA)	• 7 Apr: New Yugoslav constitution makes Tito president for life • 3 May: Haitian president Duvalier declares martial law after protests against him • Supreme Court rules in Gideon vs Wainright that states must provide attorneys for defendants who are unable to afford legal counsel (USA)	• 6 May: Amended Bantu laws further strengthen South African apartheid; eight black leaders including Nelson Mandela are sentenced to life in prison (14 Jun) • 20 Aug: US president Johnson signs the Economic Opportunity Act which commits $947.5 million to a war on poverty • Oct: East Germany grants amnesty to 10,000 political prisoners due to West German influence	• 4 Jun: US president Johnson presents his Great Society program to rid the USA of poverty • 1 Dec: USA begins the airlift of Cuban refugees • Busing of schoolchildren begins in North Carolina as a means of desegregation (USA)	• 1 Jul: Medicare health program, financed by social security payments, takes effect (USA) • Aug: Mao Zedong proclaims China's Cultural Revolution for the construction of an ideal communist state • 19 Sep: Bill introduced in South Africa to eliminate all interracial political parties	• 10 May: Road Safety Bill provides for compulsory breath tests (UK) • 25 Oct: Medical Termination of Pregnancy or "Abortion" Bill is passed by UK parliament • Birth control is legalized in France
Religion	• 20 Jan: Russian Orthodox Church is elected a member of the World Council of Churches • 31 Oct: Algerian riots marking the 1954 Muslim Rebellion claim 86 lives	• 3 Jan: Fidel Castro is excommunicated from the Catholic Church because of his anticlerical policies • 3 May: Hundreds of Muslims die in confrontation with Hindus in Bengal (Ind) • 25 Jun: US Supreme Court outlaws official prayers in school	• 3 Jun: Pope John XXIII dies and is succeeded by Paul VI (29 Jun) • 6 Jun: Martial law declared after riots protesting against the arrest of Muslim religious leader Ruhollah Khomeini (Iran)	• Mar: Malcolm X announces his intentions to split from the Black Muslim movement to form his own group (USA) • 20 Nov: Catholic Church exonerates Jewish guilt over the crucifixion of Jesus Christ	• 21 Feb: Organization of Afro-American Unity leader Malcolm X is assassinated in New York (USA) • International Society for Krishna Consciousness founded in New York	• 23 Mar: Pope and Archbishop of Canterbury meet officially for the first time, in Rome • 11 May: 100 priests protesting against police brutality in Barcelona are beaten by the police (Sp) • Vatican removes the rule forbidding US Catholics to eat meat on Fridays	• Death of Cardinal Francis Spellman, Archbishop of New York (USA)
Events and trends	• 1 Mar: US president Kennedy creates the Peace Corps of Young Americans for voluntary work overseas • 12 Apr: Major Yuri Gagarin is the first man to fly in space (USSR) • Angola begins a war of liberation against the Portuguese lasting until 1974	• Jul: Telstar satellite facilitates TV transmission between Europe and the USA • 15 Oct: Amnesty International created to investigate human rights abuses (UK) • Racial tension breaks out in the Deep South as a black student seeks to attend the University of Mississippi (USA)	• 28 Aug: 200,000 march through Washington in a civil rights demonstration (USA) • Britain is gripped by "Beatlemania" • Betty Friedan writes The Feminine Mystique (USA) • Valium is introduced by Roche laboratories (USA)	• 11 Jan: Surgeon General's Report links smoking with lung cancer and other diseases • 2 Jun: Palestine Liberation Organization (PLO) is created in Jerusalem • First Brook Advisory Clinic opens to give family planning advice to unmarried couples (UK)	• Feb–Mar: Extensive civil rights demonstrations in Alabama (USA) • UK government bans all cigarette advertising from television • First appearance of the Mary Quant-designed miniskirt, in London (UK)	• Betty Friedan founds the National Organization of Women (NOW) to fight for equal rights for women in the USA • US Food and Drug Administration report reveals no data to prove "The Pill" unsafe • London thrives as a center of world fashion trends	• 30 May: Eastern Nigeria secedes as the Republic of Biafra; the resulting civil war lasts two and a half years • 8 Oct: Revolutionary guerrilla leader Ché Guevara is murdered in Bolivia • 3 Dec: First human heart transplant successfully completed, in Cape Town (SA)
Politics	• 20 Jan: John F Kennedy sworn in as US president • 17–20 Apr: Bay of Pigs invasion of Cuba ends in disaster and embarrassment for the USA	• 3 Jul: Algerian independence won after 132 years of French rule • Oct: Crisis over Soviet nuclear missiles found in Cuba; after a US embargo and the missiles are removed	• 22 Nov: US president Kennedy assassinated in Dallas, Texas (USA)	• 7 Aug: US Congress passes the Gulf of Tonkin Resolution, allowing president Johnson to step up US action in Vietnam • Oct: Soviet leader Nikita Khrushchev is ousted and replaced with Leonid Brezhnev	• 29 Jun: US troops enter offensive for the first time in Vietnam • 11 Nov: Rhodesia announces Unilateral Declaration of Independence from Britain; Britain and the UN impose sanctions	• 19 Jan: Indira Gandhi is elected prime minister of India • 29 Jun: First US bombing of Hanoi (N Viet)	• 5-10 Jun: Israel wins a quick victory in the Six-Day War against Egypt, Jordan, Syria and Saudi Arabia

82

1968	1969	1970	1971	1972	1973
• Crops in Saudi Arabia and other Red Sea countries destroyed by locust plague • United Farm Workers Organizing Committee leader, Cesar Chavez, organizes a national grape boycott (USA)	• Use of penicillin and tetracycline in livestock feed forbidden by the British Ministry of Agriculture • US FDA forbids the injection of most antibiotics into US livestock	• Much of the US corn crop is devastated by a fungus blight • World cotton production surpasses 50 million bales		• US prohibits the use of DDT pesticide because of damage to the environment • Soviet and Chinese crops ruined by severe drought; Moscow is forced to buy 4 million tonnes of milling wheat and 4.5 million tonnes of feed grain	• In response to high prices, US farmers plant 130 million hectares of wheat, an increase of 12 million on the previous year • US president Nixon orders a temporary embargo on the export of soya beans and cotton seeds (USA)
• Jan: British Leyland Motor Corp created by a merger of BMC and Leyland Motor Corp (UK) • 14 May: French workers stage strikes in support of student protesters; worker grievances include poor state salaries and discrimination • 23 Aug: Czech workers stage a quick general strike to protest at Soviet presence • Petroleum companies discover oil on Alaska's North Slope and organize the building of a pipeline (USA)	• 17 Jan: UK government publishes *In Place of Strife*, a White Paper on industrial relations (UK) • Jun: Phillips Petroleum discovers a massive oil field off the coast of Norway • With an unusual degree of unity Italy's trade unions use strikes and violence to gain pay increases	• 2 Nov: United Auto Workers initiate a 67-day strike against General Motors plants (USA) • Nov: UK figures reveal that days lost by strikes are equivalent to the number in 1926 • Dec: Shipyard and factory workers in Poland riot over high food prices • Libya nationalizes its oil companies	• 4 Feb: Rolls Royce declares bankruptcy (UK) • 7 Dec: Libya nationalizes the holdings of British Petroleum • Postal strike in favor of 19.5% pay increase halts deliveries for 47 days (UK) • Amtrak (National Railroad Passenger Corp) takes over almost all US railroad traffic	• May: Mexican prospectors strike oil; Chiapas-Tabasco oil field is the largest in the western hemisphere • 6 Nov: British government orders a 90-day compulsory freeze on prices and wages • Chile's nationalization of major industrial firms continues under president Salvador Allende	• 5 Feb: 20,000 black workers go on strike in South Africa • 3 Sep: TUC expels 20 unions which have obeyed the new Industrial Relations Act (UK) • Oct: US oil companies Exxon and Mobil are nationalized by Iraq • Energy crisis (triggered by the Yom Kippur War) contributes to the worst worldwide economic recession since the 1930s
• Mar: Alexander Dubček's regime eases press censorship and arrests the former secret police chief (Czech) • 11 Apr: US president Johnson signs the Civil Rights Bill making it illegal to refuse housing on the ground of race (USA) • 13 Sep: Press censorship reimposed by occupying Soviet forces (Czech) • Nov: Shirley Chisholm is the first black woman elected to the House of Representatives (USA)	• Jun: Nigeria bans night flights supplying food and medicine to starving Biafrans. By November 300,000 refugees face starvation • 9 Jun: Enoch Powell proposes the repatriation of immigrants from Britain • 17 Oct: Passage of Divorce Reform Bill makes total breakdown of marriage ground for divorce (UK)	• 2 Aug: Mississippi has its first interracial marriage (USA) • 9 Oct: Italian Senate votes to legalize abortion • George Wallace, former governor of Alabama, asks other southern governors to defy federal integration orders (USA)	• 7 Feb: Referendum in Switzerland gives the vote to women • 20 Feb: Liechtenstein's male electorate denies women the vote • 20 Apr: US Supreme Court upholds the principle of busing schoolchildren to achieve a racial balance	• 22 Mar: Equal Rights Amendment passed by the US Senate • 6 Aug: Idi Amin reveals intentions to expel 50,000 Asians (Uga) • 26 Nov: Race Relations Act takes effect, making it illegal for employers to discriminate on the ground of color (UK)	• 22 Jan: US Supreme Court rules that states may not ban abortions during the first six months of pregnancy • 15 Oct: South African racial segregation is extended to cover all public gatherings • 24 Nov: Australian government enfranchises aboriginals
• 29 Jul: Papal encyclical declares any form of artificial birth control a violation of divine will (Vat) • 5–6 Oct: 100 Catholics in Northern Ireland injured in demonstrations against discrimination regarding housing and employment (UK)	• 9 May: Vatican reveals plans to remove 30 "saints" from the Catholic liturgical calendar • Aug: Sectarian riots in Belfast and Londonderry lead to military intervention by British troops (UK)	• 16 Mar: New English Bible goes on sale; one million copies are sold in the first day (UK) • Jun: Methodist Church conference in Manchester announces that women will be permitted to become ministers (UK)	• Aug: 5000 Catholic and 2000 Protestant homes burned in four days of Belfast violence; 300 suspected IRA supporters arrested (UK) • State and federal aid to parochial schools ruled unconstitutional by the US Supreme Court	• 30 Jan: "Bloody Sunday": 13 Catholics shot dead by British troops during riots in Londonderry (UK) • 14 Sep: Tonsure, the circular head shave for monks, is abolished by Pope Paul VI	• 30 new cardinals named by Pope Paul VI • Attempt made by three Cypriot bishops to defrock Archbishop Makarios when he refuses to resign as president of Cyprus
• 4 Apr: Dr Martin Luther King is assassinated in Memphis, Tennessee (USA) • May: Student rioting and protests spread to the civilian population; de Gaulle's regime is threatened (Fr) • Proctor and Gamble, Lever Bros and Colgate-Palmolive introduce enzyme detergent but the product creates environmental problems	• Feb: Human eggs are fertilized in test tubes for the first time (UK) • 17 Mar: Golda Meir becomes prime minister of Israel • 21 Jul: Neil Armstrong is the first man to walk on the Moon (USA) • 15 Oct: Millions across the USA protest against the Vietnam War	• Jan: Secessionist revolt in Biafra is crushed by Nigerian troops • Many US colleges are closed by student demonstrations over the Vietnam War • US Food and Drug Administration issues a warning that birth-control pills may produce blood clots	• 7 Jan: Announcement that long hair is now legal in the USSR • British College of Physicians compares cigarette smoking deaths to the great cholera and typhoid epidemics of the 19th century • US bans cigarette advertising from television	• 10 Jan: Surgeon-General's report reveals that nonsmokers exposed to cigarette smoke may suffer ill effects (USA) • 17 Jun: Watergate affair begins with a break-in at the Democratic Party national headquarters (USA) • Richard Leakey and Glynn Isaac find a skull which allegedly dates the first human at 2.5 million BC (Ken)	• 11 Sep: General Augusto Pinochet becomes president of Chile in a CIA-backed coup which claims 2700 lives • Steep rise in food prices throughout Europe, USA and Japan • Three-day working week ordered in Britain to conserve electricity
• May: Occupation of the Sorbonne in Paris begins a month of student rebellions supported by a general strike, demanding the overthrow of de Gaulle's regime (Fr) • 20–21 Aug: Alexander Dubček's "Prague Spring" reform movement suppressed by Warsaw Pact troops (Czech)	• Sep: Colonel Muammar Qadhafi leads a military revolt in Libya	• 9 Oct: Cambodia becomes a Khmer Republic under Lon Nol after the overthrow of Prince Sihanouk (Mar); reign of terror begins against Vietnamese citizens	• 25 Jan: Idi Amin seizes power in a military coup in Uganda • 21 Apr: "Papa Doc" Duvalier dies and is succeeded as president of Haiti by his son "Baby Doc"	• 30 Mar: The British government assumes direct control over Northern Ireland • 11 Aug: Last US ground troops withdraw from Vietnam	• 27 Jan: Ceasefire in Vietnam ends direct US involvement • 6 Oct: Yom Kippur War begins in the Middle East with a simultaneous attack by Arab states on Israel

83

In the 1960s unprecedented, rapid change began to affect many millions of people in Asia, Latin America and Africa amidst the emergence of new conflicts in their independent states. The creation of new governments and rapid industrialization swiftly increased the urban population. For masses of people ways of life changed as a result of migration to live and work in towns, often in the "informal" economy, or as agriculture was transformed by the impact of the Green Revolution. Education, newspapers, films and radio opened new horizons in both town and village, and offered moralities and family relationships that were destabilizing and, for the young, exciting.

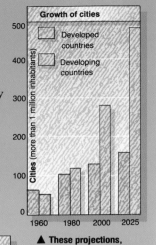

Growth of cities

- Developed countries
- Developing countries

▲ These projections, based on evidence from the 1960s, underlined the speed of urbanization that had been initiated. Increasing numbers were now coming to live in the largest cities which were becoming characteristic of developing countries.

Births and deaths 1970

Births   Deaths

Philippines, India, Venezuela, Egypt, China, Ceylon, Argentina, Japan

Rate (per 1000 population)

◄ Improved diets and a measure of public health provision cut down the infant death rate swiftly, leading to a rapid rise in populations and the growing youthfulness of developing countries, thus increasing employment problems.

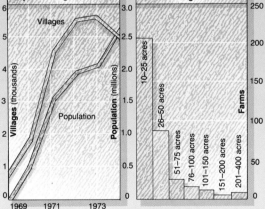

Ujamaa villages

Villages

Villages (thousands)

Population

Population (millions)

1969   1971   1973

Land holding in Ismani

Population (millions)

10–25 acres
26–50 acres
51–75 acres
76–100 acres
101–150 acres
151–200 acres
201–400 acres

Farms

▼ Successful cultivation of new high-yielding varieties of rice (HYVs) required irrigation water, fertilizers and pesticides. This meant that they were first adopted mainly by richer Indian farmers who increased their wealth and power. But small farmers in the more favored areas soon caught up. The major problems lay in regions for which the new technology was inappropriate. Poor people, mainly laborers, gained so long as employment increased — as it often did — and as greater production reduced food prices.

▲ Many countries introduced radical change in the countryside. Tanzania launched *ujamaa*, a key component in the pursuit of African socialism. The program sought to concentrate the farmers in selected villages where basic services and education could be provided for all. But force was required to persuade the farmers to move far from their fields and daily walk long distances. The services provided hardly justified the scale of sacrifice. In the end the scheme was discredited.

▲ Landholdings in Ismani in 1957 (in what was to become independent Tanzania) were quite unequal. But still roughly two-thirds of farmers cultivated more than 5 acres (2 hectares) and 30–40 percent over 10 acres (alongside the 26 farmers with over 100 acres or 40 hectares), which was much better than figures for Asia. Of course, land size does not indicate fertility or access to water or whether the land is afflicted with pests such as the tsetse fly, decisive factors for what the farmer could earn.

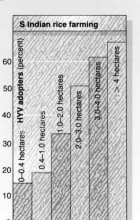

S Indian rice farming

HYV adopters (percent)

0–0.4 hectares
0.4–1.0 hectares
1.0–2.0 hectares
2.0–3.0 hectares
3.0–4.0 hectares
> 4 hectares

The 1960s were turbulent, giddy, exciting and fearful. The most powerful armed forces in the world, those of the United States, fought a brutal and bitter war in Vietnam and, while not defeated, did not win and were forced to withdraw with ignominy. China plunged into the extraordinary chaos of the "Cultural Revolution", when students mobilized as fanatical "Red Guards" attacked intellectuals and the communist establishment and were sent into the countryside to reinvigorate rural society with communist ideals. It excited worldwide interest as an experiment in mass emancipation, a vast refashioning of society by voluntary means and the self-scourging of a Communist party. It exercised enormous influence on young student activists in the West; Western intellectuals greeted Maoism as the model for social change, in the wake of the general discrediting of Bolshevism; and it inspired emulation elsewhere in Asia, notably in India. Its origins and operation were in reality less heroic than the posters and propaganda proclaimed, having to do with a power struggle in the Communist party leadership. It revealed the existence of an enormous and frustrated stratum of young people, grave discontents among workers and peasants, and a party that was apparently sclerotic.

Meanwhile much of colonial sub-Saharan Africa attained independence from colonial masters. Sometimes, as in the former Portuguese colonies, independence was only achieved through bitter wars that left countries wracked with continuing hostilities (especially Angola and Mozambique). But in others, Julius Nyerere's Tanzania (the old Tanganyika with Zanzibar) and Kenneth Kaunda's Zambia (Northern Rhodesia), there were experiments in development under the banners of "African Socialism", outlined most influentially in Nyerere's Arusha Declaration of 1967.

On the other hand emancipation seemed to be accompanied by savagery in some parts of the world: some regimes physically liquidated or exiled a significant proportion of the intelligentsia and trade union and peasant activists. The prototype was the military takeover in Brazil in 1964, followed a year later by an even more devastating one in Indonesia which led to the violent destruction of the Indonesian Communist party. So many of its supporters were killed, even among poor rural people, as to leave an imprint in the demography of Java and Bali. Eastern India experienced attempts at armed revolution on Maoist lines which deteriorated, however, in the state of West Bengal into individual acts of violence and murder and provoked a brutal response from the security forces. Educated young people, many of them facing the prospect of long-term unemployment, led this movement in India.

STRIVING FOR DEVELOPMENT

The same social group also led an insurrection in Sri Lanka in 1971 which was only put down by the government, which included communists and members of Sri Lanka's Trotskyist party, after the major powers from East and West had provided arms. There were also coups in Uruguay and in Argentina. In 1973 world social democracy and communism saw their most significant defeat in the overthrow of Salvador Allende's elected socialist government in Chile. The involvement of the United States in the fall of Allende was the most notable example of Western opposition to leftist regimes. This was the political context which gave rise to the theory that the "development" of the west had involved the systematic "underdevelopment" of the rest of the world through appropriation of resources and exploitation of labor; and that such underdevelopment continued even after the achievement of formal independence by erstwhile colonies, because of their dependence on Western capital backed by the use of power to support regimes sympathetic to capitalist interests.

African socialism

Many of the newly independent states of Africa, led by intellectuals who had been educated in France or Britain and who had been influenced there by Fabian (gradualist) socialist or communist ideas, seemed set to escape the toils of dependence on the West by embracing doctrines of "African socialism". It was not universal – Félix Houphouet-Boigny of the Ivory Coast prided himself on his conservative pragmatism and close association with France; the new Nigerian governments and President Hastings Banda of Malawi also kept their distance. But others created an ideology from diverse sources to provide an inspiration for their peoples, a theory of what made Africa unique and potentially united and as a statement of aspirations. There were many variations, but at the heart was the proposition that traditional Africa was marked by cooperative communities, mutual self-help, not the exploitation of one class by another. This society, it was alleged, was in principle already a socialist order, and provided a basis for

▼ These people in an *ujamaa* village in Tanzania seem to show some enthusiasm for village life. "Villagization" did assist provision of such "basic needs" as clean water, health care and education, though collective agricultural production was unsuccessful and soon lapsed.

Life in Latin American Shanty Towns

Rapid economic growth in Latin America in the 1960s stimulated the migration of masses of workers to the cities in search of better pay. The established classes were shocked and terrified; they needed the new workers to support economic expansion, but were most reluctant to meet the social costs, particularly in housing. Newcomers concentrated in the old dilapidated parts of the city in conditions of terrible overcrowding, turning them into slums. They replaced those born in the city and the better-off amongst them moved out to seize land, often publicly owned, to build their own houses with very much more space. They often filled up all the unoccupied areas, particularly where it was expensive to build legally.

Land occupations were often highly organized affairs, undertaken by "professionals", such as petty gangsters, who worked with corrupt policemen and local city politicians, anxious to secure reelection. The organizers found the land and, for a fee, organized the invasions and helped with building materials. Sometimes, they laid out a street plan with spaces for shops and other facilities because they wanted to attract the respectable working class to what would become a respectable residential neighborhood. The people who joined the invasions were usually young married couples with small children and reasonably secure jobs who desperately needed to escape from the slums to allow their children to grow up in better surroundings.

The original shanty towns were scarecrow dwellings of polythene, oil drums and cardboard, without water and sewerage services, subject to flooding and dust winds. Over the years many were transformed into areas with solid two-story brick and tile houses and schools and shops. The first inhabitants quickly tapped public electricity supplies (which led the electricity supply companies to recognize them so they could bill them), but had great difficulties in securing water supplies and sewage disposal, especially where dwellings were built across water courses or up steep mountain sides. Sometimes the gangsters continued to try to exercise authority and major battles were needed to oust them. There were also middle-class families who squatted – doctors, lawyers, architects – as the only way of getting an adequate amount of land when land prices had soared.

At first, governments reacted by attempting to clear areas, just to assert their capacity to reestablish order or to make way for major infrastructure projects, such as highways, bridges and parks. Much violence and great human misery were the results. In time some governments learned to tread with care. Then they provided new housing or sites with services for the displaced squatters. However, these shanty towns were usually developed where land was cheap because it was remote from where the jobs were located, so they were often quickly deserted by the original occupants and sold off to those who could afford to commute.

Eventually, many governments learned to tolerate the shanties, and some grew to considerable size, such as Netzahualcoyotl in Mexico City. The inhabitants did indeed upgrade them over time and turned them into decent neighborhoods. By 1990 a fifth of the inhabitants of the squatter settlements in the ring road round Mexico City owned cars and commuted to work in the great factory zones of the north.

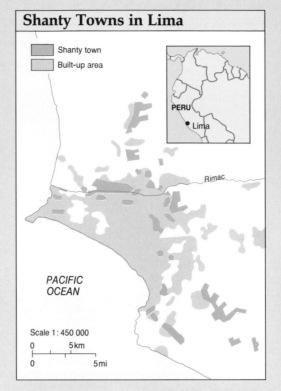

Shanty Towns in Lima

■ Shanty town
▒ Built-up area

PERU
● Lima

Rimac

PACIFIC
OCEAN

Scale 1 : 450 000
0   5km
0   5mi

◀ **Lima, capital of Peru, is not necessarily the most dramatic case of the growth of shanty towns. They spread very quickly in almost all the large cities of the Third World, ranging from thousands of families who lived most of their lives on the pavements of the central city area (as in Bombay) to solid respectable housing areas.**

▼ **Squatters occupied land that was usually empty because it was difficult to build on, such as the edge of rivers, beaches, or, as here, steep hillsides. Because shanty houses on such sites lacked adequate foundations, torrential tropical rains sometimes swept them away with considerable loss of life.**

development different from either unregulated markets or naked state power. Several important African leaders – starting with Kwame Nkrumah in the Gold Coast – saw this doctrine as flowing from their Christianity and embodied in movements of community development, self-help and local participation, particularly when married, at the level of the state, to social democracy. Thus, the desperate shortage of capital could be compensated for by the use of cooperative labor. In Nyerere's Tanzania the *ujamaa* or "villagization" program regrouped the rural population in model new villages where voluntary labor was to create schools, shops, clinics, welfare and community centers, and churches.

The practice was very different. In Nyerere's original statements of *ujamaa*, for example, the formation of the new villages and the establishment of communal production were supposed to take place on a voluntary basis and be undertaken by people themselves. But very quickly the process became subject to coercion, marking the determination of the state to control agricultural production by subjecting the peasant population to its will. Tanzania was not alone in this effort in sub-Saharan Africa, though elsewhere the same result might be sought by different means – through agricultural settlement schemes or changes in land tenure. With single parties in such states, a censored press and controlled political life, few were available to speak the truth. While the rhetoric continued, efforts to industrialize led

to state trading corporations purchasing village output at low prices and selling it abroad at high ones, and diverting the surplus into industry, the salaries of the burgeoning bureaucracy, or private pockets. But exceedingly inefficient industry could not be sustained without imports, and impoverished cultivators could not forever produce exports to pay for them.

Urbanization and work in the "Third World"

After 1950 the speed of growth of the urban population of the world quickened. In 1950 there were 300 million town and city dwellers in the developing countries; by 1980 there would be 1.3 billion. These figures of course conceal enormous variety. Latin America became dominantly urban; most Africans were still rural dwellers in the 1970s. China and India had only about 20 percent of their people living in cities in 1965, but in absolute terms this was equivalent to the whole population of black Africa or South America.

The pattern of urban growth encouraged large cities rather than dispersed small ones. The world's largest cities, such as Mexico City and São Paulo, became characteristic of developing countries rather than, as in the past, of more developed countries. At the same time big cities spread their populations over much larger areas, and almost all experienced some decline in the numbers living in inner-city areas. Sometimes, with rapidly growing smaller cities up to 100 kilometers (60 miles) away from the large city,

▲ West African women are famous for traditionally dominating market selling and trading while the men farm. It sometimes gave women an important measure of independence and self-confidence. Trucks used as buses were called "mammy wagons" because they carried so many women traders round the country. Here, in Ghana, women operate a street market.

► From the 1960s high birth rates combined with a rapid decline in infant deaths produced a swift increase in the population of the Third World at a time when population sizes in Europe, North America and Japan were almost stagnant. This was especially true of the two great population giants, China and India, which between them had nearly two thousand million people.

▼ Officially, until the 1980s, China rejected birth control and its population increased rapidly. The urban minority was highly privileged, so the government tried to prevent an increase in their numbers for fear they could not be fed. However, apart from the early 1960s – when possibly 20 million died in famine – China's food supply has kept pace with population and diets have improved.

very large metropolitan areas began to emerge, dependent on the capacity to move increasing numbers of people and volumes of goods over long distances. One of the elements causing the spread of population was the tendency for larger modern manufacturing plants to be built well away from old built-up areas, leaving them with a mass of petty enterprises in what came to be called the "informal sector".

This term began to be used in the early 1970s following the recognition that many forms of employment, involving a high proportion of the work force of Third World cities, were missed out by official employment statistics. This "unrecorded" sector of the economy included a very heterogeneous set of activities, some actually illegal, though many not: from work in small engineering workshops using relatively sophisticated machinery to black-marketeering; from "moonlighting" work done by skilled electricians to collecting garbage in the streets for recycling; from informal money-lending to shoe-shining. The most obvious characteristic that such operations have in common is that they are too small to be captured in official statistics. But this is only an

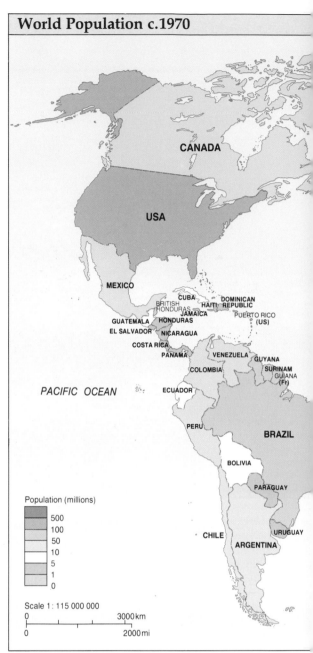

World Population c.1970

Population (millions)
500
100
50
10
5
1
0

Scale 1 : 115 000 000
0   3000 km
0   2000 mi

indicator of a more fundamental feature, which is that employment in these kinds of activities was "informal" in the sense of not being regulated by modern contracts. One of the main objectives of the organized labor movement, starting in the west in the 19th century and then spreading to the Third World, was to win legally enforceable rights to such benefits as sick pay, paid annual leave, protection against unfair dismissal, and to adequate standards of health and safety at work. The most important characteristic of work in the "informal sector" was that it is not subject to laws providing such rights.

However, it was often to the advantage of employers, in the West as well as in the Third World, to engage labor informally, because it was cheaper, unlikely to be organized and could thus be shed at will. Many activities, in manufacturing, distribution and in services, were carried on through various kinds of "putting out" arrangements: in engineering, say, by subcontracting

ALB	ALBANIA
AUST	AUSTRIA
BELG	BELGIUM
BULG	BULGARIA
CZECH	CZECHOSLOVAKIA
DEN	DENMARK
E GER	EAST GERMANY
EQ GUINEA	EQUATORIAL GUINEA
LUX	LUXEMBOURG
NETH	NETHERLANDS
SWITZ	SWITZERLAND
UAE	UNITED ARAB EMIRATES
UK	UNITED KINGDOM
W GER	WEST GERMANY
YUG	YUGOSLAVIA

to small workshops in which labor laws did not apply; in retailing through commission-selling; in the garments industry by employing women who worked at home. Even garbage picking was controlled by a small number of wealthy people who advanced money to collectors. It is not surprising, therefore, that the "informal sector" began to grow relatively as well as absolutely with the expansion of Third World cities in the 1960s.

Some development experts argued that the "informal sector" offered potential for employment-generating growth. They sought to implement programs of assistance for "small-scale entrepreneurs". There is no doubt that there have been small, informal enterprises with growth potential. But for those who were employed informally in Third World cities, though their wages were perhaps higher than they would have been in agriculture, their conditions of work and livelihood often compared very unfavorably with those of the minority of workers who were employed in the public sector or by big companies. Such workers enjoyed considerable job security – to the extent that their jobs could sometimes become a form of property and be passed on to their descendants. They enjoyed a full range of benefits, including perhaps salaries pegged to a cost-of-living index. The number of such jobs in the manufacturing sector grew only slowly because of the capital-intensive nature of much of the industrialization in the Third World. This was the result of attempts to pursue "import-substitution" strategies of industrialization, which in fact required imports of capital goods and raw materials, and set up industries which survived only because of being protected by high tariff barriers. These allowed inefficient industries catering to very restricted elite markets to survive. Such features of "underdevelopment" followed from the policies of Third World regimes as much as from the dominance of Western-based,

89

transnational capitalist corporations in the international economy.

Some social scientists argued that by the early 1970s the minority of workers in cities in the Third World who were in the "good jobs" constituted a "labor aristocracy" with strong interests in the perpetuation of the current situation and not in any struggle for social change to improve the lot of the mass of the people in their countries. Certainly the urban "working class" became, and has remained, divided by differences of job status which would often be reinforced by ethnic differences. The way in which urbanization and industrialization took place generally meant that jobs in particular industries, or in particular parts of a plant, became monopolized by people from a certain religious, regional or linguistic background. It thus became difficult for others, even with the same or better qualifications, to enter these jobs. A "principle of particularism" became established, extending even to very poor jobs. It was observed in Djakarta in the 1960s, for example, that those who survived by collecting cigarette butts came from a certain region and not from others. This kind of fragmentation of the "working class" lay behind the eruptions of violent confrontation between people of different tribal backgrounds, or as in South Asia, people of different religions.

Part of the informal sector was based in people's homes, and especially in the squatter settlements that came to surround the big cities of developing countries, or, in the case of Rio in Brazil, became interspersed with high-rise blocks of luxury apartments. Some of these so-called "informal settlements" grew to house a major part of the city's population. When such areas of illegal or irregular housing were first noticed, they were seen as a kind of physical "marginalization" of a section of the population from the established public society. However, measured against the life of the better-off minority, the poor majority had always been marginalized. There were continual interactions and exchanges, and the shanty dwellers often proved themselves capable of wielding power in the public domain. Furthermore,

► In the arid areas on the periphery of the Sahara Desert, finding and fetching water is a major activity. Social change is very remote, and most women and girls spend much time carrying water from distant sources. The arrival of cheap pumps powered by solar energy may one day change this.

▼ The Indian Punjab region was a main beneficiary of the new agricultural technology of the 1960s. As this scene in the town of Jandiali shows, much prosperity resulted. A minority of farmers became wealthy enough to own tractors as well as motorcycles and air conditioners. Punjab attracted rural laborers from the rest of the country.

quite dramatic increases in yields made possible by new cereal varieties which were especially responsive to fertilizers.

The impact of these higher yielding, modern varieties began to be felt from 1965 in the better irrigated parts of the developing world (and their successful cultivation has continued to be regionally concentrated). While some hailed "the end of hunger" as the output of foodgrains rose, other experts soon reached pessimistic conclusions. The extent of the "revolution" in agricultural production was contested and it was argued that the Biblical saying "To Him That Hath Shall Be Given" was borne out, because the water, fertilizer and pesticide requirements of the new varieties meant that they could be adopted successfully only by richer farmers. If poor farmers tried to grow them they failed to obtain much if any yield advantage because they could not afford to apply adequate amounts of the complementary inputs. Poor farmers suffered financial losses which led to increased indebtedness. There was then a tendency for these poor farmers to lose their land because of their debts to the rich people. Elsewhere, it was argued, landlords would find that it paid to evict their tenants and take over cultivation themselves. The rich peasants and landlords would also find it advantageous to invest in tractors and other machinery, leading to the displacement of labor, so that agricultural workers would lose out as well. Thus, it was felt, the Green Revolution would increase rural inequality and further impoverish large numbers of people.

By the end of the 1960s a wave of uprisings and violence swept across rural India, as in the infamous incident at the village in South India called Kilvenmani, in which 41 low-caste agricultural workers were burned alive by landlords' henchmen. An official report on *The Causes of the Present Agrarian Unrest* concluded that among the causes of such violence were the effects of changes taking place in agriculture.

There is no doubt that the introduction of new agricultural technology brought suffering to some rural people. In Malaysia's main rice-growing regions, for example, the use of tractors and combine harvesters meant the loss of their livelihoods for laborers and former tenant farmers, causing pockets of serious poverty in a relatively rich country. Elsewhere, in some cases, work burdens on rural women increased because of the continued high demand for their labor, while that for men declined. And there is no doubt that the political power of rich peasants increased. The widespread resistance from the rural poor such as seemed likely around 1970 did not occur probably because of the varying mix of welfare provision and of repression employed by Asian states. It has also become clear that there *have* been benefits from the Green Revolution, notably because of the effects of increased cereal production in lowering and stabilizing the prices of foodgrains (which account for 70 percent or more of the expenditure of the poor). Thus, because very poor people are especially dependent upon wage labor and the purchasing of food, they did benefit as consumers.

with the passage of time, the marginalized in the "informal settlements" might come to be the majority – between 60 and 85 percent in Addis Ababa, Luanda, Dar es Salaam and Bogotá. Quite often such areas lacked all services; households were obliged to buy water at high prices from private sellers, to dump garbage in the nearest available watercourse and steal electricity. Yet other millions were crammed in horrifying city slums, many families to a room. And yet others were homeless, eking out an existence by sleeping on the pavements, in railroad stations or under bridges.

The Green Revolution and rural societies
By the early 1960s it was clear that the social problems of Asia, stemming from inequalities in access to land, were far from solved. In some countries – notably India – programs intended to bring about redistribution of land had not been properly implemented, while in China, where redistribution had taken place, problems of organizing agricultural production in a densely populated, land-hungry country remained. Yet from the perspective of American foreign policy Chinese communism appeared a potent threat, capable of winning widespread support among Asia's poor people. There were political as well as humanitarian reasons for seeking to improve their lot.

This was the context in which the research foundations, endowed by two of America's greatest capitalists, J.D. Rockefeller and Henry Ford, increased their funding of agricultural research aimed at increasing the productivity of wheat and rice. Experts continued to press the importance of land redistribution, but it was clear that the existing regimes in most of Asia would not undertake it because of the importance to them of the large landowners' support. So finding ways of increasing food supplies without changing the structure of land ownership was essential. Agricultural research gave birth to what came to be called the Green Revolution – referring to the

OLD AGE

Growing old is a natural and inevitable process, however much people attempt to disguise or slow it down. What has been remarkable about the 20th century has been the increased number of people who survive into old age. A European born in 1850 might have expected to live for 40 years; now Westerners would expect on average to live for 70 years. This is not because people can live longer than they used to but largely because more survive into adulthood after the conquest of childhood diseases.

An important development in the Western world since the early years of the century has been the provision of old age pensions, starting at a formal retirement age of 60 or 65. One result is that the role of contributor to society can end abruptly. For many the chance to live freely without work responsibilities is a liberation. Often good health is maintained for 10 or 15 years after retirement and old age becomes a period of new interests and steady contentment.

For others, however, retirement brings a devastating loss of status. In a fast-changing society the skills and experiences of the old are rapidly redundant. Often income is reduced. Health problems are bound to increase gradually as the body ages. It becomes harder to accept change so that events such as moving house – perhaps into an old people's home – or the death of a spouse become all the more traumatic.

For society as a whole there is the responsibility of making the last years of life fulfilling ones. However, as the numbers of survivors increase and the birth rate falls, there are in many societies fewer young people to provide for the increasing costs of old age. This presents an enormous challenge.

In non-Western societies medical improvements have also led to longer life expectancy. In a poor agricultural society, however, old people may have a more defined role. Where change is slow, experience of the past is valuable in itself and thus confers status. Without state pensions the old may continue in productive employment simply by shifting to less arduous tasks. Even so, in a poor society old age is bound to be harsh. Some nomadic societies leave their old people to die when they can no longer contribute.

The end of human life, death, comes inevitably and every society has evolved rituals for coming to terms with it. In the West death often takes place impersonally in hospital, and many feel that traditional ways of coping have been lost. It is only recently that through the hospice movement and support groups that the West has learned again to face the reality of death.

▲ One hundred years young: Mrs Bowler of Reading, England, celebrates her birthday. Surviving to a hundred is still a rare experience – despite many medical improvements we still have not found the secret of extending human life far beyond this point.

▶▶ Exercises in the park. These Chinese old people go through a traditional exercise routine which should prolong active life. The benefits of such routines are increasingly recognized in an age when retirement can bring steady decline in body and mind.

▶ An 87-year-old woman sells lottery tickets in Tokyo. Old age does not necessarily mean ending on a scrapheap, even where old people are an increasing proportion of population. Every society has a huge underused resource in its old people.

▲ The trauma of change: an old person faced with a housing crisis is comforted by a social worker. Sudden change can be particularly difficult for the elderly.

▲ Old people's lives can lack meaning, as the faces of these old men in a home suggest. Yet enormous resources are needed to provide fulfilling alternatives.

◀ Memorials to loved ones. Since the days of the pyramids and before the urge to commemorate the dead has been a strong one in human society – even when space is limited. Here mourners in Mexico decorate the resting places of their relatives. Some societies, especially perhaps those with Latin cultures, have retained a close association with the dead whereas others have tended to marginalize death, emotionally and physically, by removing and cemeteries to discrete, hidden sites.

Datafile

The 1960s were a time of hope and experimentation in Eastern Europe and to a lesser extent in the Soviet Union. In places the "iron curtain" was lifted slightly, permitting increased East–West contact and dialogue. Communist regimes tried to legitimize their rule by promising, and to some extent delivering, increased social equality, real incomes, job security, social welfare and educational opportunities. For a while such experiments as Hungary's "market socialism" and Yugoslavia's workers' self-management aroused new enthusiasm for socialism. But hopes for reform were destroyed when the Soviet Union crushed Czechoslovakia's reform movement – the Prague Spring – in 1968–69.

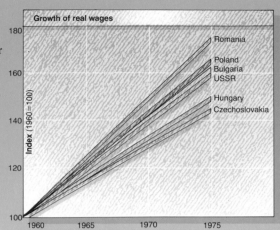

Growth of real wages

Index (1960 = 100)

Romania
Poland
Bulgaria
USSR
Hungary
Czechoslovakia

◀ For a while in the 1960s rising real wages assuaged or bought off workers' discontent, raised industrial morale and avoided repetitions of the serious workers' unrest that had shaken East European regimes in 1953–56 and the Soviet Union in 1962. In the longer term, however, the growth of real wages outstripped the supply of consumer goods, resulting in shortages, black-marketeering and hours wasted in queues for scarce goods. Ordinary people increasingly felt frustrated, disillusioned and alienated.

Births and deaths 1970

Births   Deaths

Albania, Czechoslovakia, Romania, Yugoslavia, Poland, Bulgaria, Hungary, GDR

Rate (per 1000 population)

◀ In Eastern Europe industrialized East Germany had the lowest birth rate and the highest death rate. A large proportion of its population was elderly, partly because of the mass exodus of young people before the Berlin Wall was built in 1961. Opposite combinations were found in the least industrialized areas and where there had been great losses in World War II. Wartime losses partly account for the Soviet Union's birth rate of 17.7 and death rate of 8.7 in 1970. Some regimes did improve health and life expectancy.

Living space 1970

GDR, Poland, Romania, Yugoslavia, Hungary, USSR, Bulgaria, Czechoslovakia, France, FRG

Persons per room

◀ Increased investment in the 1960s reduced housing shortages and overcrowding. But in 1970 the average number of persons per room was still much higher than in the West.

▼ Access to Western television programs in east Germany and Czechoslovakia stimulated discontent with poor living conditions in Eastern Europe, whereas the backward communications infrastructure discouraged sought-after Western investment. The gap between east and west began to deepen.

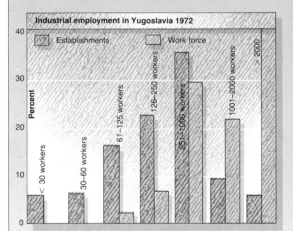

Industrial employment in Yugoslavia 1972

Establishments   Work force

Percent

< 30 workers, 30–60 workers, 61–125 workers, 126–250 workers, 251–1000 workers, 1001–2000 workers, > 2000

◀ From the 1950s Yugoslavia's industry formally embraced the novel system of workers' self-management. But in practice the envisaged growth of workers' control of industry was impeded by the sheer magnitude of firms and their consequent complexity. In spite of intentions, managers remained remote from the shop floor. By 1972 over 60 percent of Yugoslav industrial workers worked in enterprises employing over 1000 workers and the average size of industrial enterprises was several times the Western average.

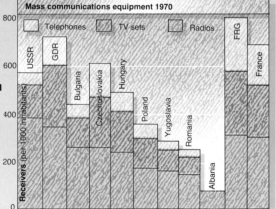

Mass communications equipment 1970

Telephones   TV sets   Radios

Receivers (per 1000 inhabitants)

USSR, GDR, Bulgaria, Czechoslovakia, Hungary, Poland, Yugoslavia, Romania, Albania, FRG, France

▶ A proclaimed goal of the Soviet regime in the 1950s and 1960s was to "catch up and overtake" the United States in consumption per head of meat, milk, eggs and other dairy produce. This goal was eventually achieved, but just at the point when Americans were becoming more aware of the health hazards caused by excessive consumption of fatty high-cholesterol foodstuffs and alcohol. The Soviet achievement resulted in increased susceptibility to heart disease, obesity, cancer and cirrhosis of the liver.

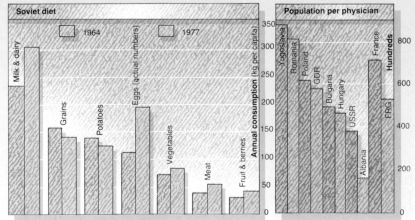

Soviet diet

1964   1977

Milk & dairy, Grains, Potatoes, Eggs (actual numbers), Vegetables, Meat, Fruit & berries

Annual consumption (kg per capita)

Population per physician

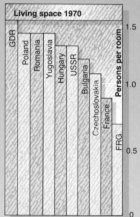

Yugoslavia, Romania, Poland, GDR, Bulgaria, Hungary, USSR, Albania, France, FRG

Hundreds

◀ By 1970 the Soviet Union and Albania boasted the world's most favorable ratios of physicians to population. But many physicians (most of whom were women) were over-specialized and had low social status, which led to poor morale and inflexibility. This contributed to a situation where a quarter of the Soviet population was hospitalized each year. The potential benefits were also offset by poor housing, insanitary water, low personal hygiene and inadequate medical supplies (even of basic items, such as dressings and syringes).

STAGNATION AND EXPERIMENTATION

The new Soviet optimism, vitality and experimentation fomented by the frenetic and unpredictable Khrushchev regime (1955–1964) was slowly suffocated from the mid-1960s under Leonid Brezhnev (1964–1982). The new "freeze" was brought about by a renewal of all-pervasive bureaucratic regulation, a reassertion of reactionary vested interests and ideological dogmatism, cat-and-mouse persecution and "show trials" of dissidents and Jews, widely-publicized violations of "human rights" and abuses of psychiatry. This climate strongly contributed to the widespread disillusionment, cynicism and corruption of the Brezhnev "years of stagnation".

The Soviet "gerontocracy" – the aging Soviet leadership of the Brezhnev era – was also a "kleptocracy", a regime that pocketed much of the people's hard-won wealth. Soviet Republics such as Georgia, Azerbaijan, Uzbekistan (where Brezhnev's notorious son-in-law was involved in billion-ruble agricultural frauds), Kazakhstan and

▼ Soviet pioneers. Soviet education aimed to instill values in children, such as love of work and devotion to Lenin. All schoolchildren were expected to join the pioneers youth organization.

Tadjikistan, together with many local fiefdoms in the Russian Federation, were run by party mafias for their own benefit. The party "Godfathers" lived like millionaires on the proceeds of illegal trafficking, political jobbery, protection rackets and connections with the "second economy". Deprived of clear conceptions of the distinctions between private and public property and private and public goods, both rulers and ruled came to regard public property and public goods as gifts to be appropriated, or used profligately. This deeply corrupting situation gave rise to an increasingly amoral and feckless society, which would ultimately sap the strength of the superpower.

The Soviet Union's agrarian problem
Agricultural output, which had expanded by 50 percent in 1953–58, failed to expand any further in 1959–63, and the 1963 harvest was a disaster. The scope for easily achievable advances had been

rapidly exhausted. When the official retail prices of meat and dairy produce were sharply increased in 1962 to help finance more sustained intensification of agriculture, there was major workers' unrest in several Soviet cities. Thereafter further improvements in Soviet food supplies were to be achieved, not by raising official retail prices but by vastly increasing state expenditure on food subsidies and on agricultural investment. In the 1970s food subsidies accounted for 10 to 15 percent of state expenditure and agriculture received 25 to 30 percent of Soviet investment. Massive resources went into this Soviet "black hole". Unfortunately, the forms in which urban food supply problems were tackled ultimately exacerbated rather than alleviated Soviet food shortages.

Reluctance to raise official retail prices of foodstuffs (for fear of provoking urban unrest), combined with the considerable growth of the disposable money incomes of the Soviet population fostered demand for foodstuffs which continually outstripped the moderate further growth of food supplies. Indeed, it was in the interest of the farm population to deliver only modest increases in production for the state distribution network and the urban sector. For so long as agriculture remained a "problem" in the eyes of the state, farmers could expect to receive greatly increased farm subsidies, incomes and investment from the state. Conversely, if they had produced enough to satisfy growing urban demand and eliminate the need for large food imports from the West, agriculture would have ceased to be a "problem" and the state would have treated the farm sector less generously.

It therefore paid the Soviet farm population to provide only the most perfunctory fulfilment of their obligations to the state or collective sector and to concentrate on their private "home improvements" and increased private production of goods (not just food, but clothing, footwear, jewelry, drinks and the like) for themselves and for high-priced "free" markets. These private activities increasingly diverted material resources from the collective and state farms, often with the tacit approval of sympathetic farm officials who were "in on the game". Thus even after agricultural output stopped growing altogether in the late 1970s and through the 1980s, the real incomes and assets of the farm population nevertheless

▲ Peasant women visiting Moscow. Between 1930 and 1970 there was a massive exodus from the Soviet countryside. The urban population expanded by about 100 million, with the result that most town- and city-dwellers were of peasant stock, and continued to be linked with the countryside by family relationships. Moreover peasants were always to be seen in cities and towns, on the main streets, at railroad stations, and behind stalls at food markets.

continued to increase, as the state desperately pumped in more and more resources in a vain endeavor to reinvigorate Soviet collective farming and as persistent urban food shortages perpetuated rich opportunities for private profiteering. Quite simply, Soviet farmers gladly accepted more and more income and state support, in return for less and less effort.

The shrewd peasantry had at last won a sort of revenge for its sufferings in the 1930s and 1940s. In contrast to more recently collectivized peasantries in China and Eastern Europe, the Soviet peasantry gradually lost interest in "decollectivizing" or dismantling a system which they had learned to work and "milk" to their own advantage and which permitted levels of profiteering, alongside an absence of individual financial responsibility and risk, that privatized agriculture could not hope to match. This explains the very muted peasant response, other than in the more recently collectivized Baltic Republics and Western Ukraine, to 1980s proposals for decollectivization or privatization of Soviet agriculture. Thus, *through* the collective farm system, the Soviet state had in the end unwittingly erected an immense social barrier to any fundamental solution to the problem of chronic food shortages.

Economic stagnation

This institutionalized imbalance of supply and demand, reinforced by shortages induced by high military expenditure and by diversion of resources to inefficient heavy industry, was at the root of the luxuriant growth of blackmarketeering, corruption, pilfering and moonlighting under Brezhnev. Persistent shortages steadily diminished the value of rising money incomes, diminished work incentives and redirected energies from work to frustrating searching and queuing for scarce goods. People's increased dependence upon access to pilfered or black-market goods increased the value of the privileged access to special shops, services and accommodation reserved for key party and state personnel, and incensed and demoralized the unprivileged masses. The latter were being fobbed off with a superficially striking growth and equalization of money incomes, at a time when money income was being progressively deprived of real significance; position and "pull" ("*blat*") rather than money increasingly determined degrees of access to scarce material and cultural goods, services, housing and amenities. Most Soviet households accumulated large savings, frustrated at the dearth of attractive things to buy, although pent-up purchasing power was also channeled increasingly into alarmingly high consumption of alcohol and cheap cigarettes, to the growing detriment of health and family life.

During the 1960s and 1970s Soviet reformers devised elaborate bonus schemes, piece rates and pay scales in an endeavor to reward "each according to his work". But the intended incentives were largely nullified by shortages and erratic supplies. The Soviet workers' attitudes to work and remuneration were neatly encapsulated in an oft-quoted catch-phrase: "You pretend to pay us, and we pretend to work."

Women and the family

During the 1960s Soviet family legislation was brought more into line with that of the West, completing the reversal of Stalin's sexual counter-revolution. The December 1965 divorce law further liberalized divorce procedures; and the 1968 Family Code increased protection and financial safeguards for divorced women and their offspring. It also substantially increased the rights and status of children born out of wedlock. The number of divorces per thousand inhabitants (0.4 in 1950, 1.6 in 1965) reached a high plateau of 3.3–3.5 (or one divorce for every three marriages) in 1976–89. Other factors besides more liberal divorce procedures were at work. Nearly half of female divorcees cited male alcoholism and/or drunkenness as the chief reasons for divorce, reflecting the massive rise in Soviet alcohol consumption in the 1960s–70s. In addition, familial child-rearing functions were becoming less important as the importance of schools, peer groups and social organizations increased and as the average size of Soviet families declined to 3.7 persons in 1970 and 3.5 persons in 1989. Indeed, the average number of children per married woman decreased to two in the course of the 1970s, as Soviet couples adjusted to life in very cramped

▼ Apartment block in Moscow. The scale and monotony of most modern Soviet apartment blocks were no doubt intended to impress and to reinforce a sense of "proletarian uniformity". But the results were soulless and oppressive.

▼ A subway executive in Moscow, responsible for rolling stock. Since World War II women have been a majority of the Soviet work force, but most have been confined to low-status manual occupations. Some rose to supervisory positions, but even the most formidable Soviet matriarchs rarely attained positions of real power and authority.

▼ The recreational facilities in Soviet towns and cities were usually limited, but most of the older cities were well endowed with elegant and extensive parks (as here), many of which had belonged to the aristocracy or rich industrialists before 1917. In addition, most cities were well provided with cinemas and large "palaces of culture" (leisure centers). But there was a shortage of small, local, more informal venues (such as bars, cafes and restaurants).

urban accommodation or decided to forgo additional children so as to be able to spend more on clothing, footwear and consumer durables, which were expensive for Soviet citizens. The restraints of religion, social disapproval and pressure from the extended family were also being eroded, even in rural areas, where family farming of "private plots" was finally overtaken by income from "collective work" as the main source of household income, reducing the economic pressures to keep rural families intact. Increased urbanization and employment opportunities for women had also made it easier for formerly dependent wives to leave their husbands. Nevertheless, far from the family disappearing under Communist rule, families still embraced 94 percent of the Soviet population in 1970, and Soviet women were still far from achieving full emancipation and equality. In the 1960s–70s, average male earnings were 50 percent higher than those of Soviet women.

Absence of freedom of association and expression largely prevented the emergence of independent women's movements in the Soviet Union. Indeed the Soviet regime claimed that there was no need for independent women's organizations, because (officially) women's equality and emancipation had already been accomplished by early Soviet family legislation, universal education and the massive expansion of female employment. Soviet women who dissented from the official view stood accused of defaming the Soviet state. But while women did make up a majority of the Soviet work force, they were disproportionately concentrated in manual occupations and so-called "non-productive services", which conferred little power or status in the Soviet Union, and there continued to be a dearth of women in positions of authority. In secondary education girls were markedly higher achievers than boys, yet fewer girls were recruited to higher education and power-wielding posts. The meager provision of labor-saving household appliances and the two to three hours per day spent in shopping queues mainly affected women, as Soviet men still saw shopping and household chores as "women's work". Soviet power was still masculine!

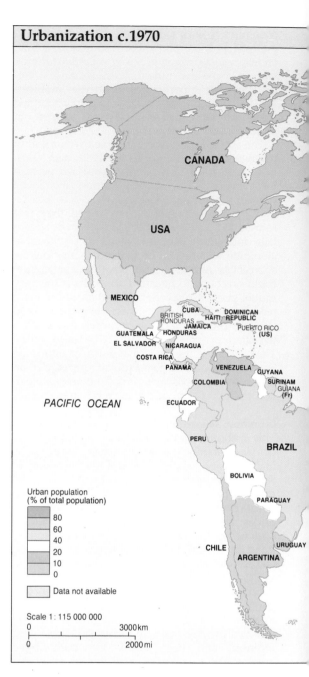

Urbanization c.1970

Urban population
(% of total population)

80
60
40
20
10
0

Data not available

Scale 1 : 115 000 000

0 ——— 3000 km
0 ——— 2000 mi

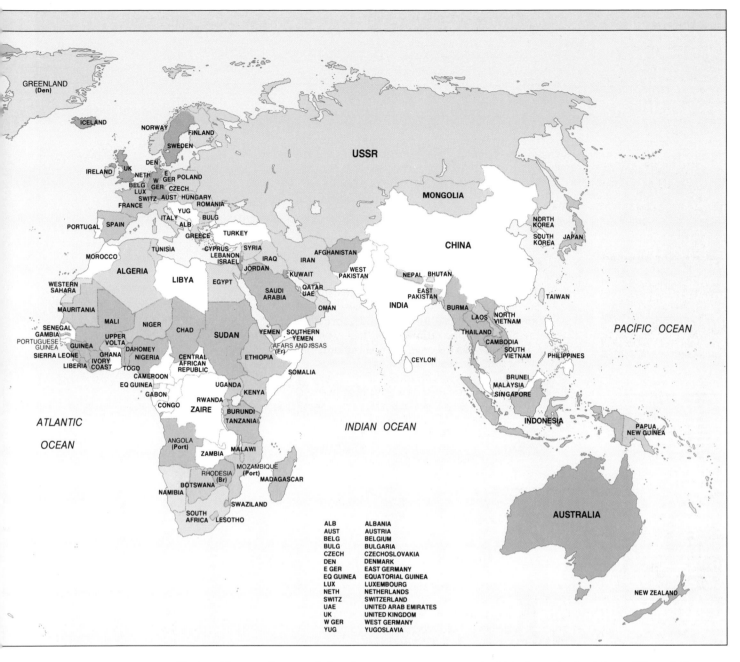

ALB	ALBANIA
AUST	AUSTRIA
BELG	BELGIUM
BULG	BULGARIA
CZECH	CZECHOSLOVAKIA
DEN	DENMARK
E GER	EAST GERMANY
EQ GUINEA	EQUATORIAL GUINEA
LUX	LUXEMBOURG
NETH	NETHERLANDS
SWITZ	SWITZERLAND
UAE	UNITED ARAB EMIRATES
UK	UNITED KINGDOM
W GER	WEST GERMANY
YUG	YUGOSLAVIA

▲ By the 1970s the industrialized West had become substantially "suburbanized", leaving inner-city areas increasingly to the least privileged. Meanwhile the Third World was already experiencing the rapid growth of some very big cities, leading to the mushrooming of shanty towns. In the Soviet Union in 1950 only Moscow and Leningrad had contained more than 1 million inhabitants, but by 1970 the number of these big cities had increased to 20.

Eastern Europe: the search for change

Throughout Eastern Europe this was a time of unprecedented growth and, until the Soviet invasion of Czechoslovakia in 1968, of optimism and rising consumption. Between 1960 and 1970 private car ownership increased fourfold in East Germany and Poland and by as much as seven times in Hungary. Eastern European societies thus experienced consumerism, albeit on a modest scale by comparison with their Western neighbors; they too were marked by the rise of service employment and by expansion of welfare services and of educational opportunity. What was different was the formal commitment in Eastern Europe to the achievement of equality, not just equality of opportunity. The extent of social mobility was higher than in the west. Half the university students in East Germany were from working-class families in the early 1960s, when in Western Europe, outside Britain and Scandinavia, the proportion was less than 10 per-

cent. Yet important status differentiation remained between professional people, party apparatchiks and ordinary workers.

Different patterns of development and change characterized the states of Eastern Europe, resulting from their histories, cultures and the varying relationships between the Communist party and the people. East Germany, with an apparently successful economy, was influenced above all by its proximity to the West and anxieties over its relationships with the Federal Republic – symbolized by the building of the Berlin Wall in 1961. It became the most orthodox ally of the Soviet Union, the one most willing to toe the Soviet line. Poland, though it experienced comparatively high rates of growth of both industrial and agricultural output, remained an unhappy society. Even more than in the neighboring countries had the Communist party failed to become at all rooted amongst the people, and there was not much enthusiasm even amongst its members.

The party remained in power only because of the threat from the Soviet Union, offending the deep sense of Polish nationalism and giving rise to recurrent unrest and powerful antigovernment mobilization amongst workers. There was more popular support for communism in Czechoslovakia and Hungary, and it was perhaps for this reason that these two states saw the most serious attempts to remold socialism in the 1960s.

Czechoslovakia's "socialism with a human face"
The need for social reform in Czechoslovakia was widely accepted, even among members of the ruling party apparatus, as the remedy for the stagnation which had set in by the early 1960s, and brought disillusionment with communism in a country where it had known strong support.

Thus the Czechoslovak reform movement of 1963–68 did not aim to jettison "socialism" and the leading role of the party. It strove to achieve "socialism with a human face" by removing hardliners, democratizing the party and relaxing censorship. In keeping with the Czechs' reputation for being the most liberal, educated and sophisticated nation in Eastern Europe, the relatively large party and non-party intelligentsia dominated the Czechoslovak reform movement.

Intelligentsia hegemony in the Czech reform movement was both a strength and a weakness. The movement was exceptionally articulate and commanded great moral and intellectual respect and authority. On the other hand, because it lacked a mass base, the Soviet-led Warsaw Pact invasion of Czechoslovakia in August 1968 was

▲ A roadside trading depot in Yugoslavia. During the time of the postwar Communist regimes, rural Eastern Europe remained relatively untouched by modern amenities. There were few automobiles to be seen and most roads were dusty dirt tracks which became quagmires in wet weather. In the Soviet Union in the late 1960s the metaled road network was not much bigger than that of the UK, a country ninety times smaller.

not answered by widespread and tenacious resistance. This was another "Revolution of the Intellectuals", like that of 1848, and it was partly for this reason that it failed.

Hungary's "market socialism"

The happiest and most unexpected reversal of fortunes occurred in Hungary under Janos Kadar (party leader from 1956 to 1988). From late 1961 onward, after repression and recollectivization had brutally but effectively reimposed party control, Kadar's regime set out to conciliate Hungary's intelligentsia, workers, peasants and even Catholics, under the slogan "Those who are not against us are with us". Censorship and travel restrictions were progressively relaxed. Most political prisoners were gradually released and rehabilitated. Police excesses were curbed and there was increased observance of due legal process and the rule of law.

In the rural sector, which still accounted for about half Hungary's population in the 1960s, the new collective farms were granted unprecedented commercial and managerial autonomy, in equally unprecedented recognition of their (hitherto ignored) formal legal status as autonomous (self-managed) agricultural producers' cooperatives. Collective farmers responded by vigorously expanding Hungary's food output and exports, including food and wine exports to Western markets. The commercial and managerial autonomy which produced successful results in agriculture gradually spread to catering, food-processing, retailing, personal services, taxis, crafts and, lastly, factory industry.

In 1968, while Soviet and Western attention was nervously fixed upon the more highly publicized and provocative manner in which broadly similar socioeconomic changes were being introduced in neighboring Czechoslovakia, the low-key Kadar regime quietly inaugurated a comprehensive and carefully prepared "New Economic Mechanism" in Hungary – and got away with it. Henceforth, industrial productivity growth, innovation and responsiveness were to be promoted by encouraging industrial enterprises to establish direct contractual relations with one another and with their final customers at home and abroad, to become self-financing and to use repayable interest-bearing bank credits in place of outright grants from the state budget. By 1971 Hungary had effectively ceased to be a command economy, even though large-scale industry remained state-owned. Managers of large enterprises also remained party/state appointees who were not empowered to dismiss workers at will. The 1967 labor code gave the unions a "regularly used" right to veto management decisions, and industrial inefficiency and overmanning were to be dealt with more by redeployment than by painful plant closures and dismissals. Yet the sheer size of Hungarian industrial enterprises was more conducive to hierarchy, inequality and workers' alienation than to the growth of workers' participation, control and contentment. In 1973 Hungarian industry averaged 1070 employees per enterprise, 10 to 20 times the average for many Western states.

Workers' Self-management

The boldest social experiment in Eastern Europe was Yugoslavia's system of workers' self-management. It drew on earlier aspirations to give workers more involvement in industrial organization but emerged from particular circumstances. Tito's postwar Communist regime had initially tried to reconstruct Yugoslavia's economy along Soviet lines, with central direction and investment in heavy industry. The attempt ended in disaster and a new approach was needed. Instead the Communists devolved decision-making to the lowest possible level, partly in the hope of averting ethnic conflicts.

In 1950 workers' councils were established in most enterprises employing over 30 workers which elected teams to manage enterprises. The teams could make appointments and decisions about investment and salaries. At first their freedom was circumscribed by central regulation but in 1965–66 new life was given to the system. The economy expanded, but so too did bad investment decisions, wage inflation and imports. The system not only produced bad management, it also failed to prevent the alienation found in other socialist countries and in large-scale capitalist business: most enterprise directors were political appointees who remained aloof from the shop-floor.

▲ Heavy industries commemorated on Polish stamps. The postwar Polish Communist regime invested in such industries, which soon poisoned the atmosphere and alienated their workers. At the same time they neglected the development potential of Polish light industries.

▼ Catholic clergy in Zagreb, Croatia (part of Yugoslavia). The Croatian Catholic church remained a powerful force under Communist rule.

Datafile

The early 1960s, while the long postwar boom continued, was a time of some moral fervor, epitomized by the presidency of John F. Kennedy in the United States. It was also a time when it seemed plausible to suppose that class conflict had come to an end and a new type of "post-industrial society" was emerging. Both the hopes of the establishment of a better society and these ideas about social change were shattered by the events of the late 1960s. Then, as economic growth faltered, America experienced a wave of social violence, of youth protest and of agitation for Black Power. In Europe the tumult of 1968 exposed deep discontents. A counterculture grew up which threatened established values.

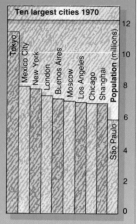

Ten largest cities 1970

▲ By now cities like Mexico City and Buenos Aires were growing very fast, drawing in migrants from rural areas to shanty towns and slums, and initiating tremendous problems of congestion and pollution.

◄ Western populations were still growing, though more slowly. In Germany the death rate exceeded that of births, foreshadowing the aging of the population which was to become a social problem in industrial societies at the end of the century.

Births and deaths 1970

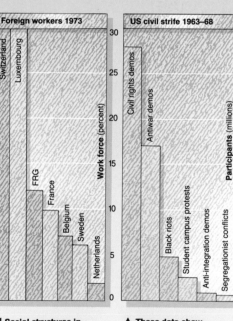

▶ Labor migration into western Europe in the time when booming economies required more workers reached a peak around 1973. Then, with recession, limitations on labor migration began to be introduced and, partly as a result, ethnic tensions increased. But Switzerland exported some of its unemployment back to Italy!

Foreign workers 1973

US civil strife 1963–68

◄ Social structures in Europe had changed rather little. In Britain there had been decline in the relative importance of the lowest ranked, unskilled workers but little change at the top of the social hierarchy. Nowhere did economic growth bring a significant narrowing of the gap in incomes between richest and poorest.

▲ These data show estimates of participation in different types of civil strife in the United States between 1963 and 1968, and reflect the violence of the time. There were most arrests associated with "negro riots" (nearly 50,000) but almost one-third as many in civil rights demonstrations which were mainly peaceful.

UK social structure

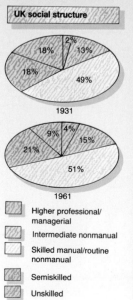

- Higher professional/managerial
- Intermediate nonmanual
- Skilled manual/routine nonmanual
- Semiskilled
- Unskilled

For many in North America and Western Europe who were young at the time "the sixties" stand out as a distinctive period, one of greatly expanding opportunity and personal freedom. Others, looking back on this time, see it rather as one of decay, marked by personal and social irresponsibility. They link this to the "overdevelopment" of the state and especially of welfare provision. These, they argue, made for both a lack of responsibility and of enterprise and initiative which came to threaten the economic base of the freedom enjoyed by the young.

The contrasting moods of the early and the later 1960s partly reflected the tempo of the international economy. During the 1960s the long economic boom of the postwar period began to falter, substantially because the stimulus to growth in the reconstruction of Europe and Japan had by now been exhausted. Both productivity and the profitability of capitalist enterprise declined after 1965. The steep rise of oil prices in 1973 only delivered the final blow to an economic system that was already staggering. The inefficient rigidities inherent in Fordist methods of organizing production in very large-scale factories, with massive investments in specialized assembly lines, started to become apparent. The capacity to deliver collective goods – social welfare – had depended upon continuous growth in productivity and thus was threatened. For the moment states preferred to incur fiscal problems in maintaining welfare expenditure, but this did not restrain the mounting pressure from those who had been excluded from the political settlement of the 1950s – groups of marginal workers outside the big unions, blacks and members of the other ethnic minority groups, women and young people. The student movements of the time reflected anxiety about the future as well as the appeal of a radical counterculture which questioned the values of industrial society.

Post-industrial society?

In the 1960s sociologists began to argue that quite fundamental changes had taken place in Western society. These they sought to describe through such terms as "the service class society", "the knowledge society" or, most influentially, with Daniel Bell's term "post-industrial society". The main elements of these ideas were that whereas the business firm had been the key institution of advanced societies, and the principal social classes those of the capitalist entrepreneurs and the industrial proletariat, now theoretical knowledge was the crucial resource. Universities and research centers were the leading institutions (the "axial structures", according to Bell), society was increasingly run by technocrats rather than by capitalists, and the majority of people were

PROGRESS IN QUESTION

The rise of technocrats and meritocrats

Challenges from students

Experiences of immigrant workers

Liberalism and civil rights

Countercultures and their trappings

Churches and society

The new feminism

employed not in manufacturing but in personal, financial and social services. The values of hard work, encapsulated in Max Weber's concept of the "protestant ethic", were being challenged by a new ethic of fun and leisure. Some saw in these new conditions the possibility of greater social integration and harmony, resulting from the erosion of class differences; others saw potential for conflict between the old, liberal, humane values and those of the new technocracy (which the British writer C.P. Snow described as "the two cultures").

There was substantial evidence for all of these ideas. At some time in the 1950s the United States had become the first nation in which more than half of the employed population was not involved in producing food, clothing, houses, automobiles or other tangible goods. The United Kingdom followed suit in the 1960s. The increasing

▼ **Boy meets girl in New York's Greenwich Village. Greater personal freedom challenged the protestant ethic in industrial countries.**

importance of white-collar jobs apparently meant that people's experience of work was becoming more fulfilling, involving personal interaction rather than subservience to machines. More and more workers were described in official statistics as "managerial, professional or technical" (29 percent of male workers in the United States in 1970), and increasing proportions of the national product of the advanced countries were being spent on "research and development" (in the United States 9 percent in 1965, with another 7 percent going on education – compared with only 3.4 percent in 1949). Even in the most "class-ridden" of all Western societies – in Britain – the way in which the remaining industrial workers shared in the general prosperity seemed to show that they too were becoming "middle class" in their values and attitudes, in the process sociologists described as that of "embourgeoisement".

Change was more apparent than real. In fact only in Britain did manufacturing workers ever, at any point in the history of industrialization, constitute a majority of the work force. The long-run trend of change in occupational structures was rather a shift from agriculture to services employment with the share in industry remaining stable over long periods. In practice a great deal of employment in services involved office work which was as much subject to routine, to hierarchical authority and to "deskilling" through the breaking down of tasks into simple, mechanical operations, as manufacturing jobs. The "professionalization" of work was often a chimera: as Bell wrote, "the word engineer is now used to describe anyone from a salesman (a 'systems engineer' at IBM) to a garbage collector (a 'sanitary engineer' in the Chicago euphemism)". Similarly the expansion of education tended to increase the entry requirements for repetitive jobs. Above all the advanced industrial societies of the West were increasingly dependent, not less so, on large-scale bureaucracies over which individuals had little control.

New estates and towns, and new suburbs where the working and middle classes lived side by side, seemed to lend credence to the notion of "embourgeoisement". But a famous study by David Lockwood and John Goldthorpe of British automobile workers found that not levels of income and consumption but work remained the definitive experience of class. The industrial worker was still dependent upon a wage, owed his relative affluence to overtime or his wife's ability to supplement the household income, and

generally held his labor to be not a vocation but drudgery. Even where working- and middle-class households lived in the same neighborhoods there was little sign of social integration. While the middle classes socialized primarily at home, working-class leisure activities continued to show strong communal characteristics, to hinge on kinship and community, on pubs and clubs, and to display a marked gender divide. Finally, the immediate impact of the secular decline of the share of the popular vote for the British Labour party after the mid-1960s was to make its supporters proportionately *more* "working class". The thesis of "embourgeoisement" was quite comprehensively rebutted.

The end of ideology?
The appearance of a more integrated society was enhanced, however, in Western Europe in the early 1960s by the ascendancy of a politics of consensus. This was described in Britain as "Butskellism", a term deriving from the elision of the name of the then leader of the Labour party (Hugh Gaitskell) with that of R.A. Butler, the principal Conservative theoretician. Both the major parties were committed in practice to much the same set of objectives, of welfarism, of increasing equality of opportunity and a "social market economy". In France the conservative government led by Charles de Gaulle was highly interventionist. In the Federal Republic of Germany the Bad Godesberg Conference of the Social Democratic party (SPD) in 1959 marked a historic change of direction. The party formally jettisoned its commitment to Marxism as an ideology and

▲ In the 1960s and 1970s employment in big office blocks such as this became more significant in people's working lives than factory jobs. There was talk of a "new service class society". But in spite of its apparently greater independence and "professionalism" a great deal of office work was as much subject to control and routine as that on an assembly line.

► Visitors at a motor show in Paris in the 1960s. Cars were more than ever a major status symbol. In the 1950s the purchase of a car and of major electrical consumer goods had become the aspiration of most citizens in the West. In the 1960s these aspirations were substantially satisfied. In Britain there were 2 million private cars in 1950; by 1964 over 8 million. Now smarter and faster cars became an increasingly possible dream.

Meritocracy

◄ "Meritocrats" at work in a high-tech factory.

In 1958 the British sociologist Michael Young published *The Rise of the Meritocracy*, a partly satirical book which showed how some social scientists understood the changes taking place in western societies. Young wrote as if from the perspective of someone working in 2033 who was trying to explain the conflicts of that time by reviewing the history of the 20th century. He argued that "The fundamental change of the last century... fairly begun before 1963, is that intelligence has been redistributed between the classes, and the nature of the classes changed. The talented have been given the opportunity to rise to the level which accords with their capacities, and the lower classes consequently reserved for those who are also lower in ability". In societies dependent on high levels of skill large numbers of those of low intelligence were hardly employable. Fortunately there was a demand for their labor as personal servants of meritocrats. Young thus anticipated the renewal of domestic service by the end of the 20th century. Because of the widespread acceptance of the "merit" principle social harmony was established, for a time, with those of lesser merit finding fulfillment in handicrafts and games. Young pointed to a darker lining in some social democratic aspirations of his own time, which seemed likely to introduce new tensions in society.

asserted that "Democratic Socialism" in Europe was rooted in Christian ethics, humanism and classical philosophy. Emphasis was placed on freedom and justice; the party favored "a free market wherever free competition really exists"; it stood for the elimination of privilege but made no mention of class struggle.

The takeover or participation in government by socialists almost all over Europe in the 1960s did not result in any dramatic changes in policy. Only in Britain did the old issue of the socialization of "the forces of production", through nationalization, remain a matter of controversy. Everywhere governments consulted different interest groups in society more extensively, following a pattern of corporatism marked out most strongly by the socialist parties in the Nordic countries. The stability of European societies was disturbed principally by strains induced by decolonization, especially in France. There de Gaulle's granting of independence to Algeria in 1962, bitterly resented by many though it was, finally caused the threat of disintegration to recede.

The events of 1968

In the calm consensus in Europe in the early 1960s few anticipated the convulsions of 1968, when for a moment France seemed at the point of revolution and there was strident social protest almost everywhere. These events lent force to the arguments of the American philosopher Herbert Marcuse that in the later 20th century the revolutionary class was no longer the industrial workers, who had been coopted into the management of capitalism, but students and the young more generally, who had the capacity to engage in social criticism and to organize on a large scale. The German students' union did not accept what was described as the "revisionism" of Bad Godesberg and remained active in social protest; Italian students in the early 1960s demonstrated against overcrowding in the universities and the rigidity of the curriculum; students in France mobilized around the same issues but were also powerfully politicized through their involvement in the struggles over decolonization and later by hostility to American imperialism in Vietnam. This was the immediate background to the events

of May 1968, when students and riot police confronted each other across barricades in Paris in an atmosphere which combined carnival and sense of fun (exemplified in the slogan "*Je suis marxist – tendance Groucho*"), with demands for university reform and for sweeping social change. When thousands and then millions of workers took part in a general strike in support of the students the Fifth Republic seemed near to collapse. But the sweeping Gaullist victory in the elections which followed in June showed that the political center had held in face of pressure from the extremes.

A survey of student participants in the revolt of May 1968 showed that for 56 percent of them the chief motive had actually been their concern over employment prospects; for 35 percent the focus was on poor educational facilities. A mere 12 percent thought of the events as a challenge to the structures of society. Student activism thus seems to have reflected some rather mundane concerns, and it was a more powerful force in France and Germany than in Britain partly, at least, because though recruitment to the elite in both countries was more dependent on academic merit than in

▲ Turkish *Gastarbeiter* ("guestworkers") in Germany. Germany was particularly dependent on immigrant workers because its own labor force was actually decreasing between 1960 and 1975. The aim was to recruit low-paid workers on a temporary basis; and it was assumed that the sending countries would benefit by the alleviation of their own unemployment problems, by remittances and by the eventual return to them of experienced workers.

Britain, the proportion of university students coming from peasant or working-class backgrounds was actually much *lower*.

The tumultuous year of 1968 thus crystallized social trends of the 1960s. There had been changes in European societies and a mood of criticism of capitalist industrialization. But old structures of power and authority persisted.

Migration and immigration

Settled and immobile, the traditional working classes of Western Europe failed to plug regional and sectoral gaps in the labor market. The problem was resolved by new waves of recruitment to the industrial work force. Young and healthy workers were recruited, with state support, mainly from southern Europe, Turkey and North Africa and at first left after short stays. They therefore claimed back little of what they paid in social insurance contributions. They also enabled the labor force to be adjusted to economic cycles. The recession of 1966–67 brought about a net loss of 800,000 jobs in West Germany, yet led to an increase in unemployment figures of only 300,000, because of the sharp fall-off in total numbers of foreign workers, euphemistically called "guest workers".

The indigenous work force was able to shift from old, declining or dying industries into new industries and the service sector. Above all, it was able to vacate the dullest, the poorest paid and the least secure jobs. Thus, the interests of migrant labor were generally underrepresented by trade union leaderships.

The presence of resident foreigners was not new to France or Germany, but in the course of

the 1960s the scale of employment of foreign workers increased dramatically. In the late 1940s there had been 1.5 million foreign workers in France; in the early 1970s their numbers had increased to 3.5 million so that they accounted for 7 percent of the total population. As early as the mid-1960s, foreign labor made up over 5 percent of West Germany's active labor force.

Problems of cultural assimilation, which were of a relatively minor order in the case of Italian migrant workers for instance, became acute especially with regard to Turkish workers in West Germany, to Algerians in France, and the relatively smaller numbers of migrant, from the West Indies and from South Asia who went to

▲ Families of Turkish *Gastarbeiter* in Berlin. Many immigrants settled down, wishing to stay a long time in the host country, though without necessarily changing their citizenship. This gave rise to problems in schools: should migrants' children conform to local cultural norms? Were local standards endangered, as some (host nation) parents feared? There were housing problems too. Segregation arose when Germans or Britons left inner-city areas and immigrants perforce settled in the places they had left.

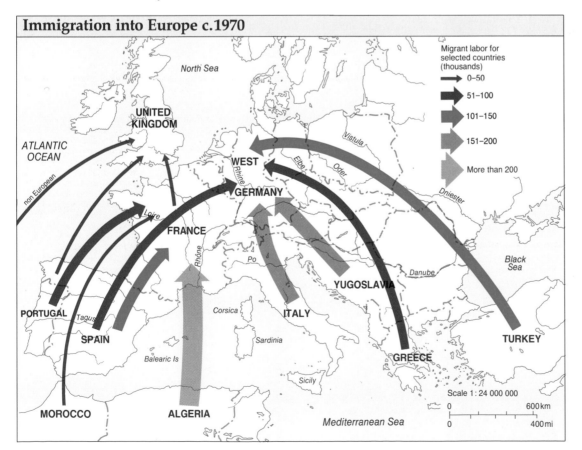

Immigration into Europe c.1970

Migrant labor for selected countries (thousands)

→ 0–50
→ 51–100
→ 101–150
→ 151–200
→ More than 200

North Sea

ATLANTIC OCEAN

non European

UNITED KINGDOM

Vistula

WEST GERMANY

Rhine

Elbe

Oder

Dniester

FRANCE

Loire

Rhône

Po

Danube

Black Sea

YUGOSLAVIA

PORTUGAL

Tagus

Corsica

ITALY

SPAIN

Sardinia

GREECE

TURKEY

Balearic Is

Sicily

Scale 1 : 24 000 000

0   600 km
0   400 mi

MOROCCO

ALGERIA

Mediterranean Sea

◄ By 1969 immigrants made up over 5 percent of the total population of Western Europe. Italians, Spaniards, Portuguese and (in Britain) the Irish were now rivaled in numbers by Algerians (in France), Yugoslavs, Greeks and Turks (in Germany) and Indians, Pakistanis and West Indians (in Britain). They shared the experience of being absorbed as a "reserve army of labor", in the least desirable jobs characterized by insecurity and poor working conditions, which had been deserted by indigenous labor. They also shared the experience of prejudice, though in varying degrees.

Britain. As West Germany's population of guest workers gradually became more settled, so the want of political as opposed to economic planning on the part of the government was exposed. Foreign workers and their families, enjoying no political rights in their "host" country and herded together in what were in effect to become ghettos, were vulnerable to prejudices activated by the experience of recession and unemployment which was to follow the oil crisis of 1973. Governments, instead of seriously confronting the issue of assimilation, resorted to restricting immigration – as Britain had already done as early as 1961. And so, intentionally or unintentionally, they seemed to legitimize the view that immigration was responsible for unemployment.

America: the triumph of liberalism

In the United States the early 1960s bear the stamp, above all others, of John F. Kennedy. His brief presidency (1961–63) encouraged the belief – not only in the United States – that a new and exciting age had arrived, and one above all of high moral purpose. "Ask not what your country can do for you", he said, "Ask what you can do for your country". This sense of purpose was extended into real accomplishment in the first years of Lyndon Baines Johnson's presidency (which began with Kennedy's assassination in 1963). In 1964 Johnson declared a "war on poverty" to carry out welfare initiatives which had been launched by his predecessor, and then announced his conception of the Great Society – "a place where men are more concerned with the quality of their goals than with the quality of their goods".

Johnson established the Medicare program of health insurance. Derided by the New England establishment as anti-intellectual, he saw through the Elementary and Secondary Education Act which provided grants for low-income pupils; and under his masterly leadership the 89th Congress, it was said, "brought to a harvest a generation's backlog of ideas and social legislation". At the same time the civil rights movement built up to a final push for racial equality. Already under Kennedy there had been a wave of desegregation of lunch counters, of "freedom rides" on interstate buses – testing a verdict of the Supreme Court that restaurants at bus stations could not discriminate against interstate travelers, and provoking violent opposition; and the southern universities were desegregated amidst bitter struggle. In August 1963 200,000 people gathered in Washington for a civil rights march, which was addressed passionately by Martin Luther King. "I still have a dream", he said, "It is a dream deeply rooted in the American Dream [that] one day in the red hills of Georgia, the sons of former slaves and the sons of former slave-owners will be able to sit together at the table of brotherhood".

King's vision came closer to being realized with the Civil Rights Act of 1964 which outlawed racial discrimination in public places, required equal access to public facilities, and prohibited discrimination in voter registration. A year later the Voting Rights Act effectively completed the enfranchisement of blacks. This was the apogee of American liberalism in the 1960s.

▲ Listeners to speeches at the great civil rights march in Washington, D.C., in August 1963. By this time the pressure from such demonstrations had pushed the administration into more resolute support for desegregation and the expansion of black voting rights; and troops had enforced court orders directing southern state universities to admit blacks. The achievement of civil rights was near.

◀ Even as the civil rights movement triumphed the black ghettoes erupted in the most destructive urban riots seen since the Civil War (1861–65). They showed the bitterness felt by blacks and signaled a new drive, not now for integration but for separatism and for self-help rather than reliance on white liberals. Some advocates of Black Power now sought to pursue a guerrilla war against white dominance.

In 1965, only five days after Johnson had signed the Voting Rights Act, the Watts area of Los Angeles erupted in racial violence, leaving 34 dead, and signaling the first of four long hot summers which revealed the depths of antiwhite bitterness in American society. Watts shocked America, for it was so much *better off* than other black neighborhoods, and had been treated as a model of race relations. The even more intense violence in Newark and in Detroit in 1967 also happened in places where blacks had apparently been relatively favored. The common pattern running through Watts, Newark and Detroit was the cry for Black Power. The civil rights campaigners' idea of white and black togetherness was spurned. A new movement rapidly developed with features that were anathema to the civil rights activists – rejection of integration and also a

◀ Tenements in Harlem. Once a genteel white neighborhood, Harlem became New York's largest black ghetto following the influx of blacks into the city early in the 20th century. In 1960 there was no part of Harlem in which more than 45 percent of housing was considered adequate. Only 7 percent of men were employed in professional or managerial occupations. It was said, "the negro has been left out of the swelling prosperity and social progress of the nation", echoing views that had already been expressed in the 1830s.

willingness to employ violence. The looting that went on in the city riots was lauded as a political act. The Black Muslims, led by Elijah Muhammed and Malcolm X, jeered at Martin Luther King, and won a lot of support amongst young black unemployed and outcasts in the ghettos of the northern cities, offering a vision of a future society in which blacks would be on top. Part of their anger derived from the view that "The black man's burden [is] the white liberal!"

Thus it was that "In the smoking ruins of the gutted cities little remained of the sanguine expectations of liberalism" (Leuchtenburg), and the hope of the Great Society was smashed by violence, leading in the end to the election of the Republican Richard Nixon as president, by the "silent majority" of the American people, who were not black, who were not young students, and who looked to a man who answered the call to "Bring Us Together Again".

Youth protest and the "counterculture"

The affluence of the 1960s brought, amidst the wave of social and political protest, what has been called a revolution in morals – of a counter-culture which in Theodore Roszak's words called for the "subversion of the scientific world view". While "modernity" sped ahead, new divisions opened up in Western society as hitherto silent social groups, ethnic or religious minorities, or immigrants demanded recognition and made their grievances felt. At universities the students' rebellion reflected the broader movement of change toward a more democratic and egalitarian society and a more humane personal and family life. Civil rights campaigns together with social critique advanced by the new left also gave feminism a new voice. In America gay rights activists began to campaign for the acceptance of an alternative sexuality.

Troubled by the prospects of a world that seemed increasingly bureaucratized and technologically driven, a new generation of young people rose to challenge entrenched institutions and the whole way of thinking on which the premises of Western consumer culture and meritocracy rested. Their protest against the establishment and its institutions and their revaluation of the value systems and symbols of authority which had prevailed in the West since the 18th century, had been foreshadowed by the so-called sexual revolution of the 1920s, and in America in particular also by a fervent critique of materialism in the same decade. After the war the "beats" of the 1950s, spreading also to Europe, picked up this theme. But it was to take that superabundance of worldly goods in the 1960s to produce a social and political protest movement which spread throughout the Western world.

The increasing presence of youth as a social and political force was crucial to this development. By the mid-1960s over half of America's population was under 30. According to a survey 80 percent of the under-35s were in some way involved in a search for "self-fulfillment", seeking an alternative life-style from that of their elders.

The icon-breaking counterculture of the young rejected the bourgeois catechism of the protestant

◀ The postwar boom in higher education created enormous problems. Since the establishment of new universities did not keep pace with the growing enrolment, most students had to be absorbed in the existing institutions. By the early 1960s the Sorbonne in Paris had almost 100,000 students. Student protest in France, as here in the Louvre, mixed issues of overcrowding and protest against an ossified university system with political grievances against the Gaullist regime.

ethic, fostering a rebellion against almost every aspect of traditional patterns of deference. The established churches which had until well into the 20th century preserved much of their importance as a mainstay of popular culture, and had continued to act as a bulwark of conservative social values, rapidly began to lose both their political and cultural influence. Official piety and church attendance were in decline. Yet religion was not. If anything, young people became more religious as they rejected the rationalism of the scientific age, replacing it with romantic, millennial or utopian dreams.

More harmful was the increasing consumption of alcohol and new experimentation with hallucinatory drugs to expand perception. Drugs

▼ Tupperware's range of plastic containers for the fridge and freezer and other uses was sold directly at home by organizing so-called "Tupperware parties", as seen here. Social gatherings of this kind, which mixed pleasure with the serious business of housekeeping, were a welcome relief for the relatively isolated housewife of the 1960s. Until the late 1960s public opinion averred that mothers should remain at home. Women generally obliged and actually tried to live up to the notion they could attain fulfillment only through rearing children and keeping house.

◄ The rediscovery of the pleasures of rituals and of festivity was an important part of the "counterculture" which erupted in America in the mid-1960s. At festivals such as this "live-in", usually held at urban parks, young people celebrated their new sense of personal freedom. When America's social reform movement came to a halt with the election of Richard Nixon toward the end of the 1960s, many of the once-utopian reformers of the counterculture turned away from their quest for fulfillment through a liberated community to fulfillment through the liberated self. This exploration and search for a true and autonomous identity later launched the "me first" protest movement.

were initially associated with performing or listening to rock music which was part and parcel of the youth revolt of the 1960s. "Acid Rock" made its appearance in San Francisco's light and sound shows. In Britain the Beatles' song, "Lucy in the Sky with Diamonds", clearly referred to the drug LSD. Drugs spread and marijuana became quite commonplace.

For many young people long hair and an unkempt appearance expressed the desire to escape the rigidity of a work-oriented existence. For the new "pot-heads" (in America) to be dirty was to be beautiful as they dropped out of school, drifting from "pad" to "pad". Alternative ways of living were found in so-called crash pads or communes, in the cities or away from them in the countryside, where the "flower children" and "hippies" of the 1960s and 1970s congregated.

Women and the family
In the new counterculture, with its focus on youth and hassle-free self-expression, there was little room for the very young or the mature or very old members of society. There was a certain cruelty in the way in which the old were declared to be obsolescent, part of that history that the young tried to shed. There was no tradition anymore, it seemed, and perhaps it is not surprising that initial bewilderment among the older generation eventually gave way to urgent calls for a return to "old fashioned decency and morality". How was one to deal with the changing position of women as they claimed the freedom to choose to have sexual experience and relationships both before, after and outside marriage; the free use of contraceptives and, if an unwanted pregnancy should occur, the right to abort? The really new

and potentially liberating ingredient in women's lives had been the breakthrough in contraceptive technology. The contraceptive "Pill", developed by American scientists in the 1950s, became commercially available by the early 1960s.

Sexuality was possibly the most important preoccupation of radical feminism: it was sexuality which made men the "intimate" enemy. In the early 1970s abortion emerged as almost the definitive issue of the feminist movement. For radical feminists it symbolized women's sexual and reproductive self-determination; for other feminists it became an issue of women's individual freedom of choice. In the end even the Vatican proved incapable of stopping the distribution of contraceptives and the legalization of abortion in Italy in 1978. In Britain and a number of American states abortion had been legalized by 1970, though only Denmark (1973) and Sweden (1975) legalized abortion on demand.

The new degree of equality and independence that women sought to achieve was seen by many as an outright rejection of both marriage and the family. The rapid expansion in the numbers of married women in the labor force after 1960, and above all their changing attitudes to work or a career, seemed to confirm this fear. Women now no longer predominantly worked because they had to, in order to supplement family income, but because they wanted to; and they wanted to even if they had children.

So for the pro-family platform this was a difficult time as women seemed to move away from their central role as wives and mothers. Anxieties deepened when the family came under attack from "abolitionists", suggesting that the family stood in the way of progress – or from radical feminists who attacked it as the basis for women's oppression. New attitudes toward sex seemed to find expression in casual relationships and cohabitation rather than life-long commit-

ment. While divorce and separation rates started their long climb upward (more than doubling between 1960 and 1975 in many countries), indicating the growing fragility of the concept of "marriage for life", marriage rates also continued to drop. The birth rate within marriage also began to fall again, soon to reach zero growth rates in a number of countries; while the rate of births outside marriage began to rise more rapidly, especially among teenagers. In 1969 in Germany 37 percent of all first-born children were conceived before marriage. Social pressure to get married when pregnant was still high (to a lesser extent in Sweden). Until 1970 the number of single-parent families remained roughly the same

▲ A central issue of the "second wave feminism" of the 1960s was rebellion against the physical assertion of male power. This included the exploitation of women as sexual objects which is also the theme of these magazine covers. Sexuality was possibly the most important preoccupation of radical feminism. It was also gainfully exploited by the media, which sometimes ridiculed feminist arguments against sexual oppression and also expressed overt hostility to the whole notion of women's liberation.

Churches and Society

After World War II the long process of secularization – the decline of religious belief – accelerated. Although the great majority of people in western societies continued to express their belief in some kind of deity, active church membership dropped. By the early 1960s only about 10 percent of the British people – mostly the elderly, women and young children – went to church at all regularly. Religious observance was not much more active in Catholic France and Italy. Amongst the industrialized countries only the United States did not conform to the trend. A survey carried out in 60 countries showed that the United States had a higher level of religious commitment than any other, except for India. Outside America the cultural role of churches largely disappeared. Outside Ireland churchmen lost their political influence.

Throughout the earlier 20th century the Roman Catholic Church, in particular, remained a profoundly conservative influence. There were glimmerings of change after the war when a very small number of "worker priests" in France had a considerable impact. They took up manual jobs and, identifying with workers, opposed the

injustice of the existing social order. But their activities were stopped in the 1950s. Meanwhile Protestant theological reform exposed the Church, seeming to suggest that its message had become irrelevant. In this context the papacy of Pope John XXIII after 1958 brought dramatic change, The Ecumenical Council which he summoned (known as "Vatican II") and which met from 1962 to 1965 reformed much of the Church's social teaching as well as rewriting liturgy and lowering old regulations. The Mass, for example, was no longer said in Latin. After the Council the Church made strides toward ecumenism and became more open even on issues such as mixed marriage. Yet it still remained resistant to the practice of birth control, to abortion and to homosexuality, all condemned by John's successor Pope Paul VI, under whose leadership the pace of reform slowed down.

Later in the 20th century the Christian churches were to become more divided, between liberal theology and a return to "fundamentals", and between the pursuit of an active social role (as in "liberation theology", for example) or a conservative one.

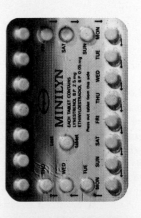

▲ Contraceptive tablets. Birth control changed dramatically in the 1960s with the arrival of the pill. In Britain it was initially issued by family-planning clinics and doctors. In America family planning as a public service was provided only to the poorest groups.

as in 1870 (10–12 percent – with national variations). After 1970, however, the single-parent family emerged as a more deliberate, intentional or less transitional life-style and the proportion of single-parent families was to double by 1980 (in America by that time to 21.4 percent of families with dependent children).

Attitudes to marriage

For a minority the significance of marriage as an institution began to diminish, demonstrating that different kinds of human sexual relationships were possible. The emergence of diverse family forms and life-styles, beginning with the "dual role perspective" (work and family) for women, single parenting, "common law" marriage or living in a commune also illustrated the fact that the very nature and range of possible ways of living together were products of social change. For many people, older (historical) family relationships became irrelevant. The so-called bourgeois family type (itself a product of social and economic change), which by 1900 had spread far beyond the middle classes to become the social norm, had centered on the mother and on the wife as a dependent. Love, the pivot of marriage,

had then had the character of a moral duty. All this was changing as the old dependents, wife and children, were now accorded new rights and women in particular achieved new independence. In Britain in 1974, for example, in over half a million couples the wife was the main earner; while in some seven million others wives contributed around a quarter of the family budget.

On the whole, however, the sexual revolution seemed not to have had all the consequences its earlier exponents claimed for it. There was no general consensus on sex roles, and traditional attitudes toward marriage remained pervasive – especially when it came to questions of fidelity in marriage. Despite the preoccupation with sex and its pleasures, sexual relationships outside marriage were not easily tolerated, by either partner. Sex may have been offered as a commodity by the amusement industry, the cinema or sex shop, but ideals of "true love" asserted themselves against "libertinism" in a number of ways. If libertinism did not materialize, then women's new independence and rights, and the reforms in divorce law toward the end of the 1960s and in the 1970s, certainly made it easier for women to make the break from marriages which had gone wrong.

▲ Feminist demonstrations such as this High School event in the United States were usually organized to raise women's consciousness of a shared struggle. Until the early 1970s consciousness-raising had a central place in feminist groups' activities, to help women to relate their personal experiences to wider issues of sexual oppression. By learning together women were to acquire a revolutionary solidarity of sisterhood. Among the more radical groups, this fueled anger and protest against male-dominated politics – eventually leading to separate organizations for women.

LAW AND ORDER

"Society" implies "order", but order is not synonymous with law. In many societies, both in the past and today, there has been no legal system, no laws, no courts, no prisons. Instead, order has been maintained by means of customary regulations and sanctions, though sometimes there have also been specialists in the settlement of disputes. With the development of large-scale societies and in particular of the nation state, standardization of law has been essential together with the development of the principle of citizenship, implying both rights and obligations. In the 20th century the extension of formal systems of law and of legal institutions has gone hand in hand with the spread of state organization. The great European colonial empires were of the greatest importance in this global change.

In many countries, however, different ways of maintaining social order continue to coexist. Thus in Papua New Guinea the institutions associated with Western law are part of the state, while in parts of the country order is still sometimes maintained between communities by means of traditional ceremonial warfare.

The principles of modern law are closely tied to the idea of the liberal democratic state. Equality of all before the law, separation of judiciary, executive and legislature, and public process are all part of what the law is supposed to be. There is also a darker side. While order may be desirable, it often implies conformity against the will of individuals or social minorities. Law also has an element of discipline which is enforced by means of punishment, and may thus be used to defend the positions of the powerful. Sometimes, as in Nazi Germany and communist states, the law has meant the defense of the position and beliefs of the party – political and ideological deviation were criminalized. In others it has been used to defend the privileges of the wealthy and powerful.

The law and the legal system are important aspects of the effective separation of the public and private realms. The criminalization of marital violence, corporal punishment of children by their parents, use of drugs, pornography – all arguably part of the "private" sphere – have been and continue to be important legal issues. While it has increasingly been recognized that different cultures may require different legal provisions, the experience of the 20th century has shown starkly that legal questions are also political questions and that the law can be used for illegitimate political ends – to discipline those who do not fit in with the mainstream of society.

▲ ▶ A stern but caring state: productive work and education are displayed in a Soviet "model" prison 1933. The aim is reform rather than punishment, preparation for return to society. This public face of Bolshevik penal theory was belied by the horrors of Soviet labor camps.

▶ ▶ A US prison, based on penal theory which confines the body and breaks the will. There is no pretense of reform here.

▶ Police in Boston in the United States. In face of protest, law and order may come down to force

◀ Legal majesty and impartiality are personified in these judges from Sierra Leone and symbolized by their special dress and remote bearing. Maintenance of these ideals in the face of powerful sectional interests is a constant struggle in all societies. The law is upheld not only by legal institutions; press freedom may be just as important. It is not yet clear whether Western legal systems work in non-Western cultures.

◀ The stark machinery of death in the United States: an electric chair. In many societies death continues to be the punishment for misdemeanors ranging through theft, murder, adultery, treason, political and sexual deviation. As with all law, the use of capital punishment may have more to do with politics than with justice or morality.

▼ Whose law, whose justice? The law in the hands of one section of society. Law has often been a means for control by a minority — by these whites in South Africa, by the party in the Soviet Union and in Nazi Germany. Censorship, the whip, the secret death, the panoply of control, a state without citizens, only degrees of prisoner — law can easily be used to build the prison state.

SEEING BEYOND THE VISIBLE

Our eyes can see only visible light, a very small part of the electromagnetic spectrum, but radiation beyond the visible range can be "seen" using specialized instruments, revealing details hidden to the naked eye. Although 19th-century scientists could detect the X-ray, infrared, and ultraviolet parts of the spectrum by photography, during the 20th century a whole new range of instruments were developed to overcome the limitations of the naked eye, making exciting new developments possible. Photography relied on the use of sensitive film to make an image, but the development of the cathode ray tube and television technology made it possible to build detectors which gave television pictures showing how things looked in different parts of the spectrum, without having to wait for film to be developed. Looking at things in other parts of the spectrum made it possible to see through opaque materials using X-rays, or, with radar, to spot enemy aircraft at great distances, day or night, cloudy or clear, by looking at them with radio waves.

Microscopy was transformed by the development of electron microscopes from the 1930s. Optical microscopes could give magnifications of 20,000 times, but when electron microscopes were eventually made they could magnify 1,000,000 times, revealing viruses and the interior of cells. By 1960 a further development, the field-ion microscope, gave the first images of atoms, magnifying 10,000,000 times.

When radar and infrared detectors were used to look at the Earth itself, the new science of remote sensing was born, and found immediate applications in weather forecasting, mapmaking, monitoring crop damage and detecting natural resources. Astronomers too found uses for such sensors, and new branches of astronomy were born. Space technology made it possible to place remote sensing satellites in orbit above the Earth, to monitor the weather and map natural resources, and send space probes to the farthest reaches of the Solar System.

A key development was the introduction – originally for military use – of computer image processing from the 1960s. When applied to remote sensing, greatly improved pictures could be created, revealing even more detail of the Earth and planets. Applied to X-ray technology, "body scanners" could be built which revealed hidden details of the human body.

Improved techniques also made it possible to see things that happened too fast for the eye. By 1908 photographs were being taken of fast-moving splashes of liquids, and by the 1970s it was possible to "freeze" waves moving at the speed of light.

"Seeing" was no longer restricted to using the electromagnetic spectrum. Sonar, developed during World War II to detect submarines by sound waves, was developed into a way of making pictures of the seabed, and, in the 1950s "ultrasound" which detected objects in a watery environment such as the womb, was first used to see inside the human body.

► Electron diffraction microscopy was developed in the 1930s. An image is formed by putting a beam of electrons through the specimen and studying the ways in which the beam is diffracted. This image is formed by the crystallic structure of the atoms of pure silicon. In the 1980s several other techniques of microscopy were developed to reveal detail at the atomic level.

▼ The scanning electron microscope gives a three-dimensional image of the specimen (such as *Staphylococcus* bacteria, shown magnified 5,000 times).

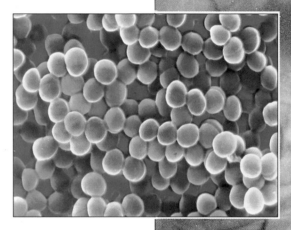

▼ A false-color image of the planet Neptune, (eighth planet from the Sun) photographed by the space probe Voyager 2 in August 1989.

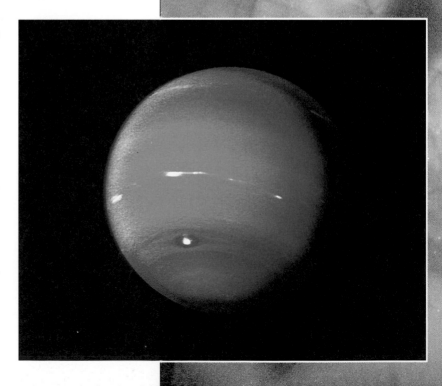

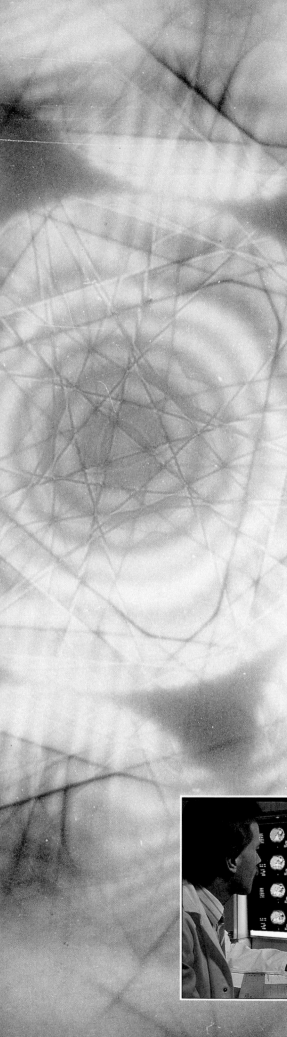

◄ Radar carried on high-flying aircraft can be used both for navigation and for tracking weather phenomena such as hurricanes. This example was photographed off Mexico in 1955. A radio beam is emitted from the aircraft, and is reflected back by the water and ice particles in the clouds. Since the introduction of meteorological satellites, such tracking is now usually done from space.

▲ High-speed photography can reveal details that happen too fast to be observed by the naked eye.

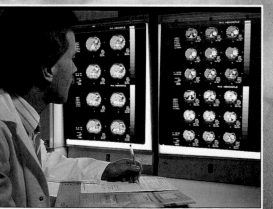

◄ In the 1970s and 1980s new techniques of non-invasive imaging of the interior of the human body. CAT scanning involves a series of X-ray images taken all round the body; a computer collects the information and constructs a "slice" through the body tissues, differentiating between bone, fat and muscle. This technique is valuable for the location of tumors and blood clots.

THE
REVOLUTION
OF YOUTH

Time Chart

	1961	1962	1963	1964	1965	1966	1967
Film	• Release of Walt Disney's *101 Dalmatians* (USA) • *Judgment at Nuremberg* released, directed by Stanley Kramer (USA) • Release of *Last Year at Marienbad*, directed by Alain Resnais (Fr) • *West Side Story* released, directed by Robert Wise and Jerome Robbins; Natalie Wood starred (USA)	• *Lawrence of Arabia* (director, David Lean) brought Peter O'Toole to stardom (UK) • Release of *Dr No*, directed by Terence Young – the first James Bond movie starring Sean Connery (UK) • *Jules et Jim* released, directed by François Truffaut (Fr) • 5 Aug: Marilyn Monroe found dead of a drugs overdose (USA)	• *Cleopatra* (director, Joseph Mankiewicz) brought Richard Burton and Elizabeth Taylor together (USA) • Release of *8½*, directed by Federico Fellini (It) • *Tom Jones* released, directed by Tony Richardson and starring Albert Finney (UK) • Release of *Dr Strangelove*, starring Peter Sellers and directed by Stanley Kubrick (UK)	• Release of the Beatles' first movie, *A Hard Day's Night*, directed by Richard Lester (UK) • Release of *Zorba the Greek* (director Michael Cacoyannis) starring Anthony Quinn (Gr) • *My Fair Lady* released, directed by George Cukor and starring Audrey Hepburn and Rex Harrison (USA) • Sidney Poitier became the first black actor to win the Oscar for Best Actor (USA)	• Release of *Dr Zhivago*, directed by David Lean, with Julie Christie and Omar Sharif (UK) • *The Knack* released, directed by Richard Lester and starring Rita Tushingham and Michael Crawford (UK) • Release of *The Sound of Music*, directed by Robert Wise and starring Julie Andrews, with a score by Rodgers and Hammerstein (USA)	• Release of *Un Homme et une Femme*, directed by Claude Lelouch (Fr) • Paul Scofield starred in *A Man for All Seasons*, directed by Fred Zinneman (UK) • *Torn Curtain* was Hitchcock's 50th movie (USA) • Release of *Who's Afraid of Virginia Woolf*, directed by Mike Nichols and starring Elizabeth Taylor and Richard Burton (USA)	• Catherine Deneuve starred in Luis Bunuel's *Belle de Jour* (Fr/It) • Release of *Bonnie and Clyde*, directed by Arthur Penn and starring Warren Beatty and Faye Dunaway (USA) • *Elvira Madigan* released, directed by Bo Widerberg (Swe) • *The Graduate*, directed by Mike Nichols, starring Dustin Hoffman (USA) • 8 Jul: Death of Vivien Leigh, from TB (UK)
Media	• Production of the satirical revue *Beyond the Fringe* (UK)	• Feb: *The Sunday Times* introduced Britain's first newspaper color supplement • 11 Jul: Live TV transmitted from Europe to the USA by Telstar	• 22 Nov: President Kennedy's assassination was televised (USA) • 23 Nov: The first episode of BBC TV science fiction series *Dr Who* broadcast (UK)	• 28 Mar: Radio Caroline, the first pirate radio station operating from the North Sea, began to broadcast • Jun: Comedian Lenny Bruce arrested (USA)	• 8 Feb: Cigarette advertising banned on British TV	• Premiere of science fiction serial *Star Trek* (USA) • 15 Aug: Closure of the *New York Herald Tribune* announced (USA)	
Music	• 28 Sep: Bob Dylan caused a stir, playing in Greenwich Village (USA) • Sep: Chubby Checker's *The Twist* started a dance craze (USA) • Dec: Clarinettist Acker Bilk's *Stranger on the Shore* reached no 1 (UK)	• 30 May: Benny Goodman played in Moscow (USSR) • The Beatles signed with EMI, and released *Love Me Do* (UK) • Release of Bob Dylan's *Blowin' In The Wind* (USA)	• Fans screamed at the Beatles in a huge London Palladium concert (UK) • The Beatles' *I Want To Hold Your Hand* sold 1 million copies before release (UK) • Rolling Stones' first record, *Come On* (UK) • 11 Oct: Edith Piaf died aged 47 (Fr)	• 15 Jan: The world's first discotheque, *Whisky-a-Go-Go*, opened in Los Angeles (USA) • Aug: Death of country star Jim Reeves (USA) • 10 Oct: Ravi Shankar played at New York's Town Hall (USA)	• 11 Jun: The Beatles received MBE awards from the Queen (UK) • Release of *The Sound of Silence* by Simon and Garfunkel (USA)	• Mar: *Uptight* was Stevie Wonder's first hit (USA) • May: The Beach Boys' *Sloop John B* entered the charts (USA) • Van Morrison left R&B group Them to pursue a solo career (UK)	• May: *Purple Haze*, by Jimi Hendrix, at no 3 (USA) • 18 Jun: The first large pop festival was held at Monterey, featuring Hendrix, Janis Joplin, The Who (USA)
Fashion and Design	• IBM Selectric typewriter produced by designer Eliot Noyes (USA) • Oleg Cassini was appointed Jackie Kennedy's official dress designer (USA) • First couture minis presented by Marc Bohan at Dior and André Courrèges (Fr)	• Apr: Opening of the Seattle World's Fair, the Century 21 Exposition (USA) • Council of Fashion Designers of America founded • Camera Nazionale della Moda Italiana founded (It) • Mary Quant won the first Bath Museum of Costume "Dress of the Year" award (UK) • Yves Saint Laurent opened his fashion house (Fr)	• Issey Miyake showed his first fashion collection in Tokyo (Jap) • Pierre Cardin produced his first ready-to-wear collection (Fr) • London fashion taken to America by chainstore JC Penney	• Apr: New York World's Fair opened (USA) • Terence Conran opened his first Habitat home furnishing store (UK) • Barbara Hulanicki's Biba boutique opened in Kensington (UK) • Vidal Sassoon created his geometric "five-point cut" (UK) • André Courrèges and Pierre Cardin produced "Space Age" fashions (Fr)	• Former architect Paco Rabanne created a plastic dress (Fr) • Nov: Model Jean Shrimpton's miniskirt shocked racegoers at the Melbourne Cup (Aus) • America's first Mod store, Paraphernalia, opened in New York	• Fashion designer Jean Muir formed her own company (UK) • Experimental design studios Archizoom and Superstudio founded in Florence (It) • Twiggy was the Face of '66 (UK) • Hemlines dropped, as the midi was shown in London and Paris	• A totally inflatable plastic chair was designed for Zanotta Co. (It) • Apr: Expo '67 opened in Montreal (Can) • First injection-moulded plastic chair designed by Joe Colombo (It) • Laura Ashley opened her first London shop (UK) • Beatle John Lennon's Rolls Royce was given a psychedelic "coat of many colors" (UK)
Sport	• 6 May: Tottenham Hotspur won the FA Cup and the League title, the first team to do so this century (UK)	• Jul: Dawn Fraser (Aus) became the first woman to swim 100m in under 1 minute • Sep: Rod Laver (Aus) became the first man since 1938 to win the tennis Grand Slam	• Sir Adetoklunbo Ademole became the first black African IOC member • Feb: René Lacoste patented a metal tennis racket (Fr)	• 29 Jan: Opening of ninth Winter Olympics, at Innsbruck (Aust) • Aug: South Africa banned from Olympics because of apartheid • 10 Oct: Opening of the first Olympics to be held in Asia, in Tokyo (Jap)	• 1 Jan: Stanley Matthews was the first professional footballer to be knighted (UK) • 1 Feb: Ron Clarke (Aus) broke 5000m world record twice in three weeks • East and West Germany decided to compete separately in the 1968 Olympics	• 4 Sep: Racing driver Jack Brabham (Aus) won the world championship in a car he had built, the first man to achieve this • Dec: Francis Chichester completed the world's longest nonstop solo sea voyage, from Plymouth, UK, to Sydney, Aus, in 107 days	• 4 Jan: Donald Campbell died in an attempt on world water speed record (UK) • 15 Jan: Inaugural Super Bowl match between Football League champions (USA) • 30 Apr: Muhammad Ali (Cassius Clay) was stripped of his world boxing title
Misc.	• Yuri Gagarin was the first man to go into space and back (USSR)	• 22 Oct: President Kennedy ordered the Cuban missile blockade	• Martin Luther King's "I have a dream" speech, in Washington (USA)	• The first US pilot was shot down and captured in Vietnam	• Jan: Skateboards became a craze	• Aug: The Chinese Cultural Revolution announced	• 150,000 marched in protest against the Vietnam war (USA)

1968	1969	1970	1971	1972	1973
• Release of *If*, directed by Lindsay Anderson (UK) • *Funny Girl* (director, William Wyler) gave Barbra Streisand her first starring role (USA) • Paul Newman directed his wife, Joanne Woodward, in *Rachel, Rachel* (USA) • Release of *2001 – a Space Odyssey*, directed by Stanley Kubrick (USA)	• John Wayne won his only Oscar, for *True Grit*, directed by Henry Hathaway (USA) • Release of Federico Fellini's *Satyricon* (It) • Paul Newman and Robert Redford starred in *Butch Cassidy and the Sundance Kid*, directed by George Roy Hill (USA) • Release of *Romeo and Juliet*, directed by Franco Zeffirelli (It) • *Easy Rider*, directed by and starring Dennis Hopper, also with Peter Fonda, epitomized the "acid culture" (USA)	• Release of *Days and Nights in the Forest*, directed by Satyajit Ray (Ind) • Release of *Patton* (director Franklin Schaffner) (USA)	• Release of Stanley Kubrick's *A Clockwork Orange* (UK) • Dirk Bogarde starred in *Death in Venice*, directed by Luchino Visconti (It) • Release of *The French Connection*, directed by William Friedkin (USA)	• Liza Minelli and Joel Gray starred in *Cabaret*, directed by Bob Fosse (USA) • Release of Tarkovsky's *Solaris* (USSR) • *Last Tango in Paris* (director, Bernardo Bertolucci) released; Marlon Brando starred (USA) • Release of *The Discreet Charm of the Bourgeoisie*, directed by Luis Bunuel (Sp) • Release of Francis Ford Coppola's *The Godfather*, starring Marlon Brando (USA)	• Release of *Day for Night*, directed by François Truffaut (Fr) • *The Exorcist* released (director, William Friedkin) (USA) • Release of *Fear Eats the Soul*, directed by Rainer Werner Fassbinder (Ger)
• *Hawaii Five-0* pilot program shown (USA) • ABC news special "How Life Began" showed *in utero* pictures, and film of a birth (USA)	• Premiere of *Monty Python's Flying Circus*, on BBC TV (UK) • 10 Jan: *New York Saturday Evening Post* closed • 18 May: Apollo 10 sent the first live color TV pictures of the Earth	• Amateur radio stations helped with communications in the Peruvian earthquake disaster • 9 Nov: David Frost's LWT program disrupted by Jerry Rubin and Yippies sprinkling Frost with flower petals (USA)	• Soviet TV broadcast the BBC costume drama series *The Forsyte Saga* • The editors of the underground magazine *Oz* on trial for obscenity (UK)	• Dec: The last issue of *Life* magazine (USA) • *Cosmopolitan* launched in the UK • Two feminist magazines launched, *MS* in America, and *Spare Rib* in the UK	• BBC presented *War and Peace* (UK) • 500 million worldwide watched the wedding of Princess Anne and Mark Phillips (UK)
• 22 Jun: Judy Garland died, aged 47 (USA) • 7 Jul: Rolling Stone Brian Jones died aged 25 (UK) • Joni Mitchell's first album *Song for a Seagull* (USA) • Premiere of hit hippy musical *Hair* (USA) • The Beatles formed Apple Co. (UK)	• 15 Aug: 400,000 attended the Woodstock pop festival (USA) • Sep: The Isle of Wight festival was Britain's biggest • Nov: Hells Angels stabbed a fan to death while the Rolling Stones played at the Altamont festival (USA)	• 10 Apr: Paul McCartney quit the Beatles (UK) • 18 Sep: Jimi Hendrix died of a drug overdose aged 27 (USA) • 4 Oct: Janis Joplin died of a drug overdose aged 27 (USA) • Release of Simon & Garfunkel's *Bridge Over Troubled Water* (USA)	• 3 Jul: The Doors' Jim Morrison died aged 28 • 1 Aug: A concert to raise money for victims of flood and civil war in Bangladesh was organized by George Harrison and friends	• 17 Jun: *Fiddler on the Roof* hit a record 3225 straight performances (USA) • 30 Aug: John Lennon and Yoko Ono played Madison Square Gardens (USA) • Premiere of *Jesus Christ Superstar*, by Tim Rice and Andrew Lloyd Webber (UK) • The Moog synthesizer patented	• 26 May: Carole King played to 70,000 in Central Park (USA) • Release of *Killing Me Softly With his Song*, by Roberta Flack (USA)
• Shoji Hamada awarded the Order of Culture medal for reviving the art of ceramics (Jap) • The Beatles' Apple boutique was psychedelically decorated by the Dutch group Fool (UK) • Zandra Rhodes formed her own fashion house (UK) • Calvin Klein started his own fashion business (USA) • Balenciaga retired from couture (Sp)	• Mar: Concorde 001, the supersonic airliner, made its maiden flight (UK/Fr) • Japan Industrial Design Promotion Organization established • Fashion designer Rei Kawakubo (Jap) founded Comme des Garçons • The musical *Hair* popularized Afro hairstyles	• Mar: Expo '70 opened in Osaka (Jap) • Fiorucci launched his designer jeans (It) • Kenzo (Jap) opened his fashion shop, Jungle Jap, in London (UK) • Ergonomi design group founded (Scan) • *Women's Wear Daily* coined the term "hot-pants" (USA) • *Harpers & Queen* magazine launched (UK)	• Intel Co introduced the microprocessor (USA) • The Crafts Council set up (UK) • Publication of *Design for the Real World*, the book by Victor Papanek which inspired design for the handicapped and the "third world"	• New York's MoMA presented an exhibition in recognition of the contribution of Italian avant-garde designers (USA) • Frei Otto designed a lightweight tent-like roof for the Munich Olympic stadium (Ger) • Fashion retailer Joseph Ettedgui (Mor) opened a London store (UK)	• IBM's Selectric self-correcting typewriters featured an ergonomically designed keyboard (USA) • Nov: Le Grand Divertissement, Versailles, was a showcase for the collections of five leading French and five US fashion designers (Fr)
• Feb: Winter Olympics held at Grenoble (Fr) • Sep: South Africa cancelled MCC winter tour because Basil d'Oliveira was on the team • Oct: Mexico City Olympics: altitude was a problem for many athletes; two US athletes sent home after giving the Black Power salute during the 200m award ceremony	• May: Graham Hill (UK) won the Monaco Grand Prix for a record 5th time. • Nov: Anti-apartheid demonstrators disrupted the South African Springbok rugby team's British tour • 20 Nov: Brazilian soccer star Pele scored his 1000th goal	• May: South African cricket tour of the UK cancelled, and SA banned by the IOC from the 1972 Olympics • Jun: Tony Jacklin was first British golfer for 50 years to win the US Open • Jun: Brazil was permanently awarded the soccer World Cup trophy, after winning it for the third time	• 26 Dec: Rod Laver (Aus) became the first tennis millionaire • Princess Anne named Sportswoman of the Year (UK)	• 2 Feb: Winter Olympics opened in Tokyo (Jap) • 26 Aug: Opening of Munich Olympic Games, at which US swimmer Mark Spitz won seven gold medals (Ger) • 5 Sep: Arab guerrillas attacked Israeli building at the Olympic village; 17 killed (Ger) • Sep: Bobby Fischer became first US world chess champion	• 31 Mar: Red Rum won the Grand National in record time (UK) • Aug: 180 arrested for soccer violence (UK) • Jackie Stewart, champion racing driver, retired on the eve of his 100th Grand Prix (UK)
• 4 Apr: Martin Luther King assassinated (USA) • 5 Jun: Assassination of Senator Robert Kennedy (USA)	• 20 Jul: Neil Armstrong was first man on the Moon • First *in vitro* fertilization of human egg cells, (UK)		• Idi Amin seized power in Uganda	• 30 Jan: "Bloody Sunday" in Belfast (UK) • 17 Jun: Watergate break-in (USA)	• US troops quit Vietnam

Datafile

The affluence of the 1960s and early 1970s brought a renewed confidence in modernity and technology, this time coupled with an emphasis on the young, and an impatience with tradition. In fashion, this brought a revolution that threatened to sweep away the established systems for the creation and dissemination of fashion; in design the sense that everything would soon be replaced by something newer led to a celebration of impermanence itself. Furniture was made of plastic and paper; and the idea of built-in obsolescence became widespread for most consumer durables. Fashion and design, together with music, seemed ready to revolutionize the world.

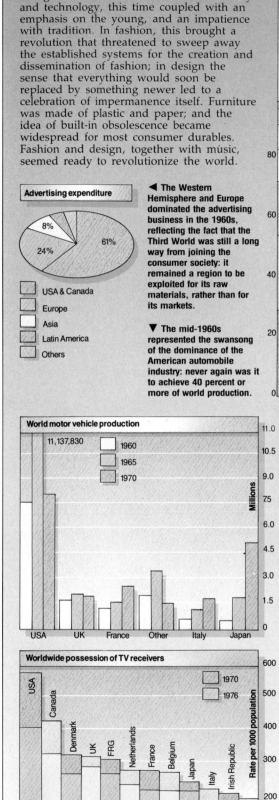

Advertising expenditure

- USA & Canada
- Europe
- Asia
- Latin America
- Others

◀ **The Western Hemisphere and Europe dominated the advertising business in the 1960s, reflecting the fact that the Third World was still a long way from joining the consumer society: it remained a region to be exploited for its raw materials, rather than for its markets.**

▼ **The mid-1960s represented the swansong of the dominance of the American automobile industry: never again was it to achieve 40 percent or more of world production.**

World motor vehicle production

11,137,830 — 1960, 1965, 1970

USA UK France Other Italy Japan

Worldwide possession of TV receivers

1970, 1976

USA, Canada, Denmark, UK, FRG, Netherlands, France, Belgium, Japan, Italy, Irish Republic, Hong Kong

Rate per 1000 population

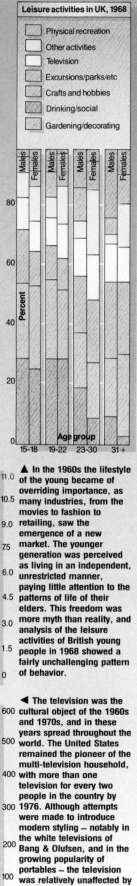

Leisure activities in UK, 1968

- Physical recreation
- Other activities
- Television
- Excursions/parks/etc
- Crafts and hobbies
- Drinking/social
- Gardening/decorating

Males / Females

Percent

Age group
15-18 19-22 23-30 31+

▲ **In the 1960s the lifestyle of the young became of overriding importance, as many industries, from the movies to fashion to retailing, saw the emergence of a new market. The younger generation was perceived as living in an independent, unrestricted manner, paying little attention to the patterns of life of their elders. This freedom was more myth than reality, and analysis of the leisure activities of British young people in 1968 showed a fairly unchallenging pattern of behavior.**

◀ **The television was the cultural object of the 1960s and 1970s, and in these years spread throughout the world. The United States remained the pioneer of the multi-television household, with more than one television for every two people in the country by 1976. Although attempts were made to introduce modern styling – notably in the white televisions of Bang & Olufsen, and in the growing popularity of portables – the television was relatively unaffected by the new design ideas of the period.**

The music and youth subcultures of the 1950s and early 1960s generated a number of dress styles, especially in Britain. That of the teddy boys never lost its outlaw status, but the mod fashions of a slightly later period, which originated among art students, fertilized mainstream fashion and created a new cheap instant high fashion. It was designed from the beginning to be mass-produced and to be worn by the young, yet still the product of individual artists; inspired by the teenager, it was not yet "street fashion" as such.

This style was popularized, first in Britain, later in the United States, by television pop-music shows, later still by new women's magazines catering to specific sections of the market, and especially to the under-25s. In catering for this new clientèle, younger than the previous fashion market, manufacturers were almost bound to produce youthful styles; but the new youth styles were taken up everywhere, by fashion writers in *Vogue* and in the more staid newspapers as well as in the trendier magazines. At the beginning of the 1960s the youthful – and soon the positively infantile – styles seemed to express the optimism of the "affluent society", the joy of consumerism, and even a kind of innocence, as the old, rigid hierarchies of deference and the stifling sexual puritanism of Western culture after World War II began to dissolve. Simple shift dresses, sometimes with childish raised waistlines, flat shoes with cream or black stockings, tight ribbed sweaters, pinafore dresses and long or short straight hair and "Christopher Robin" fringes replaced the over-sculptured cuts of the fifties. All these expressed not just a rebellion of youth, but a general reaction to the hierarchic modes of the previous decades. Subsequently associated with the "permissive society" or the breakdown of sexual restraint and family values, short skirts initially seemed to express the innocence of a new generation growing up with the hope of a thaw in the Cold War.

The new fashions testified that the New Look and its aftermath had never been adequate for the lives that women – and not just young women – were leading in the 1950s and 1960s. Although the new youth fashions are often said to have been the brainchild of British designer Mary Quant, there is a sense in which they originated from within Paris, the heartland of French *haute couture* itself.

Paris and London

After World War II Chanel had been in eclipse, (owing in part to her wartime association with a Nazi officer), but in 1953 she decided to re-open the doors of her salon. Her first collection seemed to be a disaster – the simple little dresses and suits were quite out of tune with the carapace-like

THE SWINGING SIXTIES

creations of Dior, Balenciaga and Pierre Balmain, and the show was panned. Yet within a year the American ready-to-wear manufacturers had seen the potential of the Chanel suit, and the design went into mass production. Chanel claimed she was no longer interested in designing for the few, but for the woman in the street. With its simple jacket and skirt and its signature of braid trim and gold chain necklaces, an off-the-face hat and bag with a chain handle, the Chanel suit became the uniform of the smart American business or career woman. Jackie Kennedy was wearing such a suit when her husband was assassinated, and the Chanel mode of simplicity was the inspiration for the mainstream fashions of the early sixties.

Another Parisian, André Courrèges, introduced the two most revolutionary fashions of the 1960s: the miniskirt and the trouser suit. His futuristic designs expressed the optimism of the space age. But it was Mary Quant who did more than anyone else to bring this youthful style of fashion to the mass market. Her designs displayed an amalgam of influences: the Mods, the London art-school scene of the fifties – already bohemian and avant-garde – and French *haute couture*. She described her fashions as "mod" and classless, "pop" fashions in a time of pop songs and pop art. But although she herself was an original artist, with her husband she married her talent for design to an awareness of the latest American mass-production and merchandising techniques. Improved sizing was one innovation; another was her original presentation, first in her own shop Bazaar, in the King's Road, Chelsea, where the displays were young and zany instead of still and lifeless, and in her use of pop music during the showings of her collections; another was in her use of original materials. In the space-age sixties, synthetic materials could be translated into high fashion. The use of shiny PVC for raincoats and hats was her most successful experiment, but she later used "old-fashioned" synthetic crêpes and satins in the "off" colors of the 1930s and 1940s – maroon, burnt orange, eau de nil and salmon pink – for droopy blouses and minidresses that began to have a "retro" feel about them, rather than invoke pure modernism.

As she successfully launched into cosmetics in

▼ In 1967 the fashion esthetic changed – from the bright Mary Quant image to a hippy or ethnic style with hallucinatory overtones. Style became – for both sexes – soft, droopy and "feminine": long hair, full sleeves, flared trousers. Boutiques such as this one in London were drenched in color and music.

the second half of the sixties – and as she and her models wore the geometric hairstyles created by Vidal Sassoon – she, like Chanel before her, initiated a total look. Significantly, one of her most successful products, a foundation cream called "Starkers", was advertised as looking so "natural" that it was as if you were wearing nothing (ie your face was stark naked), but by this time the cult of the natural – in reality, no more natural than any other fashion – was in full swing. The name "Starkers" was a typical use of the upper-class slang of an earlier period. This language – "super", "smashing" – united with the language of the criminal fringe – "dolly-bird", "my old man" – is revealing not so much of any classlessness of the period as of a knowingness about class and a new kind of snobbery, "trendiness", which rejected the middle-class and "square" in favor of the glamor of both the upper and the lower classes. It was also a childish language, of the school playground and the 1930s schoolgirl story.

By the mid-1960s the British designers had snatched the fashion initiative from Paris, but it was not immediately clear that this was the beginning of a waning in the dominance of the Paris "system". That system had presupposed that women formed one homogeneous group, all equally receptive to the same fashion styles, and divided only by whether they purchased original models, expensive copies or cheap adaptations.

The advent of youth fashions, which had begun, tentatively at first, in the 1950s but escalated in the 1960s, indicated that there was instead a variety of consumer groups, each aspiring to something different and distinctive.

Fashion and the counter-culture

Various specific fashion styles developed within counter-cultural groups, often organized around pop-music styles and bands, and these became a growing influence on *haute couture*. The hippy look of flowing scarves, loose, flowery robes and flowing sleeves and trousers was widely copied. But "hippy" dressing was a critique of the very fashion system it both plundered and influenced. The counter-culture of the late sixties also loved second-hand clothes. Quite apart from cheapness, recycling clothes was part of a tactic of bricolage and of self-sufficient living on the margins of capitalism, which demonstrated their opposition to the wastefulness of the consumer society. They snapped up old "frocks" from the thirties and forties, tailored men's and women's jackets and suits, and antique hats and shoes. A Chelsea dress shop called "Granny Takes a Trip" epitomized the late sixties esthetic, with punning reference to hallucinogenic drugs as well as to the rifling of the past for "old-fashioned" styles. In addition, the political concerns of the student movement of the period brought various forms of

► The British model Twiggy, (Leslie Hornsby) who began the trend for very young models, was nominated the *"Daily Express* face of the year" in 1966. She was then a sixteen-year-old weighing 90lb (41kg) and perfectly suited the clothes of the period. With her androgynous haircut, she epitomized the waiflike, childish look which miniskirts, high waists, very short or very long hair and as here, schoolgirlish fashions gave women in the mid-sixties.

▼ As well as the hippie-based fashion for frills, beads and long hair, men's fashions in the 1960s looked back to the teddy-boys of the previous decades, and through them, to the turn of the century. Double-breasted jackets, pointed collars and tight trousers, whether straight or flared, gave a sharp but informal look.

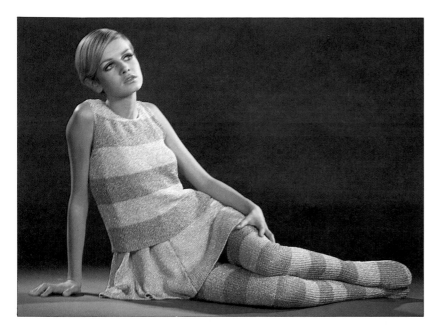

dress from exotic cultures into Western fashion, in an attempt – perhaps contradictory – to celebrate rather than exploit the Third World.

Instead of a Paris-dictated line of artistic evolution imitating the manner in which other art forms developed, fashion became knowingly self-conscious. Designers seemed to acknowledge more openly that fashion is all about novelty and change for the sake of change. Although pastiche and the rifling of history for decorative and fashion motifs has been part of fashion at least since the early 19th century, the scale of the borrowing was intensified in the esthetics of "retro-chic".

One of its early innovators was Biba of London. Biba's creator, Barbara Hulanicki, started in 1964 with a mail-order service selling dolly dresses at rock-bottom prices to the newly fashionable teenagers of the period. By the late sixties she had branched out into art nouveau/art deco fantasy shops where you could buy feather boas, sleazy thirties' pyjama suits in cream or flesh-colored

Fashion Photographers

Between the wars, and even more in the 1950s, the love affair of black-and-white photography with high fashion gave birth to the frozen perfection of the fashion image. The sharp lines, dark shadow and white light dramatized the angular, exaggerated creations of the New Look period particularly well. American photographer Richard Avedon captured the self-dramatization, the confidence, sophistication and self-mockery of *haute couture* in his work for *Harper's Bazaar* in the early fifties. Avedon and others loved to place their glacial or cavorting models in bizarre or incongruous situations.

By 1960 a new generation of photographers was seeking inspiration from the grainy images of the new cinematic realism of British films such as *Saturday Night and Sunday Morning* or *Room at the Top*. Their work displaced line drawing as the main medium for fashion illustration, but was at times even more mannered, while the search for novelty could lead to downright eccentricity in choice of angles or location. At times the fashion photograph seemed less to attempt to convey information about the latest styles than to capture the mood of an ensemble, or even to suggest a whole lifestyle. The fashion photographs of the 1960s made of high fashion a performance, a street event, a triumph of the will. They also transformed photographic models into celebrities and stars, while the photographers themselves – David Bailey, Lord Snowdon, John French – became household names, heroes of the swinging sixties. Michelangelo Antonioni's film *Blow Up* – often taken to epitomize "Swinging London" – involved just such a fashion photographer as its main character. In the 1970s, the imagery became even more mannered and eccentric, or else banal. Black models appeared more frequently, but models tended to become ever more precocious, while some photographers, notably the German Helmut Newton, flirted with an imagery drawn from soft pornography.

► **The Rolling Stones, photographed by John French.**

▲▼ The Biba look that flourished in London in the 1960s provided a total design environment that repackaged Hollywood art-deco and art-nouveau imagery for sixties' youth. The vast store itself opened in 1973 but was not viable. Biba's distinctive styling included packaging, the actual store (including, especially, the showcases for the goods on sale), mail-order material and the clothes themselves.

satin, wide-shouldered, dumpy forties' dresses, and endless period accessories, all available in a range of "dirty" shades from old rose to chocolate. Her final gamble was to fill the whole of an old department store – which retained its original art-deco carpets and fittings – with clothes, accessories, furniture and even food in the Biba style. She over-reached herself, and her magic emporium was gutted, to be replaced by chain-store predictability.

All this was part of a wish to replace the products of the consumer society with objects and artefacts that had a craft rather than a commodity relationship with the owner. Although, for example, the fashion for crocheted garments was initiated by the fashion industry in Britain in 1963, this was often introduced in popular women's magazines as an opportunity to make your own. Waistcoats and shawls made from crocheted multi-colored squares, fairisle and other patterned sweaters, hats, macramé belts and other do-it-yourself alternatives to consumerism were featured in new magazines such as *Honey*, aimed at the young, trendy mass market of relatively affluent women in their early twenties.

The use of exotic motifs in alternative fashion was highly eclectic. One such fashion was a band tied round the head in the manner of American Indians - much later to become a fashion for gay men in San Francisco. Another was the kaftan, which matched a fashion for long skirts on women. Despite the hippy trail to the Indian subcontinent, Indian fashions never really caught on; men would wear African-style shirts and students the PLO-type Arab head scarf, but the adoption of Third World styles was gestural rather than serious. For some young women the early 1970s was a period of fashion refusal, in an attempt to find an alternative mode of dress that moved away from obvious self-objectification as much as from *haute-couture* discomfort. In the United States this was more likely to be achieved by styles based on sportswear; in Britain a kind of dusty picturesqueness was achieved with the combination of home-knits with jeans, dungarees and long skirts in Laura Ashley old-fashioned prints.

Soon *haute couture* was introducing ethnic borrowings into its twice-yearly shows. The appetite of the mass clothing market for new styles was so intense that rebel fashions were quickly taken up, but without their political content.

Perhaps it was inevitable that the adoption of clothing from cultures in which garments were relatively unchanging was superficial, since after all, these alternatives were all about style. The styles themselves signaled rebellion or disaffection from the dominant culture; since, however, that culture was highly organized around styles and their changes, to adopt a stylistic alternative was still to remain part of the culture which expressed change, dissidence and difference in these symbolic terms.

Design and ephemerality

The democratization of design became a reality for the first time in the economic boom years of the 1960s, as goods with a strong visual content reached a more youthful audience. Through increased consumption young people in Europe and the United States began to manifest their newly acquired wealth and to assert their "alternative" values. From the motor-bikes, motor-scooters, transistor radios and record-players of the early youth sub-cultures through to the fashion items, graphics, furniture and other lifestyle accessories of the pop sixties, they demanded artefacts which provided them with a means of identifying themselves with each other. Many designers responded to the challenge: in Britain, Mary Quant, Foale and Tuffin, Ossie Clark, John Stephens and others provided clothing for the new youth market. Graphics designers Martin Sharp and Michael English produced posters and other pieces of two-dimensional ephemera to accompany the pop music now so central to the new culture. Even furniture designers responded to the new values of expendibility, producing, by the middle of the decade, pieces of furniture which were knock-down, throw-away or blow-up.

More importantly, perhaps, where consumption itself was concerned, the pop revolution brought with it a dramatic change in retailing patterns. New boutiques sprang up aiming their goods – from fashion to ephemera – at the youth market specifically. In doing so, they emphasized the role that the visual and lifestyle aspects of their products play in consumption, stressed individualism rather than anonymous mass production, and focused as much on the visual context of the goods as on the goods themselves. Boutiques relied on peoples' buying products for reasons other than those of utility and low price.

This new approach to retailing moved, quickly, beyond the area of fashion into other lifestyle goods. In 1964 the British designer/retailer Terence Conran opened his first Habitat store, its furnishings and household goods appealing to young, educated, fashion-conscious consumers. Selling objects ranging from brightly colored enamel trays and mugs to French Provençal crockery to items of pine furniture, Habitat concentrated less on the individual product than on the total environmental effect of putting together, in a single space, a wide range of objects which expressed the same "taste" values. A careful selection of goods which together created a visually unified ensemble proved a clever way of selling customers a complete lifestyle even if they left the

▲ The Habitat catalog, offered a lifestyle "improved" by good design, relying on brightly colored domestic fittings and goods such as tableware imported from France or Italy.

▼ The geodesic dome was the most spectacular achievement of the alternative design movement of the 1960s in which Victor Papanek and Buckminster Fuller argued for appropriate use of materials and energy.

◀ The most "avant-garde" interiors in the 1950s and 1960s depended on the twin influences of European modernism — characterized by such materials as black leather, chrome and glass — and the more humanistic esthetic which was emerging from Scandinavia, particularly Sweden, epitomized by its use of natural, light woods — pine and birch — and simply decorated textiles. This interior, with its swivel chairs and exposed pine, captures the spirit of that epoch, emphasizing the essential, uncluttered airiness of the postwar domestic environment, and the fusion of the interior furnishings with the architectural space that contains them. Every detail contributes to the whole and the elements fuse into a totality which represented an optimistic vision of the modern world and the future.

▲ Robin Day's polypropylene stacking-chair, manufactured by Hille in 1963, was the first of its kind to utilize this new material. Envisaged as a chair for such places as large auditoria, football stadia, and lecture rooms, the ease with which it could be carried, stacked and linked made it enormously popular. Day's design was widely emulated and remains, even today, one of the most ubiquitous objects in the public environment.

shop with only a single item. Habitat was the first store to sell goods on the basis of "good taste" to a mass market, and in so doing it set an important precedent which was to become increasingly influential.

The "good design" movement
By the mid 1960s the concept of design as a commodity "added" to consumer objects to increase their value had become economically and culturally integrated into all the capitalist countries of the industrialized world. Design differentiated products in competition with each other, or else served as a form of national self-identification on the world market.

During the 1950s the reconstructed economies of Germany, Italy and Japan, had sought to restore themselves in international trading through identifying their goods with a particular product esthetic. For the most part, only goods aimed at

a fairly exclusive, wealthy international market were overtly described as incorporating "design", often with the name of a well-known designer attached to them. Only those companies which aimed their goods at the top end of the market made sure that they were seen by the media as being design-conscious. Others, with a mass market in mind, concentrated more on minimizing the price of their products than on their esthetic content.

The "good design" movement of these years became a clearly defined cultural phenomenon, supported by museum collections, exhibitions such as the Milan Triennales, and conferences, competitions, awards and glossy magazines. A very tightly delineated design culture grew out of this network, and as long as it remained in the hands of an international elite it was easy to identify its ideological function and cultural effects. Synonymous with the concept of good taste, it preferred minimalism to ostentation and elegance to vulgarity. Well designed products became increasingly identified with a cosmopolitan, middle-class, well-educated lifestyle. Some furniture and electronic equipment manufacturers – Olivetti and Cassinini in Italy; Hille in Britain; Bang & Olufsen in Denmark; Braun in Germany; Sony in Japan; and IBM in the United States – established their identities through their commitment to design and largely depended upon it for their commercial success.

The national styles of these goods varied one from another, however, and the modern design movement in Italy had the greatest international impact. Industrial and cultural reconstruction in the years since 1945 had encouraged close collaboration between consumer-goods manufacturers and a group of highly creative architect-designers. The economic boom of the years 1958–63, combined with a forward-looking attitude towards new materials and a commitment to an aggressively modern esthetic with its roots in sculpture, resulted in the proliferation of goods for home and office which were associated with a sophisticated, cosmopolitan lifestyle.

Italy's ability to compete favorably in international markets stemmed primarily from its policy of paying low wages to its workforce rather than from investing in advanced technology. Italian design was limited to those goods which depended on low technology – furniture, household appliances – rather than the more complex electrical and electronic products to which Japan was dedicating its energies. Forbidden by the terms of the postwar settlement to develop an armaments industry, Japan had come to dominate the consumer electronics market, in part because of American industry's preoccupation with military contracts.

"Italian design" became linked, in the minds of many, with glossy plastic tables and chairs, sumptuous leather armchairs and sofas, sculptural lamps in steel and marble, and other items of household and office equipment which appealed more on the basis of their elegant forms than their technological sophistication.

The exclusivity of Italian design gave rise to an alternative design movement in that country, to challenge the glossy, status-ridden image of mainstream fashion. Linked to social and economic factors such as the students' revolution of 1968, the anti- or counter-design movement sought to reunite design in Italy with the cultural base which had inspired it in the early postwar years. Kitsch, stylistic revivalism and irony were used in an attempt to take design out of the hands of industry and to reposition it within the mass culture. Radical architectural groups based in Florence presented Utopian visions of the future which were destined for the art gallery rather than the factory floor.

The alternative design movement

In the early 1970s a growing consciousness of the distance between Western conspicous consumption and underdevelopment in the Third World encouraged a number of designers to rethink the social and moral functions of design.

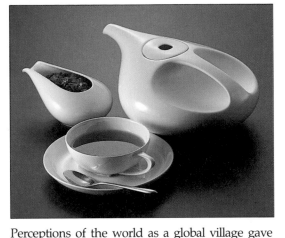

Perceptions of the world as a global village gave designers a different idea of their role than as the adjuncts of manufacturing industry. Victor Papanek's 1971 book *Design for the Real World* was one stimulus behind this movement to re-direct design into the service of the underprivileged, whether the impoverished of the Third World or the old and infirm in the West.

Papanek argued that for too long designers had been concerned with little more than creating "toys for adults". He proposed a number of areas in which designers could contribute to relieving hardship in underdeveloped countries, among them "communication systems, simple educational devices, water filtration, and immunization and inoculation equipment."

By the mid 1970s a number of Third World design schools had taken responsibility for working not only on goods aimed at western export markets but also on projects which directly helped their own population. At the National Institute of Design at Ahmedabad in India, students worked on a symbol system for contraceptive education; an artificial limb which allowed disabled people to pursue their accustomed lifestyle, and on a range of other goods designed specifically for an Indian market. However, such work remained marginal to mainstream design and failed to undermine the main economic function of design in the century, as the guarantor of added value for goods aimed at a mass society.

The Danish company Bang and Olufsen's "Beogram 4000" record player was among the most minimal and sophisticated examples of its kind to emerge in the 1970s. In sharp contrast with the complex, high-tech, value-for-money machines with which Japaneese manufacturers were flooding world markets, Bang and Olufsen opted for a more up-market look which appealed to a smaller, more discriminating group of consumers. This was reflected, inevitably, in the price of the product.

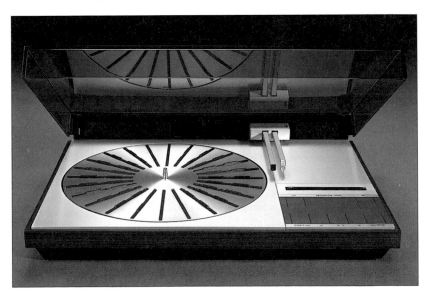

Datafile

Even though Hollywood spent the 1960s floundering without much sense of what its domestic audience would pay to see, it maintained its hold over foreign markets, and American television followed its example, offering developed and Third World countries programming at a much lower cost than their own television industries could provide. If the new technologies of communication were turning the world into a "Global Village," it was one in which only some would speak, and those who did were likely to have an American accent. In 1968 the American film industry abandoned its Production Code, ushering in a wave of "realism" that looked to critics like explicit sex and violence.

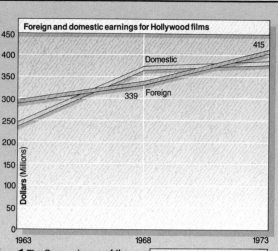

Foreign and domestic earnings for Hollywood films

◀ In the 1960s foreign sales became an equal source of revenue for Hollywood to its home market, and although the exact proportion varied, foreign and domestic earnings remained roughly level throughout the next decade. This encouraged independent producers and major companies to make films abroad, where costs were often cheaper than in the United States. By 1970 films made by American companies somewhere other than Hollywood accounted for as much as 60 percent of total American output.

Academy Awards for Best Film of the Year

1961	West Side Story	United Artists
1962	Lawrence of Arabia	Columbia
1963	Tom Jones	United Artists
1964	My Fair Lady	Warner
1965	The Sound of Music	Fox
1966	A Man for All Seasons	Columbia
1967	In the Heat of The Night	United Artists
1968	Oliver!	Columbia
1969	Midnight Cowboy	United Artists
1970	Patton	Fox
1971	The French Connection	Fox
1972	The Godfather	Paramount
1973	The Sting	Universal

◀ The Oscar winners of the 1960s reflected Hollywood's stagnant imagination; only one was not based on a book or musical. There was a sharp change in 1969 as the Academy caught up with Hollywood's pursuit of the youth market. *Midnight Cowboy* was directed by an Englishman, John Schlesinger, but its sleazy tale of New York street-life was a sharp departure from the kinds of movies previously rewarded by the Academy. *The French Connection* was the first crime movie to be voted Best Picture.

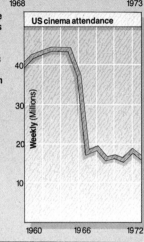

US cinema attendance

◀ Cinema attendance continued to fall steadily during the 1960s in the United States. The studios remained uncertain about what would attract audiences, and as the blockbuster phenomenon developed, they lurched headlong from one expensive project to another. Many of their difficulties were caused by the studios' continuing reluctance to accept that the family audience had been permanently lost, and that they now had to gear production exclusively to a younger market.

Feature film imports

Hollywood's largest foreign markets

◀ In 1974, 15 countries accounted for 74 percent of all Hollywood's foreign earnings. The American film industry was dependent on foreign markets; however, American pictures kept half the world's movie theaters open. In addition, all the major international distribution companies were American; even when distributing British of French films in other foreign markets, they were taking their share of the profits, and American companies were also frequently the financial backers of French, Italian or British films.

◀ American films recovered 40 percent of their production costs in Europe, while European films recovered only 10 percent of theirs in the United States. The Middle East and Asia showed a preponderance of American product only a little less than that in Latin America, while the Australian market was still dominated by Hollywood until the mid-1970s, when its government promoted a new national film industry. Only the Eastern bloc remained effectively closed to Hollywood's influence.

▶ American television repeated Hollywood's conquest of the world. At times it was almost total: in 1969, in the event billed as "the greatest show in the history of television", 723 million people watched Neil Armstrong take the first steps on the Moon. To some extent, Europe immunized itself from transatlantic pollution by quotas to limit the amount of American programs which could be screened, but such luxuries were not available to Third World countries, whose native industries were undermined.

Imported programs on television

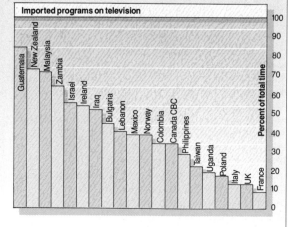

THE NETWORKS AND THE NEW WAVE

By 1960 television had "liberated" cinema by taking over its function as mass entertainment. Without a clear idea of what its post-television role should be or how to satisfy its increasingly disparate audience, Hollywood was in limbo for much of the next decade. The old studio moguls were either dead, in retirement, or battling to maintain a tenuous control over their companies. With them had gone confidence about production. The strategy of high-budget costume epics that had sustained Hollywood through the 1950s came crashing down with the extravagant failure of *Cleopatra* (1963), at $40 million the most expensive film ever made. The film's colossal losses nearly bankrupted Twentieth Century–Fox; the lesson both it and the rest of the industry chose to learn came from the movie that restored the studio's fortunes, *The Sound of Music* (1965). Made for $8 million, it grossed $78 million in the United States and Canada alone.

The industry was lured by the prospect of such returns into ever greater recklessness, spending extravagantly on visible production values in the hope that the "money on the screen" would draw in audiences. Sometimes it worked spectacularly well. Together with the re-release of *Gone with the Wind, Doctor Zhivago* (1965) kept MGM solvent for the second half of the decade. But in 1969 only one film in ten showed a profit. In the second half of the 1960s the studios resembled gambling addicts in the terminal stages of their illness, locked into a pattern of borrowing heavily from banks to finance another blockbuster that they hoped would defy the rules of movie profitability and solve the company's financial problems at a stroke. With the successive failures of lavish musicals such as *Star!, Hello Dolly* and *Dr. Doolittle*, Fox lost $78 million in 1970, and nearly bankrupted itself again.

Hollywood now derived more than half its income from abroad, with the European market supplying 80 percent of that total. Economically dependent on their international appeal, American films became more cosmopolitan, or mid-Atlantic, in their appearance. Thrillers developed convoluted plots that toured the landmarks of European capitals and pushed aging American male leads – Gregory Peck, Cary Grant – into affairs with younger European women such as Sophia Loren. "Runaway" productions made in Europe had the advantages of government subsidies and lower production costs. Epics such as David Lean's *Lawrence of Arabia* (1962) were given international casts to enhance their appeal to European distributors.

These meanderings were signs of Hollywood's uncertainty. The industry's lack of financial self-confidence led to the studios being bought by major American conglomerates for well under their market value. Universal was bought by MCA, a former talent agency, Paramount by Gulf and Western (steel, mining, plastics), United Artists by Transamerica Inc. (insurance), Warners by the Kinney Corporation (car rentals, building maintenance, funeral parlors), and MGM by Kirk Kerkorian, a Las Vegas hotel magnate. Bought for their real estate and undervalued film libraries, and for the possibility of windfall profits in good years, the companies became small elements in much larger corporations. In 1974 Paramount's film rentals amounted to only 3.5 percent of Gulf and Western's revenues.

As the studio system disintegrated in a morass of agents, deals and "packaging", the machinery which had once regulated Hollywood production crumbled. The Production Code had survived more or less intact through the 1950s, but became increasingly untenable against the industry's need to cater to a more permissive audience hostile to anything it could label "censorship". The Code was finally abandoned in favor of a ratings system in 1968.

The year 1967 was a pivotal one in Hollywood's development. Audience figures increased for the first time since 1946, partly because of the massive success of *The Graduate* and *Bonnie and Clyde*, each made for $3 million and returning more than ten times its cost. The significant increase in

▼ Many producers blamed *The Sound of Music* (1965) for nearly destroying Hollywood in the mid-1960s. It was such a huge hit that every studio tried to copy it, investing in big-budget musicals that failed disastrously at the box-office.

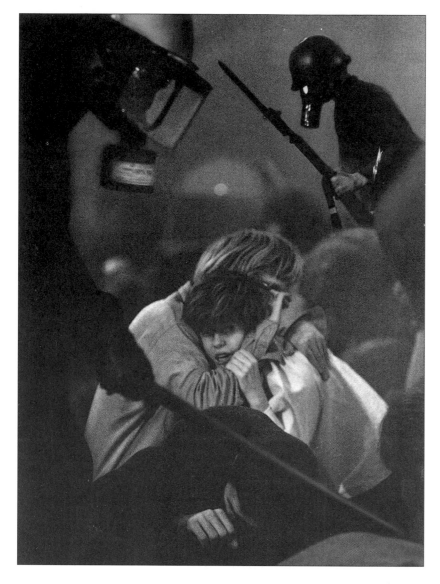

attendance was among 18- to 25-year-olds, and the studios began to search for new product to cater to this young audience. *Easy Rider*, made in 1969 for $400,000, grossed $25 million, bringing into being a new genre, the youth film, and a new system of low-budget independent production, based on the model pioneered by Roger Corman, who had specialized in "schlock" movies for the drive-in market.

Films for the young
The Hollywood "Renaissance" of the early 1970s followed an influx of a new generation of managerial talent – Richard Zanuck, Robert Evans, Alan Ladd, David Picker. The success of *Easy Rider* sent them scurrying in search of untried directors who could turn a low-budget "personal" film into both artistic masterpiece and commercial success. Production companies such as BBS and Pressman-Williams emerged to provide the brief

▲ ▶ In the late 1960s Hollywood tried to capture the youth audience, inspired by the success of the French New Wave directors, including François Truffaut. *The Graduate* (1967) was one of the first Hollywood films to succeed, wrapping Dustin Hoffman's aimless adolescent rebellion in selfconscious stylishness. Three years later, after the police violence at the 1968 Democratic Convention in Chicago, *The Strawberry Statement* (above) took the radicalism of youth revolt and student protest more seriously. A more acceptable form of rebellion brought Robert Redford stardom in the early 1970s. In *Butch Cassidy and the Sundance Kid*, (above right) Redford and Paul Newman presented their anti-social activity as a form of comic play for them and the audience.

Art Cinema and the New Wave

In France, a New Wave of filmmakers, many of them former critics, emerged in 1959 when Francois Truffaut's *400 Blows* won the Best Direction prize at the Cannes film festival. As critics on the magazine *Cahiers du Cinéma*, Truffaut, Claude Chabrol, Jacques Rivette and Jean-Luc Godard had attacked the dominant tradition in French film of respectful adaptations of "quality" novels, and asserted that the true creators of cinema were its directors. As directors, they experimented with subject matter and technique, producing films dealing with more complex and daring themes than the conventional sentimentalities of Hollywood.

This experimentation would not have been possible without an audience prepared to regard cinema as an art form comparable in esthetic merit to the theater. This new audience – young, middle-class, educated and internationally minded – welcomed a cinema that provided the stylistic innovation and thematic substance of literary modernism, for evening entertainment. Critics in the press and specialized film journals now championed the director as author, and this individualization of creativity made "cinema" critically respectable, something the bourgeois

delusion that in the Hollywood renaissance anything might be possible. Movies made for the youth market – *Medium Cool, The Revolutionary, The Strawberry Statement* – even suggested that Hollywood might be capable of an explicit political radicalism as well as an increasingly explicit depiction of sex and bloodshed.

Those moral guardians who feared that the Code's collapse would usher in the demise of decency were not far wrong. As Hollywood grew increasingly explicit in its treatment of sexuality, so the pornography industry grew less peripheral. In 1972 *Deep Throat* became the first piece of hardcore "porno-chic" to play in regular movie theaters as well as in those that showed only "adult" rated films.

By 1973 the Hollywood Renaissance had collapsed. It had become possible, however, to take American cinema seriously. In the early 1970s courses in film began to be available at American universities, and to use the words "film" and "art" in the same sentence was no longer the mark of an oddball or a film publicist.

Television in the sixties

It would be some time before anyone tried to make the same case for American television, which had changed little from the way Newton Minow, chairman of the Federal Communications Commission, had described it to its producers in 1961, as "a vast wasteland".

Minow had just been appointed to his post by John F. Kennedy, and many in his audience might have expected gentler treatment from a president who had been elected, they believed, on the strength of his appeal on television.

Television obliged politicians to become performers in a way radio never had. Kennedy, youthful, authoritative and almost handsome enough to play the lead in a TV doctor series,

seemed perfectly cast. Pursuing a policy of accessibility to the camera, he held live press conferences, delivered an ultimatum to Khrushchev via television during the Cuban missile crisis, and encouraged his wife to take the nation on a *Tour of the White House*. The impact of his assassination was intensified by the fact that he was not just the President, but a television celebrity whom the viewing public had been encouraged to feel they knew through the intimacy of the medium. For the four days between the assassination and the funeral all three networks suspended their regular schedules and carried no advertising.

By 1960 half the population of the United States depended on television as its prime source of news. Network prime time had settled into a mixture of half-hour comedy shows and hour-long action/drama series. Drama, like comedy, was constructed around a repeatable situation, usually provided by a professional activity. Lawyer- and doctor-shows provided an ideal format for hour-long stories featuring guest stars as clients or patients, but the same formula was used for series on teachers and social workers.

The formula had its limitations. The central characters had to remain unchanged by the episode's events, in order to be in their proper places by the following week's episode. The serial form provided the programming stability necessary to deliver viewers to advertisers on a regular basis. Networks tried to carry their audiences from one show to the next, employing the principle of Least Objectionable Programming. This meant that the majority of viewers who simply watched television, rather than selecting specific programs, would watch whichever show they disliked least. The unit of television viewing was not the individual program but the daytime or evening schedule as a whole. As a result, television placed little emphasis on the

You will see on US television a procession of game shows, violence, audience participation shows, formula comedies about totally unbelievable families, blood and thunder, mayhem, violence, sadism, murder, western badmen, western goodmen, private eyes, gangsters, more violence and cartoons and, endlessly, commercials – many screaming, cajoling, and offending ... Gentlemen, your trust accounting with your beneficiaries is overdue. Never have so few owed so much to so many.

NEWTON MINOW 1961

audience could care about. After 1960, enough people cared about cinema to constitute a market sufficiently large to support a personalized cinema that delighted in idiosyncratic stylistic touches, particularly if they were used to embellish sexual or psychological content.

The development of a general market for the cinematic form of self-conscious modernism established by Ingmar Bergman, Federico Fellini and the French New Wave gave room to further experimentation. In such films as Alain Resnais' *Last Year at Marienbad* (1961) and *Je T'Aime, Je T'Aime* (1968), orthodox chronology was abandoned in favor of stylized meditations on the uncertainties of time. It also opened up a Western market for East European films for the first time since the 1920s. The Hungarian director Miklos Jancso and the filmmakers of the Czechoslovak New Wave formed part of the European art film movement, until the Russian invasion of Czechoslovakia brought the "Prague Spring" to an end in 1968.

▶ Federico Fellini's *Satyricon* (1964).

distinction between fact and fiction. In sports and game shows it offered its audience an engagement with an endless dramatic experience, in which consequences and conclusions mattered less than the exuberance of competition, choice and performance. Television had a peculiar capacity to dissolve distinctions between comedy, drama, news and commercials.

Television's other typical form, the talk show, perfected its formula in the early 1960s with *The Tonight Show*, hosted by Johnny Carson. Talk shows packaged personality as a commodity, but all television employed it; even newsreaders became celebrities.

Vietnam, the first rock 'n' roll war, was also the first television war, with combat footage on the nightly news. Johnson tried assiduously to manage television coverage of the war, pundits debated endlessly about whether television had "brought the war home" or had trivialized it as just another interruption in the stream of commercials, and whether the scenes of carnage and the reports of American atrocities had numbed its audience or had increased anti-war sentiment or street violence. Television reporting was brutally attracted to scenes of violence and dissent – they made good pictures. By the end of the 1960s political groups denied conventional access to the media had recognized the staged act of violence as an effective means of gaining attention. Terrorism happened for the television camera.

Johnson's successor, Richard Nixon, saw the media as his enemy. Although his 1968 campaign

was an object-lesson in the packaging of a candidate's image, his attitude had been indelibly marked by his failure in the televised debates with Kennedy in 1960. Even before the Watergate Senate hearings topped the ratings in 1974, Nixon and his staff regularly denounced television's "nattering nabobs of negativism."

In common with most Western television systems, the Federal Communications Commissions Fairness Doctrine enforced the provision of equal time for the expression of opposing views on any given issue. Its effect was to secure the middle ground for television itself, and to make its presenters the arbiters of political dispute. Television's credibility relied on its apparent neutrality, something that marked it out from the partisan allegiances of newspapers.

By the late 1960s television news was expected to be profitable as well as prestigious. *CBS Evening News* cost $7 million to produce in 1969, and made a profit of $13 million. The need for pictorial content meant that television took to "managing" the production of news in ways reminiscent of the "yellow press" at the beginning of the century (see page 34). Needing to deliver stories with both drama and immediacy, journalists passed from gathering news to creating it, in the form of predictable and manageable events such as press conferences and publicity stunts.

Television news stimulated an ever-growing cynicism and disaffection with politics by its emphasis on dissent and disagreement. At the same time the medium itself became the vehicle for the

▲ **Richard Chamberlain as *Dr Kildare*, which premièred in 1961. Lawyer- and doctor-shows provided an ideal format for stories featuring guest stars, but they had their limitations. *Dr Kildare* could never marry, just as the *Rawhide* cattle drive could never end.**

► **Vietnam was the first television war. Some commentators believed that Lyndon Johnson decided not to run for re-election after Walter Cronkite, anchorman of *CBS News* and "the most trusted man in America", declared in March 1968 that the United States might not be able to win the war. But the presence of television had not deterred South Vietnam's police chief from shooting a bound Vietcong suspect in the head on camera during the Tet offensive the month before. Neither, later that year, were the student protestors at the Chicago Democratic convention protected from the nightsticks and billyclubs of Mayor Daley's rioting police force by their chants of "The whole world is watching".**

normal. It existed to sell viewers to advertisers, and advertisers were little interested in showing their wares to black ghetto-dwellers, for example, who might want the proffered consumer goods but lacked the wherewithal to purchase them. Television's largest advertisers – the manufacturers of automobiles, cosmetics, food, drugs, household goods and, until 1971, tobacco – wanted the networks to supply them with a middle-class audience for their sales pitch.

In the late 1960s the American networks discovered that a detailed study of the audience provided them with a way of selling advertising time at higher prices by selecting programs aimed at a wealthier, educated audience. Fewer shows were aimed at middle-aged, middle-class viewers in large towns and rural areas. More programming was directed at a younger, urban audience with more money to spend. The controlled irreverence of *Rowan and Martin's Laugh-In*, launched in 1967, was one gesture toward this audience.

American television and the wider world

In the early 1970s there was a renaissance of comedy on American television, much of it coming from Americanized versions of British programs. *All in the Family* (1970–77) took its formula and characters from the BBC's *Till Death Do Us Part*, first screened in 1964. *The Mary Tyler Moore Show*, the first sitcom to feature an independent woman as its main character, also began in 1970.

In 1969 the Public Broadcasting System (PBS) was established as a network of mainly educational stations funded partially by the federal government and partially by subscription. PBS imported much British television: the BBC's adaptation of *The Forsyte Saga* was a major ratings success in 1970, outstripped in 1974 by the surreal comedy of *Monty Python's Flying Circus*.

The main flow of television business went the other way. Before 1960, as part of an aggressive marketing strategy, American television was dumping entertainment product in Europe, Australia and the Third World at rock-bottom prices. In 1970 the BBC could buy American drama at less than one-tenth the cost per viewer-hour of producing it themselves. To some extent, European television protected itself from transatlantic pollution by quota systems, which limited the amount of American programming that could be screened. German broadcasting had been strongly influenced by the BBC model after World War II, and a national television had begun service in 1953. From the early 1960s German television supported filmmakers in producing plays and films which ventured outside the American-dominated conventions of the international film and television industries. While they produced an impressive body of work, they failed to raise the technical level of production and limited their foreign sales, which kept their cultural production marginalized.

President de Gaulle saw state domination of French television as a necessary counter-measure to the opposition expressed towards him in the French provincial press. Despite reorganization in the wake of the demonstrations of May 1968, the *Office de la Radio et Télévision Française* (ORTF) re-

▲ *Monty Python's Flying Circus* was the most successful British television export to the United States. With its catchphrase "and now for something completely different", it constantly parodied other television forms.

◄ In the early 1960s Johnny Carson's *The Tonight Show* perfected the talk-show formula, inviting the audience to spend time in the company of the celebrated (like Cassius Clay) while they discussed themselves.

mained firmly and openly in support of the conservative political status quo. Television in France and in Italy, where *Radio Televisione Italiano* (RAI) had a programming monopoly similar to that of ORTF, transmitted more informational and cultural programming than Germany or Britain.

Britain preserved its reputation for the "least worst television in the world" by actively promoting minority programming and "quality television". The BBC established its second channel in 1964 to maintain the ethos of public service broadcasting while allowing BBC1 to move downmarket into more direct competition with the commercial ITV. The adaptations, documentaries and one-off television plays that gave British television its envied reputation for quality all upheld the tradition of things English and literary. Documentaries sponsored the dissemination of knowledge, while literary adaptations of the classics and semi-classics of English literature reproduced the "worthiest" remnants of British culture. One consequence was that, as in Germany, television absorbed writing and directorial talent that might have contributed to a cinematic renaissance. The vapid British cinema of the later 1960s was evidence of the effectiveness of this.

Datafile

After 1960, international competitive sport developed a contradiction between the ideals of free competition between individual sportsmen and women representing their countries, and the reality of sport as an adjunct to international politics. Sport was never free of politics, and it became increasingly absurd to claim that it should be. Nevertheless, many of those who continued to argue for keeping sport free of politics were themselves administrators of international sport.

Many Third World countries found that success in sport could provide them with international prestige, and the sporting boycott was developed, particularly by opponents of apartheid in South Africa. It proved effective as a means of bringing the issue to public attention around the world. Those who argued that sport and politics should not mix also tended to claim that sporting contacts were generally beneficial in resolving conflict.

► The European and South American Cup was effectively the competition for the world's leading club, played between the winners of the competition for each continent's championship the previous year. The game was played less physically in Latin America than in Europe, which led to controversy during the 1960s.

► Sport was used to encourage people to participate in community life in many socialist countries. In Cuba the sports industry increased dramatically after Castro's revolution, with factories producing sports goods springing up everywhere. The Cuban baseball became the internationally accepted standard.

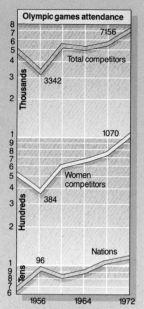

Olympic games attendance

▲ During the 1950s and 1960s the Olympic games were more widely sited than ever before, visiting Melbourne in 1956, Tokyo in 1964 and Mexico in 1968; and more nations competed. The altitude of Mexico City (2300m above sea level) led to the criticism that it was an unsuitable site for middle- and long-distance running.

World Club Championship	
1960	Real Madrid (Spa)
1961	Penarol (Uru)
1962/3	Santos (Bra)
1964/5	Intermilan (It)
1966	Penarol (Uru)
1967	Racing Club (Arg)
1968	Estudiantes (Arg)
1969	AC Milan (It)
1970	Feyenoord (Hol)
1971	Nacional (Uru)
1972	Ajax (Hol)
1973	Independiente (Arg)

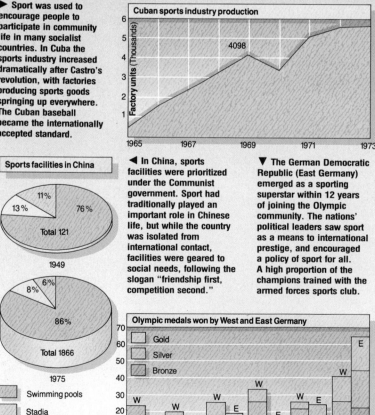

Cuban sports industry production

Sports facilities in China

◄ In China, sports facilities were prioritized under the Communist government. Sport had traditionally played an important role in Chinese life, but while the country was isolated from international contact, facilities were geared to social needs, following the slogan "friendship first, competition second."

▼ The German Democratic Republic (East Germany) emerged as a sporting superstar within 12 years of joining the Olympic community. The nations' political leaders saw sport as a means to international prestige, and encouraged a policy of sport for all. A high proportion of the champions trained with the armed forces sports club.

Olympic medals won by West and East Germany

Swimming pools
Stadia
Gymnasia

Russia was a founder member of the modern Olympic movement, but after the Russian Revolution of October 1917, no Soviet team took part in the Olympics until 1952. Initially, there was an explicit rejection of "bourgeois" sports: the Soviets boycotted important Western competitions. Instead, a centrally organized government program of national fitness, "physical culture" and sport for the masses, free of charge, was designed to create in every citizen a sense of emotional identity with the aims of the Soviet state, as a way of uniting the diverse nationalities and cultures of so vast a country.

After World War II, sport assumed a focal position in Soviet foreign policy, as a way of injecting a spirit of nationalism at home and gaining international prestige abroad. The Soviet Union emerged as a world sporting power after the 1952 Olympics, the last year in which the United States won more gold medals than the Soviet Union.

Sport and the Cold War

The Soviet presence, and their unequivocal acknowledgement of the political nature of sport, exposed the contradictions between the idealist philosophy of the Olympic Charter and the postwar actuality of intense sports competition being used as a weapon of international propaganda. The Olympics, in particular, embodied the Cold-War ideological struggle between the Eastern and Western blocs. By the late 1950s, a number of writers were lamenting the way sport had become "war without weapons".

The Soviets used sport explicitly as a vehicle to nurture solidarity with Third World nations, providing sports buildings and equipment, free of charge, and sending experts to train gifted athletes and arrange tours, displays and teaching. The Soviet Union provided sport aid to Eastern Europe and Cuba, developing a system of mutual assistance, with friendly sports meetings, athletic scholarships, and exchanges of coaches, advisors and specialized knowledge. By comparison, Western countries persisted in a haphazard and more traditionally amateur approach to sport, Western athletes had to negotiate for opportunities and compete for finance.

The conspicuous achievements of Eastern-bloc athletes fueled controversy about the pursuit of excellence and the degree to which socialist sports systems embodied the political interests of their governments or the individual interests of the citizens who comprise those societies. The 1950s started a process of re-appraisal of Western sports policies, moving towards an increase in state intervention, with the recognition that efficient mass systems of sport must be established to maximize available talent. The Soviet insistence on free access for all to sport as the basis of a

SPORT AND THE THIRD WORLD

fundamentally non-elitist system was, however, much less rigorously followed. In 1953 evidence about the fitness levels of American schoolchildren provoked Cold War anxieties about the physical condition of young people. In a 1960 article "The Soft American" in *Sports Illustrated* President-elect Kennedy proposed a national fitness system to invigorate the American nation in order to meet the Soviet challenge.

The USSR's success in using sport as a vehicle for social progress was particularly attractive to Third World countries, although lack of facilities prevented them providing comprehensive sports systems. With indigenous games traditions eroded by colonial contact, Third World nations struggling for self-identity saw modern sport as an excellent opportunity to foster patriotism through the celebration of national heroes. After the emergence into international sport of Asian and African countries, sport became a global idiom, uniting people from disparate cultures. Associations and competitions specifically for Third World countries were inaugurated to extend opportunities to Third World athletes, but all new moves – the Asian Games, the Pan American Games, the Mediterranean Games – engendered political controversy. Ironically, the more obviously politicized sport became, the more vehement were the refusals of Olympic purists to acknowledge this. In 1956, six nations withdrew

▼ Massed pageantry at the 1957 Moscow Festival. The USSR ended its boycott of major Western sports competitions by attending the 1952 Olympic Games in Helsinki, and used sport as a means of developing international friendship throughout the period.

from the Melbourne Olympics, for reasons connected either to the conflict in Suez or the invasion of Hungary earlier in the year.

The politicization of sport

With the nation state the primary unit of international sport, nationalism provided the most conspicuous form of political interference. Sophisticated ceremonial, ritual displays of nationalism, pageantry, medals and tables of results became intrinsic to all big international competitions, and the media exploited the volatile nature of sport to promote feelings of patriotism and rivalry, often carrying racist overtones. Competition was treated as a drama of national emotions, survival, and political and ideological superiority.

The Olympics were the most political event; propaganda, protests, boycotts and terrorism became commonplace. Western powerbrokers in international sports federations such as the International Olympic Committee (IOC) sought to maintain their control over the definitions under which sport and politics interact, as socialist and Third World countries, with little reason to accept the ideology of competitive individualism that Western nations attached to the forms of modern sport, increasingly participated and constantly challenged the bland assertions of Western terms of reference. The patronizing praise bestowed by European and American commentators on

athletes such as Kipjoge Keino for gaining Kenya's first Olympic gold medal in 1972, served to reinforce the neo-colonialist attitude of the West toward Third World countries. At the same time it served as evidence that sport is meritocratic, that individuals with supreme ability will surface, regardless of obstacles.

Countries with limited economic resources copied many of the characteristics of sport that evolved in the developed world. Controversy arose about the morality of nations burdened with poverty and debt investing in a sporting elite, or even in a sports policy and program. Western cultural influence, whether in media, food, music or sport, tended to benefit Third World elites, and at the same time the promotion of imported sport from the developed world turned people away from their own traditional sports and games.

When countries other than those Western industrial powers that had been in charge of international sport since the early years of the 20th century sought to redefine the relationship between sport, ideology and power, the contradictions became inescapable. A "socialist-inspired" answer, based on the philosophy that sport in the developing world should be an expression of new-found independence and "an instrument of emancipation from imperialist fetters", was symbolized by the first and only Games of the New Emerging Forces (GANEFO) in 1963. This competition stimulated more conflict with the sporting establishment: GANEFO records were not recognized and GANEFO athletes were banned from Olympic competition. From that time, the Eastern bloc and Third World countries sought more representation in existing international organizations. In 1963 Sir Adetoklunbo Ademola of Nigeria became the first black African member of the IOC. By voting with members of developing countries, the Eastern bloc started to threaten the grip of the Western world on international sport.

The suggestion that, since sport is self-evidently political, the political terms of engagement must be acceptable before agreeing to the rules of competition emerged most strongly in the 1960s over the issue of apartheid and southern Africa. The anti-apartheid sports movement, which sought to prevent all sporting contact with South Africa, gained momentum after African countries founded the Supreme Council for Sport in Africa (SCSA) in 1966. In the same year Afro-American athletes and civil-rights activists pressured the US Olympic Committee to oppose South African participation in the Olympics. By 1968 the boycott movement created widespread opposition to sporting links with South Africa: the new nations of black Africa, the Caribbean, Islamic and Communist countries threatened to boycott the Games.

In 1970 South Africa was banned from the Olympic movement. Avery Brundage, president of the IOC, reluctantly acknowledged, "We have to face the facts of life – political powers have more to say than we do." He believed that conceding to one demand that breached the fiction of sport's separation from politics would only lead

◀ Frenchman Jean-Claude Killy was the hero of the 1968 Winter Olympics, becoming the first man to win three gold medals in the downhill and slalom events. He was responsible for an upsurge of interest in winter sports, and particularly promoted the development of the French Alps as Europe's main center for them.

▼ When US 200m medallists Tommie Smith and John Carlos lowered their eyes and raised their black-gloved fists in silent protest on the victory rostrum at the 1968 Mexico Olympics, media coverage enabled them to focus the eyes of the world on the Black Power movement in the United States.

to increasing politicization. His fear was realized four days before the opening ceremony of the 1972 Olympics, when 27 African nations, some other countries outside Africa and some American black athletes threatened to pull out of the Games if Rhodesia, with a similar racial policy to that of South Africa, was allowed to compete. Brundage described this pressure as "naked political blackmail", but in 1975 Rhodesia was expelled from the Olympic movement, and Zimbabwe was accepted after independence. In 1976 Tanzania, and then a further 19 African countries along with Guyana and Iraq pulled out of the Games because the IOC refused to ban New Zealand athletes. The New Zealand All Blacks Rugby team had toured South Africa at the time of the Soweto riots, and the New Zealand government had ignored an appeal from SCSA to cancel the tour. This "third party boycott" introduced a new dimension: it was in opposition to a country collaborating with apartheid sport.

More than once, a different interpretation of politics has tragically intruded into Olympic sport. At Munich in 1972 17 people, 11 of them Israeli athletes, were killed when Palestinian Black September guerrillas took hostages at the Olympic village. Linking this with the boycotts, Brundage insisted, "The Games must go on...The IOC has suffered two savage attacks within the past few days – one on the Rhodesian situation, in which political blackmail was used, and now this."

Sport and the media

As an increasing number of countries came to participate in international competition, sport became a global phenomenon in another sense. Satellite television, new developments in electronic technology and rapid and relatively inexpensive travel made televised sport as a form of popular entertainment accessible throughout the world. As late as 1960 American network television was not yet providing full weekend sports coverage, and CBS bought the American television rights to the Rome Olympics for a mere $500,000. Network interest had, however, already improved the fortunes of American football, turning it from baseball's poor relation into the dominant American media sport.

In Europe, as in America, established national sports and large-scale international competitions were the first beneficiaries of television, but rivalry between television networks increased the variety of broadcast events. Sports organizations that had initially resisted television coverage out of fears of lost ticket sales came to recognize the potential revenue in television rights. By the mid 1960s CBS was paying the National Football League $14 million a year for exclusive television coverage, and was pioneering a further development of television's relations with sport by buying its own baseball team, the New York Yankees.

Television came increasingly to select people's experiences of local, national and international competitions. The development of video technology facilitated the presentation of sport as entertainment by the selection of key moments to be replayed. This also made possible the instant "action replay" and allowing studio experts to analyze the play and criticize the judges, superseding the old style of commentary which had attempted only to inform about the run of play and to convey some the the excitement of the event. In 1964 color cameras were used to transmit live pictures of the Olympic Games in Tokyo via satellite to audiences around the world. People in Europe, North and South America, Asia and Africa saw the imaginative flair and efficiency of the first Olympic Games to be held in Asia. Champions from other countries became household names. Sport became a prime subject for the world communications of McLuhan's "global village" to watch, to witness, and to argue over.

▲ Millions of television viewers saw Yoshinori Sakai, born on the day of the Hiroshima atom bomb, carrying the Olympic flame for the 1964 Tokyo Games.

◄ Soviet gymnast Olga Korbut captivated the world with her performance at the 1972 Munich Olympics. Although individual sporting heroines have long been highly visible, few of the countries entering the competition since the early 1950s have fielded female athletes – for religious, historical and cultural reasons. Of the 121 nations taking part in the 1972 Olympics, only 61 entered female competitors. Asian and African women were almost totally absent.

SPORTING SUPERSTARS

In the 1960s there emerged two sportsmen – both black men from unpromising backgrounds – who each won vast fortunes and became amongst the best known faces and names in the world. The two of them challenged many conventional assumptions about the place of the sportsman in modern society.

Born in 1940 in the small town of Três Corações in the state of Minas Gerais in Brazil, Edson Arantes do Nascimento (Pelé) began playing professional soccer for the Santos club at the age of 16. Two years later he attended his first World Cup Finals in Sweden.

In a career spanning 20 years and over 1300 games, Pelé established unparalleled scoring records. Late in a career which had witnessed three World Cup Final victories for his native Brazil, he became the focus for the expansion of the game in North America. His pre-eminence as a sporting legend made him a powerful symbol of the possibilities of sport as an avenue to social mobility in the 1970s. He was the highest- salaried team athlete in history and probably the richest.

Pelé's success attracted attention to Brazil itself,and his team. He showed that a Third World country could compete against and challenge economically "advanced" nations.

In 1960, two years after Pelé had appeared in his first World Cup Final, Muhammad Ali (then Cassius Marcellus Clay Jr.) won the Olympic light heavyweight boxing gold medal at Rome, at the age of 18.

In twenty years, Ali rose from the obscurity of Louisville, Kentucky, to global prominence. As a sporting role model for young blacks he explicitly confronted racial stereotypes.

His audacity in promoting his own ability, his successful challenge for the world heavyweight championship in 1964, his conversion to Islam, his stand against the Vietnam War and the regaining of "his" world title all thrust him into the center of world sport.

In the 20th century American boxers have monopolized the world heavyweight championship. The pre-eminence of black champions since 1956 has fueled racist sentiments. Ali himself saw boxing as "the fastest way for a black person to make it in this country". As his career developed, many people were prepared to pay vast sums to see him beaten.

In 1966, Ali claimed conscientious objector status because of his Black Muslim beliefs. He was convicted of draft evasion, stripped of his world titles and had his boxing licence revoked. In 1970, the United States Supreme Court unanimously reversed the conviction and Ali was allowed to fight again. In 1971 he fought Joe Frazier for the world heavyweight title and lost in 15 rounds. Three years later he defeated George Forman in Kinshasa, Zaire, to regain the world title and in the process earned $5,450,000. In the six years after his return to boxing, Ali earned an estimated $26 million; but shortly after his retirement he was diagnosed as having suffered brain damage from his boxing career.

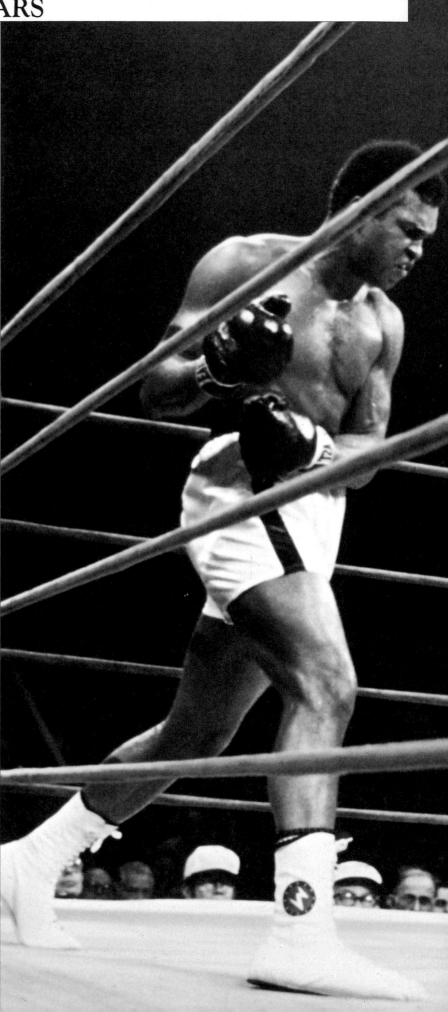

► ▲ Brazilian soccer genius Pelé, photographed right in 1970 after his team's third World Cup win, was remarkable for the power and accuracy of his kick and his uncanny skill in anticipating other players' moves. His soccer prowess brought Pelé international fame – his face was everywhere in 1970, even on stamps.

▼ Early days in the career that proved "rags to riches" could be achieved outside Hollywood – the camera froze Cassius Marcellus Clay Jr in this sparring pose in 1954, when he was just 12 years old. Six years later, Clay won Amateur Athletic Union, Golden Gloves, and Olympic Games championships. He turned professional the same year, adopting his Muslim name of Muhammad Ali in 1966. The change of name signified a change in the way in which he was seen: he now appeared a genuine threat to white America.

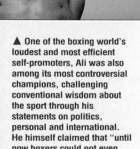

▲ One of the boxing world's loudest and most efficient self-promoters, Ali was also among its most controversial champions, challenging conventional wisdom about the sport through his statements on politics, personal and international. He himself claimed that "until now boxers could not even speak; now they can think."

◄ Seen in action with fellow world champion Joe Frazier, Ali was unusually light on his feet for a heavyweight. In a pop song commemorating his 1974 World title bout in Zaire, he was said to "float like a butterfly, sting like a bee". At his peak Ali was probably the fastest and most skillful heavyweight of all time.

Datafile

In the 1950s popular music had played, as one of its key functions, its part in the self-assertion of the young; in the 1960s this developed until it was central to the lives and even the politics of many people. Some viewed this as grafting extraneous elements on to music, but the ability of popular music to articulate personal, cultural and political experience had been developing throughout the century.

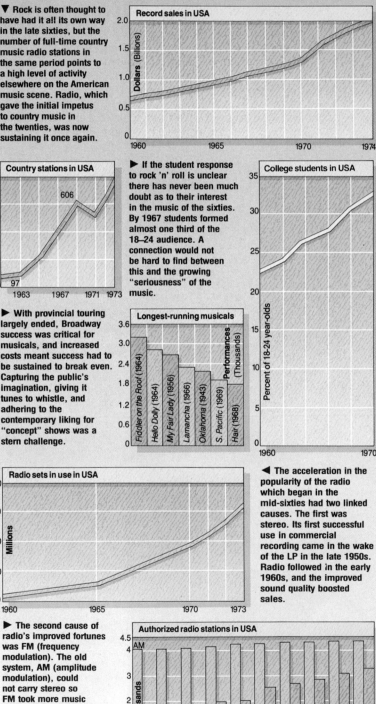

▼ The rise in record sales in the United States, during the 1960s reflected the growing vitality and importance of popular music across the entire social spectrum, as well as the increasingly large disposable income available to the young.

▼ Rock is often thought to have had it all its own way in the late sixties, but the number of full-time country music radio stations in the same period points to a high level of activity elsewhere on the American music scene. Radio, which gave the initial impetus to country music in the twenties, was now sustaining it once again.

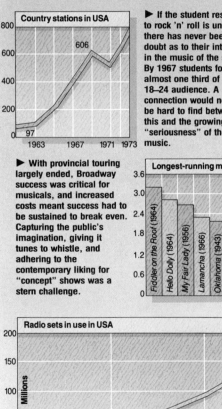

► If the student response to rock 'n' roll is unclear there has never been much doubt as to their interest in the music of the sixties. By 1967 students formed almost one third of the 18–24 audience. A connection would not be hard to find between this and the growing "seriousness" of the music.

► With provincial touring largely ended, Broadway success was critical for musicals, and increased costs meant success had to be sustained to break even. Capturing the public's imagination, giving it tunes to whistle, and adhering to the contemporary liking for "concept" shows was a stern challenge.

◄ The acceleration in the popularity of the radio which began in the mid-sixties had two linked causes. The first was stereo. Its first successful use in commercial recording came in the wake of the LP in the late 1950s. Radio followed in the early 1960s, and the improved sound quality boosted sales.

► The second cause of radio's improved fortunes was FM (frequency modulation). The old system, AM (amplitude modulation), could not carry stereo so FM took more music broadcasting, while AM stations specialized in spoken words. By the mid-1980s the two systems stood in parity.

The sixties were to see American popular music receive an unprecedented degree of attention. They began inauspiciously enough, dominated by the inoffensive sounds of "Philadelphia schlock". This was a neutralized, watered-down version of rock 'n' roll. This music accepted the emancipating changes wrought by Elvis and others in the fifties, but, unlike theirs, remained transparently artificial and commercial in intent. The music was predictable and unambitious, and, in reaction, many people began to seek something "authentic", untainted by commerce.

The folk revival

Throughout the postwar period a small nucleus of musicians had followed a path that ran counter to the prevailing tastes of young and adult markets alike. They sustained and developed the part of the rural folk tradition (white and black) that had made a point of articulating its social grievances. This urban musical left wing was a mixture of an educated white middle class (Protestant and Jewish) and a "genuine" ex-rural proletariat. Combining a fundamentalist approach to folk music with a form of political radicalism that drew heavily on the bitter experiences of the unions in the interwar period, their songs expressed two basic needs – the need for roots, and the need for change – in one form. The music of Pete Seeger, Woody Guthrie, the Almanac Singers and others demonstrated the stark contrasts between the phoneyness of contemporary popular music and the honesty of the traditional sounds, between the duplicity of current politics and an idealistic vision of justice. This radical and libertarian thrust of the folk revival found political form in the association between the music and the civil rights movement in the United States, as well as the anti-nuclear movement in Europe in the early sixties.

A major contribution to popular music of the ensuing "folk revival" lay in the increased importance of the lyrics, and the fact that the folk singer usually wrote his own material. Here one particular figure embodies both the achievements and the paradoxes of the genre. Bob Dylan's songs, delivered in tones more nasal even than those used by earlier rural singers, specialized in a "shimmering collage of literary metaphor, alliteration and imagery" which musicians of an earlier age would have found incomprehensible. In the context of early sixties' pop, though, this music opened immense possibilities for the use of language, and gave a sense of cultural tradition.

Dylan's lyrics and his delivery also had the effect of moving the music firmly away from dance and providing the basis for the more intellectual reception of popular music characteristic of the later sixties. Once again, therefore, a tension

MUSIC CAN CHANGE THE WORLD

became apparent, between music as supporting the domination of the explicit, literate tradition, and music as expressive of alternative, implicit ideas. Now, however, the poetry seemed to come "from within", as if it were a companion the music had long sought; it was also frequently identified, if not always unequivocally, with politically radical sentiments, and this considerably broadened the range of subject matter. Furthermore, Dylan's complex lyrics were so lacking in the traditional qualities of popular music that they proved virtually unusable by the vested interests of the music industry.

The sense of possessing qualities equal to but set apart from those of established culture was an important element in the counter-culture of the later 1960s. But as increasing store was set by poetic texts, however radically they might be interpreted, the music was in danger of being cut off from its source of inspiration. As singers

▼ The link between music and radical politics, as renewed by Dylan and Joan Baez was fundamental to activists such as these in Washington D.C. in 1968.

became prized for originality, and originality led to complexity, complexity negated the political point (just as it negated the symbolic simplicity of the singer-and-his-guitar).

A second major contribution of the folk revival was the creation of an audience whose members identified themselves as a community. Until now, even the most committed notions of audience solidarity had centered on sharing the status of being deviants from the social norm; milder forms of teenage commonality had been limited largely to tastes in entertainment. The audience for Dylan, Joan Baez and Phil Ochs began to see their music as the first, essential step in the forging of a whole way of life.

A basic tenet of this lifestyle was antipathy to "commercialism" and the trappings of mass consumerism. Here the political contradictions soon became apparent – contradictions that dogged the fully-fledged counter-culture later in the decade.

Many adherents found themselves torn between the desire to spread a cultural and political message, via folk music, and the fear that the channel used to do so – the communications market-place – would taint the musical tradition through commercial exploitation. Successful dissemination brought with it the risk of betrayal: "Folk music," wrote *Sing Out* editor Irwin Silber in 1964, "is the voice and expression of generations of ordinary folk who were on familiar terms with hard work. Success is the 'American Dream', the middle-class confusion of illusion and reality."

Dismayed by the appearance of the personality cult, that most hated aspect of "rat-race culture", diehards saw no gains in the coming together of folk and commerce: "The fundamentally healthy content of the folk music tradition (is) lost in the caverns of Tin Pan Alley". From the perspective of popular music, rather than folk, however, the encounter was significant: it marked the beginning of a "creative space" or division between art and image, or between the artist's authentic voice and the product that reached the market-place. Later musicians would find this space a fruitful area in which to explore and dispute meanings.

To younger folk-revival musicians – and perhaps to Dylan especially – by 1964 the limitations of the idiom, of its audience, of its saleability, had become too clear to overlook. Wholly unexpectedly, the impetus to switch direction and absorb the sounds of rock (as rock 'n' roll had now come to be known) came from a country that, according to critic Charlie Gillett, "had made no previous significant contribution to popular music in the 20th century".

Popular culture in Britain

In the early 1960s British popular culture emerged from the long winter of postwar austerity, rejuvenated by the assertive claims to attention of the young working class. Responding to prime minister Harold Macmillan's 1958 election message, "You've never had it so good", previously unregarded groups began to demand consumer cultural goods designed specifically for them. Just as rock 'n' roll had provided a commodity around which the American teenage market could be defined in the 1950s, the Mersey Beat – a raucous and driving form of rock that emerged from Liverpool in 1962–63 – signaled the arrival of the young British consumer as a commercial cultural force. But, as so often in Britain, their arrival was touched with class division. To be young, affluent and rebellious was not enough. As John Lennon later put it, "A working-class hero is something to be". Unexpectedly, this new kind of British cultural artefact proved highly exportable, and provided a major stimulus to popular culture all over the world.

Superficially at least, the radicalizing effects of rock 'n' roll seemed to have worn thin by 1960. Bland American "high school" sounds predominated. Britain's own Elvis clones, such as Cliff Richard, had turned into entertainers for all the family, while its imitation Sinatras continued to prosper both on records and on the airwaves. Though this apparent decline was due in part to a moral and/or cultural backlash, it had much to

▲ "Beatlemania" entered the language after the crowd scenes that followed the group's Palladium show in October 1963. These unprecedented displays of hysteria were greeted by a widespread incomprehension, but expressed a special sense of belonging. The appearance of badges and other fan club symbols confirmed this underlying message. A whole sub-industry of miniatures and similar icons began to appear. American standoffishness to the Beatles' music and its attendant paraphernalia melted with their arrival on American soil in February 1964, an occasion which marked a decisive shift in the fortunes of British popular culture abroad (opposite above).

do with ingrained aspects of national life and character. One of these was a readiness to live with maiden "Auntie" BBC's paternalism. British record companies were content – if not enthusiastic – to sell rock 'n' roll, but BBC resistance severely restricted airplay. The only alternative – the commercial radio station Radio Luxembourg, broadcast from mainland Europe – was very popular with teenagers (especially at 11 pm on a Sunday night for the Top 20), but that popularity did not translate itself into wholesale dissatisfaction with the BBC's music policy until 1964, when a rash of "pirate stations" broke out, broadcasting unlicensed from ships moored just outside territorial waters. The pirates introduced an American style of disk jockey to an enthusiastic British audience.

Beneath the surface there was an unprecedented amount of popular musical activity. The steadily increasing popularity of the dance-hall as a venue for "sweet Saturday night" created a demand for bands at a local level. The existence of such bands was in large measure the product of a short-lived skiffle boom. This hybrid of American blues and folk music and British music hall was an offshoot of the fashion for traditional jazz ("trad") of the mid- and late fifties. It had three important consequences: it gave a considerable push to the evolving process of musical

"democratization"; it raised the guitar to pre-eminence; and it introduced a direct link to the roots of black American music.

One further reason for rock 'n' roll's fading into entertainment had been that British listeners had no means of recognizing, let alone comprehending, the context within American culture from which it sprang, and therefore heard it in a vacuum. By the early sixties, however, skiffle had led many to an interest in black rhythm & blues, often via records brought over by sailors and American servicemen. From this they began to form a sense of the depth, significance and vitality of Afro-American musical culture, and of the unexplored potential within rock 'n' roll.

The surge of British "beat" music which followed the meteoric rise of the Beatles (from number 19 in the charts in December 1962 to unchallenged supremacy by the late summer of 1963) was greeted with much national wonderment on all sides; the grassroots activity which lay behind it had passed unobserved. This outbreak of energy and creativity from overlooked people in ignored regions – notably Liverpool and Newcastle – suggested that the country might still be alive after all.

The new music overwhelmed the British teenagers. As well as transforming the British Top 20, it engendered a spate of hysterical enthusiasm

from the public – musicians such as the Beatles were greeted by screaming teenage girls every time they were seen in public. "Beatlemania" may, in part, have been generated by the popular press. But its chief importance lies in the fact that for the first time girls took a leading role in the formation of popular culture. British girls had not enjoyed the same opportunities as their American counterparts to participate in creating and enjoying the stardom of their heroes. For them, "the sounds of pop were deeply associated with a largely 'bedroom culture' of pin-ups and a Dansette record-player". Beatlemania not only permitted this adulation to come into the open, it also provided girls with the chance to impose themselves in some way upon events around them.

In the wake of the Beatles, pop music held center stage in fashionable culture for the first time. But as it did so other groups were emerging from deeper explorations of rhythm & blues with a more profoundly unsettling music. The Rolling Stones, the Animals and others appealed to a wide section of the youth audience who felt that society's cuddly adoption of the Beatles and "beat" had undermined the element of opposition which was fundamental to the music. On the other side, sentinels ever on watch for moral degeneration began to clear their throats at the

▲ Society's trick of adopting what threatens it could not be repeated with the Rolling Stones. The arrogant sexuality of Mick Jagger and the erotic message of a song like *Satisfaction* (1965) went beyond ready assimilation. Even when held in check for television audiences, it could cause a riot in the studio.

145

▶ The brilliance of Jimi Hendrix's guitar would have set him apart even within the context of black music. By moving into rock, he opened up a unique opportunity: to integrate his innovative, blues-derived, technique with the possibilities offered by rock technology. The results were astonishing. But for Hendrix himself the tensions of being a black superstar were tragically destructive: he died of a drugs overdose in 1970.

▼ However much rock might attract ideas of revolution, put on a California beach it seemed merely part of a fun 'n' health program. Even the exiled London bus, a hostage to the demand for "authentic" British culture, helped surfers to ride the waves, not make them.

Stones' way of mixing middle-class bohemianism with a troubling and arrogant display of very un-British eroticism.

Britain and California conquer the world

The Beatles-led British invasion of American airwaves and record stores in the 1960s influenced all aspects of the American popular music scene. In Britain and the United States, few towns were without their amateur groups, almost all of whom attempted to write some of their own material. Self-penned songs were unusual for the mainstream of popular music, but held no fears for folk revivalists; what struck them most forcibly was the immense, unsuspected capacity of this new form of rock 'n' roll for personal expression.

The greatest impact of British music may not have been on "creative artists", however, but on the music industry. The industry had grown bored with the popular-music scene in the early 1960s. The Beatles in particular reawakened its interest. The reinvigoration of popular music recording brought with it a search for new ways of marketing, and a scramble for new performers to meet the demand. The Beatles pioneered the idea that the long-playing record (LP) should be more than a discrete collection of unrelated songs. This encouraged the industry to move much of its popular music production into that area – a shift

◀ Girl groups such as the Ronettes were often seen later in the decade as being merely a pop representation of black femininity. But they showed again how blacks could take on an aspect of the mainstream "game" – in this case an artless teenage glamor – and simply do it better.

▲ With the appearance of Janis Joplin a remarkable reversal had taken place: black girls now had command of showbiz glamor, and a white girl sang the blues. Part of Joplin's achievement was in countering stereotypes of femininity, claiming sexuality as a common denominator, not the exclusive right of the beautiful. Nonetheless her music relived the familiar blues singer's paradox of assertiveness and suffering.

made permanent a little later in the decade by the arrival of the "concept album" (usually attributed to *Sergeant Pepper's Lonely Hearts Club Band* – 1967). And the simple but effective notion of reducing the traditional number of tracks (and hence the royalties) meant that LPs could be sold at the same price but bring in more revenue for the music industry.

To an audience that took its music with a growing seriousness, the LP was confirmation of the status of that music. It also proved particularly attractive to the ever-increasing number of FM (frequency modulation) radio stations in the United States. This system of broadcasting, conceived in 1933, was based on a fuller range of frequency than AM (amplitude modulation), and was characterized by its ability to filter out intruding noises. Finally taking hold in the 1960s, FM stations steadily grew in number, helped by several related factors such as the introduction of stereo sound in about 1960 (stereo systems soon came complete with FM); the consequent improvement in LP quality; and the adoption of the LP for rock records. Beginning in San Francisco, FM stations became closely associated with "progressive" rock.

California dreamin'

It was to California that the focus of musical attention shifted in the middle of the decade. The state had a laid-back image, at a time when ex-Harvard professor Timothy Leary was extolling the virtues of turning on, tuning in, and dropping out with the aid of hallucinogenic drugs, but this was only partly responsible. The tradition of racially integrated audiences on the West Coast had produced a rich undercurrent of musical culture, out of which emerged the only "indigenous" music that could rival British beat in its ability to inject new life into popular music.

The relaxed, celebratory nature of "surf music", as purveyed by bands such as the Beach Boys, seemed deplorably hedonistic beside the tense concern of the "folkies" in New York's Greenwich Village, but surf music, like British beat, demonstrated the vitality of the country's musical traditions, and the rich possibilities still within them for the development of distinctive styles. One important feature of the West Coast scene was the role of the record producer. The work of Phil Spector in particular gave the producer unprecedented significance, and created a core of session musicians with a wealth of hard-earned experience. These factors, and the West Coast's film and entertainment industry (and its dollars) all encouraged the westward migration of American musicians.

The emergence and fate of the counter-culture in California's two major cities, Los Angeles and San Francisco, and its spread across much of the nation, has been much discussed. Music was consistently to the forefront of this complex of esthetic, political and social aspirations, where mysticism rubbed shoulders with revolution, where a sharply focused anti-materialism was allied with a much fuzzier, drug-induced belief in the ease of "self-discovery". And although the counter-culture asserted its dislike of commerce, the

Soul and Tamla Motown

"Soul" – by the late fifties the word had a rich resonance in black society. As the fervent optimism and vocal intensity of gospel was joined with the secular energy of r & b, a powerful idiom emerged in which individual expression and the social activity of dance combined. Songs like Otis Redding's *Respect* – especially as performed by Aretha Franklin – or James Brown's *Say It Loud* took the music into a more political area.

Commercial confidence was vital, too, and no-one showed this better than Berry Gordy, Jr. His Motown company, formed in 1960 and based in Detroit, not only pioneered black ownership in the music business, but operated a system of in-house production which ensured that all stages of a record's life remained within the company's control. The Tamla Motown "sound", epitomized by the Supremes and the Four Tops, was patronizingly described as "pop-soul"; Motown was too inventive, however, to be constrained as a mere hybrid of black music and white commerce.

involvement of music, musicians and record companies soon compromised this stance.

Los Angeles provided the first venue for the familiar encounter between music and business in its new guise. Though a little slow to begin, the city's record companies soon recognized the market potential of "folk rock", following the success in 1965 of the Byrds' distinctive studio-sound version of Dylan's *Mr Tambourine Man*. In late 1965 *Variety* magazine coined a celebrated headline, "Folk + Rock + Protest = Dollars". The trend was epitomized by the contrived "protest" of the chart-topping single *Eve of Destruction* by Barry MacGuire in 1965. Record companies eagerly followed such successes and musicians could begin to look for what they had admired in the Beatles, that combination of creative independence and financial reward. But Los Angeles moguls had other strings to their bows: before long they marketed the Monkees – a family version of the Beatles for television consumption. Concurrent with rock's growing sense of maturity and independence, the Monkees' fame was a reminder of the continuing importance of the teenage pop market.

Farther up the coast, meanwhile, San Francisco maintained a certain disdain for the material culture that so exercised Los Angeles. The absence of record-company involvement in the music scene there permitted San Francisco's music to develop along its own, less market-conscious lines. Crucially, in the words of critic Dave Laing: "The San Francisco musicians worked from a sense that they were part of something more significant than an entertainment industry." In dances and, especially, in multi-media light shows, music's sense of community was joined to psychedelia, the visual and aural experiences paralleling those obtained from the newly popular (and still legal, until 1967) drug, LSD.

By early 1967, with no small contribution from the news media, the San Francisco area was being celebrated as the center of the new lifestyle. "Flower-power", that intoxicating antithesis to all that was conventional, attracted would-be hippies from all over, and also had a sweet smell of dollars to a record industry not averse to striking an anti-Establishment stance. There was a price to pay on both sides. Never before had record companies granted their performers such latitude; never had they laid their own principles open to mockery. Yet for the performer there was no escaping the fact that, try as the companies might to seem streetwise and create the illusion of shining revolutionary ideals, to sign up with a record company was fundamentally to join the "system".

It was nevertheless intriguing that the major companies went as far as they did. The counter-culture was essentially a movement of and for the middle-class male. Its ideas of liberation, especially when crudely understood as "from work, for sex", struck resonant chords across a broad spectrum of American male society, whose members sought to take advantage of the freedoms being won by the counter-culture.

The middle-class nature of the movement is also evident in the development of two closely related ideas and practices: rock music as art, and rock criticism. As musicians' solos grew more ambitious, and their lyrics more involved, it became obvious that there was a role for the interpreter, outside the existing trade and fan magazines. Rock criticism grew out of the "underground press", which had developed a profound mistrust of the commercial and had singled out rock as expressing most clearly the ideals of the youth movement. As practised in the newly founded journals such as *Rolling Stone* and *Creem*, it operated at least partly on a circular argument: rock's growing seriousness made criticism necessary, and criticism's existence proved rock's seriousness. The step from "serious" to "art" was a small one, especially when aided by the well-known parallel between the esthetics of modern bohemianism and those of the 19th-century Romantics, whose revolutionary achievements in art, politics and life criticism had been enshrined sky-high.

The academic study of popular music, while often bedeviled by the contradictions implied in much sixties' rock criticism, owes it many debts. Not least is that of having articulated the links between culture and politics. On the public level, this connection was made most clearly by the responses of the counter-culture to the Vietnam War (and especially to police intimidation of demonstrators) and to the continuing racial unrest. Short-

▲ Indian classical musician Ravi Shankar's first impact on Western music was on jazz rather than rock. But it was through his involvement with rock that he and the sitar became well known, and this marked an important early stage in the opening up of Western ears to "world" music. Rock's first attempts to incorporate Indian music, as evidenced by the Beatles' *Norwegian Wood* (1965) were made without any direct contact with Indian musicians or understanding of the music's meaning. Shankar taught Beatle George Harrison, and brought a greater proficiency to his subsequent use of Indian music, but the approach remained superficial and made Shankar and other Indian musicians uneasy.

lived though these responses were, they pointed to a breakdown of the barrier that had traditionally separated politics from life. "The personal had become political", and this was a profound achievement for the counter-culture of the 1960s.

Rocking round the world

The counter-culture was not confined to California; and many of the most dramatic political moments of the radical politics were seen in Europe. Rock music played its role in this movement, though its position was still rarely clear cut. One unifying factor, however, behind the protests of students around the world was their hostility to the United States' involvement in the war in Vietnam, and the young in Europe looked primarily to America to supply the images and music of the alternative politics.

As British music continued to develop a status equivalent to that of America, the sixties saw the domination of the English language as the *lingua franca* of the the youth culture. French and German bands sang in English as often as in their own languages, and adopted the model of Anglo-American rock in preference to indigenous popular music. The rock festival, developed in the United States as an experiment in alternative living centered around rock music, was likewise imported wholesale into Europe.

◄▲ By 1967 "rock" had consciously distanced itself from "pop". It even mounted an invasion of Broadway, the nudity of the musical *Hair* signaling rock's confidence in its "inner" qualities. That confidence, visible also in the ascendancy of the LP, was founded in large part on the increasing representation of recording-studio technology (though the effects on *Sergeant Pepper* itself were achieved by producer George Martin's prizing of nine tracks out of a four-track machine). The other source of confidence was the musicians' growing ability to develop and sustain more grandiose ideas. In the blues-based improvizations of Cream and the "space rock" of Pink Floyd (concert image) the late sixties saw this tendency at its most effective.

ROCK FESTIVALS

For a few years, the large, outdoor rock festival – an idea borrowed from the tradition of folk and jazz festivals begun in the 1950s and from San Francisco's "human be-in" gatherings or "happenings" – became a symbolic expression of the counter-culture. The Monterey Festival of June 1967, usually seen as the first, set both the musical and the idealistic tone. The effect of so much good music, from Jefferson Airplane to Jimi Hendrix, was confirmation of rock's stature: fees were kept low and profits were donated to charity, thus giving musicians, audiences and organizers a sense of common cause.

But from the start the festivals were asked to carry the ideals of fraternal community while in part their actual effect worked against that concept. The very act of exposing San Francisco's most idealistic musicians to wider audiences planted the seeds for the break-up of that musical community. And each succeeding festival witnessed to some degree the uneasy co-existence of distant visions, anticipated political upheaval and immediate marketing hard-sell.

In the mind of the general public the festivals provided clear evidence of the threat posed by a radical youth movement. It was not just their political rhetoric, nor the widespread use of drugs; it was the sheer weight of numbers.

The sixties' largest festival took place at Woodstock in upstate New York on 15–17 August 1969, with an estimated attendance of 450,000. Despite all predictions of catastrophe the occasion provided an overwhelming display of camaraderie, and in doing so gave its name to a generation. It was also an enormous financial undertaking, with substantial payments to the performers setting them apart from their "brothers and sisters" in the audience. The organizers claimed Woodstock made them bankrupt, but after all the assets were counted, including film and record rights, it seems likely to have yielded a handsome profit.

Woodstock raised hopes of a new beginning. But by the end of the year, the "dream" seemed over. Widespread violence occurred at the Altamont Festival in December, and a youth was knifed to death during a Rolling Stones performance. This was taken as an assault on the very spirit of the counter-culture itself.

But in the course of time idealism re-surfaced. Wedded to political causes with wider popular support it shaped a festival where, with the benefit of global communications hook-ups, frustration with the prevailing ideology of self-interest could find positive expression. In this sense Live Aid, the 1985 trans-world concert to raise money to combat famine in Ethiopia, seemed to many the true inheritor of the spirit of Woodstock. To others it seemed to have inherited the paradoxes of the festivals, and added new ones. In this view the implausibility of rock stars and the music business displaying genuine altruism was compounded by the belief that rock and pop's very existence as a capitalist phenomenon made it part of the reason for the famine in the first place.

▲ The natural imagery beloved of festival-goers was taken to represent peace and love. Linked with magic, it provided another metaphor. Summoning up a witchdoctor, if not intentionally, invoked one of rationalism's oldest adversaries.

▶ Given fair weather, open-air venues provided ideal settings for the growth of a sense of community. Outside the constraints of the concert hall, too, one could believe that both the music and the new spirit knew no boundaries.

▼ The counter-culture's links with the "Beat" generation was evident in the presence of poets such as Allen Ginsberg at San Francisco "human be-ins" in 1967. Ginsberg's aim "to let my imagination go, open secrecy and scribble magic lines from my real mind" found a sympathetic response.

▲ Technology could never quite capture the feeling of "what it was like" to attend a festival, but it could, and did, help spread the word about them. To festival organizers the camera's presence sometimes had more to do with money than messages.

▲ One month before Woodstock, in July 1969, the Rolling Stones played a free concert in London's Hyde Park, featuring Ginger Johnson's African Drummers (left). The spirit of the event was encapsulated in the release of hundreds of butterflies, in memory of former Stone Brian Jones. Less than six months later the Stones gave another free concert, but this time in response to allegations of greed and overpricing during their US tour. The notorious event, at Altamont Raceway in California in December 1969, was marked by violence and, finally, the murder by Hell's Angels (nominally in charge of security) of a young black man in the audience, Meredith Hunter (above).

ART GALLERIES AND EXHIBITIONS

Artists need their work to be displayed and, with the decline of private patronage, bought, whether by institutions or by individuals.

Until the foundation in the 1920s of the first museums specifically devoted to preserving and displaying the rich variety of trends in modern art, the selection of esthetically radical works proved hard for traditional museums, such as the Louvre in Paris, which had their collections founded on the works of established Old Masters. And, as artists continued to challenge the boundaries of art, some brought *objets trouvés* into the gallery and frequently commanded high prices with them; even the museums of modern art found themselves drawn into controversy about their selection and purchasing policies.

Just as an object can "become" art by being placed in an environment – such as a purpose-built gallery – in which it is seen as art, so the galleries themselves have taken on a key function in defining the trends and categories of art criticism. The way in which pictures are hung, and the works with which they are juxtaposed, have an effect on the way the viewer "reads" them. Since the 1960s there has developed an important trend – the special exhibition – bringing together comprehensive or representative works from around the world, in a selection determined by the exhibition organizers, for commercial or academic ends. Exhibitions – such as the Post-Impressionism exhibitions organized in London in 1910 and 1912 – can add a completely new term to the vocabulary of art criticism.

Alongside the prestigious exhibitions and metropolitan museums, the municipal or local art gallery has become an ever more common feature worldwide. Such galleries provide a channel for two-way communication, between the mainstream of the world's art scene, and the local art of the region.

▶ London's Royal Academy annually shows thousands of works by lesser-known artists; many more fail the selection procedure. Preservation of works of art, many of them deteriorating fast, forms an important part of a gallery's work.

▶▶ Purpose-built galleries, such as the Museum of Contemporary Art in Los Angeles, provide spacious but sometimes forbidding accommodation for works of art. Some galleries seem to insulate the art from the outside world; others place it in a more natural setting.

▼ The exhibition catalog provides a permanent record of an exhibition and may become a weighty and scholarly volume or, as here, a work of art in its own right. This catalog, for an exhibition at New York's Museum of Modern Art, had a hinged, metallic cover.

▶ Marc Chagall at a retrospective exhibition organized in honor of his 95th birthday. Such exhibitions can survey the lifetime's work of a single artist, bringing it together under one roof for the first time, and allow the reassessment of his entire achievement and of the relative quality of each individual work.

▶▶ The public curiously inspect the items on display in an American museum of trash. In a gallery even discarded plastic can be seen as objects of pure color and form.

BIOGRAPHIES

Aaron, Hank 1934–

US baseball player. One of the best hitters in the game, over 23 professional seasons from 1952 he established several records. Over 3298 games his totals include 775 home runs, 1477 extra-base hits and 2297 runs batted in 12364 times at bat. With a lifetime batting average of 0.305, his 3771 hits and 2174 runs scored were at that time exceeded only by Ty Cobb. He played mainly for the National League Boston (later Atlanta) Braves. His last two seasons were with the American League Milwaukee Brewers.

Achebe, Chinua 1930–

Nigerian writer. Achebe, an early graduate of Ibadan University, went on to two English universities. From 1954 he worked for the Nigerian Broadcasting Corporation, becoming external broadcasting director in 1961. Also in 1967, he set up a publishing company with another writer. He taught at the University of Nigeria from 1967, with a brief interlude in the USA (1973). His first novel, *Things Fall Apart* (1958), deals, like all his work, with the clash between African tribal culture and colonial innovation. Achebe's moderation on this theme, and the value he placed on the English language, cost him some popularity at home. He also wrote short stories, and the essays *Morning on Creation Day* (1975) which deal with the political implications of writing.

Ali, Muhammad (Cassius Clay) 1942–

US boxer. Clay boxed from the age of 12, and in 1960 won an Olympic gold medal. In 1964 he knocked out Sonny Liston to become world heavyweight champion. He then became a Black Muslim and changed his name to Muhammad Ali; for his refusal, on religious grounds, to join the army, he was stripped of his title in 1967 and given a five-year prison sentence; but in 1970 the Supreme Court quashed his conviction. In 1974 he beat Joe Frazier and then George Foreman, to regain his title. After losing to Leon Spinks in 1978, he beat him the same year to become the first heavyweight boxer to win the world title three times. He retired in 1979, but attempted a comeback a year later. Ali was distinguished by lightning reflexes and great coordination, as well as his humorous showmanship and gift as a self-publicist. In 1984 he was diagnosed with "punch-drunk" syndrome – or brain damage.

Allende (Gossens), Salvador 1908–73

Chilean president. Politically aware from an early age and arrested while at medical school for "revolutionary activities", in 1933 Allende helped found the Chilean socialist party which broke away from the Soviet-orientated Communist party. He was elected to Congress in 1937, served as health minister (1939–42) and was elected to the Senate in 1945. In 1970 Allende stood in the presidential elections for the fourth time, as Popular Unity Candidate, and won narrowly. The Christian Democrats agreed to his ratification on condition that he preserve Chile's multiparty democracy. He aimed to create a socialist society in an undeveloped country while maintaining a liberal form of parliamentary agreement, and so nationalized the large copper mines, previously partly US-owned, without compensation, and ended Chile's diplomatic and economic boycott of Cuba. He brought most of the mining and manufacturing industry under state control and gave over farmland to peasant cooperatives. He increased wages, froze prices and, to overcome the ensuing fiscal deficit, printed money. In 1972 Allende increased his majority slightly but met with middle-class opposition to his policies. The threat of further nationalization caused strikes, inflation soared, food was short and street violence spread. In September 1973 Allende was killed during a violent coup by the military and anti-Marxist opposition.

Bailey, David 1938–

British photographer and film director. A self-taught photographer, his first pictures were accepted by *Vogue* magazine in 1959, when he was only 21. His method was to work with only one model – at first, Jean Shrimpton, and later Marie Helvin – and his fresh lively style of fashion portraiture made him one of the most successful and durable British fashion and beauty photographers. He produced several books, most notably *Nudes*.

Baldwin, James 1924–87

US writer. A revivalist preacher at the age of 14, Baldwin soon lost his faith. By 1945 he had published essays; in 1948 he won a major literary fellowship, and moved to Paris, where he lived until 1956, afterward alternating between Europe and the USA. *Go Tell it on the Mountain* (1953), based on his experience of revivalism, brought him fame. In *Giovanni's Room* (1956) he addressed homosexuality which, along with racism, was a lifelong theme in novels and essays. From 1957 he was active in the Civil Rights movement, and focused more and more in his writing on the racial issue; he was recognized as the literary voice of black America. Martin Luther King's assassination shattered Baldwin's hopes of a peaceful resolution to the problem of racism, and from then on he was bitterly resigned to violence; the bitterness shows in *The Fire Next Time* (1963).

Ball, Lucille 1911–89

US actress. In the fifties the star of one of TV's most successful comedy shows, *I Love Lucy*, she was America's greatest female clown but major Hollywood stardom evaded her. She had begun playing bit parts in movies in 1933, later graduating to support and co-star roles with Bob Hope and Red Skelton. The TV production company she and husband Desi Arnez created eventually controlled RKO, and on divorce in 1960 she became president of a business grossing an annual $25 million. She eventually sold to Gulf and Western, and continued starring on TV, in *The Lucy Show*.

Baltimore, David 1938–

US molecular biologist. After graduating at Swarthmore College he did postdoctoral research at Massachusetts Institute of Technology, the Einstein College of Medicine, and the Salk Institute (1963–68). He was appointed associate professor of biology at MIT, becoming full professor in 1972 (from 1982 also director of the Whitehead Institute). He discovered how the polio virus propagates itself and how its main constituents DNA and protein are formed. In 1970, however, he announced a discovery of greater importance. According to accepted belief, DNA was converted to protein by way of an intermediate RNA (ribonucleic acid). The first stage of the conversion was known as transcription, the second as translation. It was further believed that this was an irreversible process. Baltimore showed, however, that, at least in some tumor viruses, the first-stage, or transcription process was reversible: RNA can be converted to DNA by the enzyme reverse transcriptase. In 1975 Baltimore shared a Nobel prize with H.M. Temin, who had discovered reverse transcriptase independently.

Bandaranaike, Sirimavo 1916–

Sri Lankan prime minister. The daughter of wealthy parents, she married in 1940 and was diligent in supporting her husband's political career, as well as working as a volunteer to improve the condition of women in Sri Lankan society. After the assassination of her husband in 1959, the Sri Lankan Freedom Party (SLFP) won a majority in the elections, and Mrs Bandaranaike became the new SLFP leader, and the world's first woman prime minister. She improved health and educational facilities, promoted native religion and culture, and brought private schools into the state sector. But because she also nationalized some of the rubber industry and the western-controlled oil industry, the USA stopped aid to Sri Lanka, whose economy was weak. The SLFP split over a coalition with a Marxist group, and lost power in 1965, but regained it in 1970 as the senior partners in the United Front coalition. Abroad, Mrs Bandaranaike resumed her policy of nonalignment. Domestically, she expelled the US Peace Corps, and announced more nationalization. The pace of this was slow, however, and unemployment was rising. In 1971 she withstood an attempted leftist coup, but left office in 1977; she remained a member of parliament.

▼ Franz Beckenbauer

▼ Susan Bell

▼ Abebe Bikile

Barnard, Christiaan Neethling 1922–

South African surgeon. After studying medicine at the Universities of Cape Town and Minnesota he set up in private practice, eventually becoming a specialist cardio-thoracic surgeon in the University of Cape Town (1958) and subsequently (1961) head of cardio-thoracic surgery. He became interested in open-heart surgery and the possibility of replacing diseased hearts with healthy hearts from accident victims. He successfully performed a heart transplant operation in 1967, although the patient died 18 days later from complications. Later, he pioneered the replacement of diseased heart valves with artificial ones.

Beckenbauer, Franz 1945–

West German football player. Captain of the national team that won the European championships in 1972 and the 1974 World Cup, he also captained Bayern Munich to win three European Cups and four national titles. From 1976 to 1980 he played for the New York Cosmos. Returning to West Germany, he played for Hamburg until 1982. In the late 1980s he was manager of the West German national team.

Béjart (Berger), Maurice 1927–

French choreographer and opera director. At 14, Béjart attended ballet school in Marseilles and in 1945 studied in Paris, then London. He began to choreograph with the Swedish Ballet in 1952. In 1953 he cofounded *Ballets de L'Etoile* (later *Ballet-Théâtre de Paris*). His *Symphonie pour un homme seul* (1955) was the first concrete music ballet. In 1959 his *Le Sacre du printemps* was a critical triumph, and he set up the *Ballet du XXme siècle* in Brussels. From 1961 he also directed opera and incorporated jazz and acrobatics into his choreography. *Messe pour le temps présent* (1967) incorporated Eastern philosophy and audience participation (in meditation). In 1970 he founded a theater research center, MUDRA, in Brussels. The Béjart Ballet was later based in Lausanne.

Bell, Susan Jocelyn 1943–

British astronomer. A Glasgow University graduate, she did postgraduate research at Cambridge, later held a research fellowship at the University of Southampton (1968–73) and was research assistant in the Mullard Space Science Laboratory, University College, London (1974–82). At Cambridge she worked with Antony Hewish, a radio astronomer who had completed in 1967 a radio telescope specially designed to observe the scintillation of stars. In the summer of 1967 they observed an unusual signal at a wavelength of 3.7m (12.1ft) – it corresponded to a sharp burst of radio energy at short regular intervals. This was the first known pulsar. Pulsars are believed to be rapidly rotating neutron stars whose radio emission is perceived intermittently as they rotate.

Bellini, Mario 1935–

Italian industrial designer. Graduating from the Milan Polytechnic in 1959, he collaborated with Olivetti from 1963, and also worked with motor companies like Fiat, Lancia and Renault. His major contribution to modern design is the Olivetti ET101 electronic typewriter – allegedly modeled on the shark. His Praxis typewriter was modeled on the angled lectern used by Roman scribes.

Berio, Luciano 1925–

Italian composer. Berio, a musical child, left law school to go to the Milan Conservatory, graduating with honors in 1951. He worked as an opera coach and conductor, and took a composition course with Dallapiccola at Tanglewood, USA in 1952; there he first experienced electronic music. In 1954 he joined the staff of the Italian state radio, cofounding the Studio di Fonologia Musicale, an electronic music studio, and becoming its director in 1959; he also cofounded *Incontri Musicale*, a journal of avant-garde music. *Perspectives* (1956) was his first electronic composition. He continued to write experimental works for all kinds of instrument, and for voice, chorus and electronic equipment. From 1965 to 1971 he taught at the Juilliard School, New York, and later directed the electronic section of IRCAM, in Paris. His wife (from 1950), soprano Cathy Berberian, sang many of his works; their collaboration continued even after their divorce in 1965, and her brilliance favored Berio's adventurousness in vocal music, in which he often made articulation a factor in compositional structure. *Sinfonia* (1968), using quotations from other composers, like Mahler, and text from Levi-Strauss, marked his emergence as a popular composer; it was commissioned by the New York Philharmonic, and premièred in New York, with the Swingles singers; its avant-garde collage technique was quite new. He often used literary texts. His stage pieces include *La Vera Storia* (1982). *Opera* (1970) quotes from his own works and from classical opera. In 1976 he became artistic director of the Accademia Filarmonica Romana, and completed *Coro* for chorus and orchestra.

Bertolucci, Bernardo 1940–

Italian film director. He was Pasolini's assistant on *Accattone!* (1961) and directed his first feature in 1962. The second (1964) had a critical success, but it was 1970 before *La Strageia del Ragno* and *Il Conformista* established his reputation. Later films include *Last Tango in Paris* (1972), *1900* (1976), *La Luna* (1979) and *The Last Emperor* (1987).

Beuys, Joseph 1921–86

German sculptor. After studying at Düsseldorf Academy of Art, Beuys taught there from 1961 until his dismissal in 1971. Prominent in the Anti-Form movement, Beuys created "assemblages" of

refuse and found objects. After being greased and wrapped in felt by Tartars who had rescued him from the snow after a wartime plane crash, he favored felt – he traveled to America wrapped in felt for his piece *Coyote* (1974). In the 1960s he began to conduct public rituals, and organize "happenings", often involving the disarrangement and restoration of his works. His intentions were to release emotional trauma and communicate healing. He stood for parliament in 1976 and represented West Germany at the Venice Biennale.

Bikile, Abebe 1932–78

Ethiopian marathon runner, the first black African athlete to win an Olympic gold medal. One of Haile Selassie's Imperial Guards, he had run only two marathons in his life before winning in record time at the 1960 Rome Olympics. He won again in 1964, after only six weeks training, but a leg injury forced him to drop out of the Mexico City Olympics. A car accident in 1969 left him unable to walk, and he took up paraplegic sport.

Black, Sir James Whyte 1924–

British pharmacologist. After graduating in medicine at St Andrews University in 1946 he held academic positions there and in the Universities of Malaya and Glasgow. He subsequently held industrial positions with ICI (1958–64), Smith, Kline and French (1964–73) and Wellcome Research Laboratories (1978–84) and was then appointed professor of analytical pharmacology in London University (1984). His development of beta-blocking drugs was based on the fact that some hormones act on the heart by attachment to beta-receptors. By blocking these, the effect of the hormones and the load on the heart can be reduced. His second major discovery (1972), of drugs for the treatment of gastric ulcer, had a similar basis, in this case reducing acid production. He received a Nobel prize in 1988.

Boulez, Pierre 1925–

French composer and conductor. After studying higher mathematics, Boulez studied at the Paris Conservatoire with Messiaen and Leibowitz. He started composing in 1945; in 1946 he became musical director of the Renaud-Barrault theater company. His early style is forceful and expressive; he moved gradually from dodecaphony to total serialism, as in *Structures* (1951–61). Boulez worked worldwide as a teacher and a conductor. He used "mobile form" – elements of ordering left to choice – in his *Third Piano Sonata* (1957), and *Pli selon Pli* (1957–62). In 1975 he became director of the Institut de Recherches et de Coordination Acoustique Musique (IRCAM), a center in Paris for the development of electronic music; his *Répons* (1981) introduced the 4X music computer, developed at IRCAM, which was subsequently used by many other composers.

155

▼ David Bowie

▼ Willy Brandt

▼ Leonid Brezhnev

Bowie, David 1947–

British singer, musician and actor. Born David Hayward-Jones, he had been working with a mime troupe, studying at a Buddhist monastery in Scotland, and running an arts laboratory before the major success of his album *The Man Who Sold the World* in 1970. The most articulate and provocative of the "glam-rock" artists of the early 1970s, he abandoned the style mid-tour in 1973, going on to explore other musical idioms, notably soul and electronic music. He also starred in films such as *The Man Who Fell to Earth* (1976) and *Merry Christmas, Mr Lawrence* (1982). He continued recording, and manipulating his personal style; he wrote film scores, including *Labyrinth* and *Absolute Beginners* (both 1986). His duet with Mick Jagger from the Live Aid Concert, *Dancing in the Streets* (1985) was a massive hit.

Brandt, Willy 1913–92

West German chancellor. Returning to Germany after the fall of Hitler, Brandt was elected to the federal parliament in 1949. In 1957 he became the Social Democratic mayor of West Berlin and an international figure, described as the "German Kennedy", during the building of the Berlin wall. Having run three times for the chancellorship, in 1966 he became vice-chancellor and foreign minister in a coalition with the Christian Democrats. He was elected chancellor at his fourth attempt in 1969 in the new Social Democrat-Free Democrat coalition, and remained in office until 1974. He revalued the German mark and concentrated on foreign affairs. A signatory to the nuclear nonproliferation treaty, in 1970 Brandt joined with the Soviet Union in calling for the rejection of military force and the recognition of current European boundaries. He signed a nonaggression pact with Poland in 1970 establishing a mutually acceptable border, and in 1971, the year he was awarded the Nobel Peace Prize, was a party to the "big four" treaty to determine the status of Berlin. A campaigner for a united Europe, he helped to expand the European Economic Community, and after his resignation headed the Brandt Commission, which in 1980 produced a report, *North-South: a program for survival*, demanding a redistribution of wealth between the northern and southern hemispheres.

Brel, Jacques 1925–78

Belgian-born French singer and songwriter. He began writing *chansons* in 1950 and was performing at the Trois Baudets theater in Paris by 1954. He soon became an international star, and in the 1960s toured both the USA and the USSR. His lyrics contained a mordant satire on modern morals, set to sophisticated melodies far removed from formulaic pop or folk. *Ne me Quitte pas* (*If you Go Away*) is his best known song. He also wrote an opera called *Le Voyage dans la lune*.

Brenner, Sydney 1927–

South African-British molecular biologist, pioneer evaluator of the genetic code. After graduating in the University of the Witwatersrand he spent some time in Oxford before joining the British Medical Research Council's Molecular Biology Laboratory in Cambridge in 1957: he was appointed its director in 1980. By 1953 Francis Crick and J.D. Watson had demonstrated how genes reproduce themselves and carry genetic information: specific amino acids that become linked to make up proteins are coded by triplets of bases, known as codons, in the DNA chains. Brenner showed that these triple codon sequences do not overlap. He also determined that there were no breaks (punctuation points) in the sequence of bases.

Brezhnev, Leonid Ilyich 1906–82

Leader of the Soviet Union. Benefiting from Stalin's purges and Khrushchev's favor, Brezhnev rose steadily in the Ukrainian party hierarchy. After World War II he was the Moldavian party leader (1950–52), served on the CPSU (Soviet Communist party) central committee and in the Politburo (1952), before his demotion on Stalin's death. He became once more a member of the Presidium (ex-Politburo) in 1957. Titular head of state from 1960, he finally became a party leader in 1964, briefly sharing power with Kosygin after the fall of Khrushchev. Brezhnev delegated much responsibility and concentrated his attention on foreign affairs and the suppression of internal dissent. Although opposed to liberalization at home he increased the emigration of Soviet Jews and tried to improve conditions for farmers and consumers. Abroad, he pursued a policy of détente while amassing conventional forces and using the Red Army to uphold Communist regimes in neighboring countries (Czechoslovakia 1968, Afghanistan 1979).

Brook, Peter 1925–

British theater director. Brook began directing as a 17-year-old undergraduate at Oxford, with *Dr Faustus*. After spending two years at Birmingham Repertory Theatre, he directed *Romeo and Juliet* at Stratford (1947). In the 1950s he worked also in Europe and the USA, and directed a celebrated *Titus Andronicus* with Olivier (1955). In 1962 he joined the Royal Shakespeare Company (RSC). Inspired by Artaud's work, Brook ran an RSC Theatre of Cruelty season, and, also in 1964, won the New York Drama Critics' directing award for his production of Marxist playwright Peter Weiss's *Marat/Sade*. After a very successful version of *A Midsummer Night's Dream* (1970), Brook set up the International Center for Theater Research in Paris, based on the ideas of Polish director Jerzy Grotowski, and toured Africa and Asia. In 1988, he directed a vast and ambitious film of the Indian holy book, *Mahabharata*.

Brundage, Avery 1887–1975

American industrialist and sports administrator. After training as an engineer, in 1915 he set up the Avery Brundage Company, a construction firm based in Chicago. But he is chiefly remembered for his involvement with the International Olympic Committee, which he joined in 1936 and led from 1952 to his retirement in 1972. A keen amateur sportsman in his youth, he struggled to keep the Olympic Games free from professionalism and political interference.

Buñuel, Luis 1900–83

Spanish Mexican film director. In the 1920s, after founding Spain's first film club. Buñuel explored the work of Sigmund Freud before collaborating with Salvador Dalí on the surrealist films *Un Chien andalou* (1928) and *L'Age d'or* (1930), which have not lost their power to shock. Buñuel fell out with Dalí over the latter's support of Franco. His documentary film on Spanish poverty, *Las Hurdes* (1932) was banned by the government and Buñel worked in obscurity dubbing foreign films for 17 years, settling in Mexico in 1947, until *Los Olvidados* (1950) won the Cannes film festival Grand Prix. He continued to make surreal satires on the Establishment, especially the Church and the bourgeoisie, including the French-made *Nazarin* (1958), and *Viridiana* (1960) Palme d'or winner, which like several other of his films was banned in Spain, *The Exterminating Angel* (1962) and *Belle de Jour* (1966), starring Catherine Deneuve, which won the Venice Golden Lion award. In *That Obscure Object of Desire* (1977), two actresses played the heroine. His autobiography, *My Last Sigh*, was published in 1983, when he also received the Grand Cross of the Order of Isabel la Catolica, awarded by a relenting government just before his death.

Callas (Kallogeropoulos), Maria 1923–77

US soprano of Greek parentage. After studying at Athens conservatory, she played Tosca in Athens (1941) but her début in the international eye was in 1947 at La Scala, Milan, as La Gioconda in Ponchielli's opera. She joined La Scala company in 1950 and won especial renown in the title roles of *Tosca, Norma*, and *Lucia di Lammermoor*. She appeared internationally in these roles and a repertoire stretching from Italian bel canto (by Bellini, Donizetti, and Rossini), which she revived, to Wagner. Known for the brilliancy of her dramatic interpretations and her perfectionism, she was a genius. After the end of her marriage, in 1959, her relationship with Greek shipping tycoon Aristotle Onassis attracted much attention. She retired, as her voice was losing its clarity, in 1965, and gave master classes at New York's Juilliard School (1971–72). She emerged from retirement for a final world concert tour in 1973, which sadly confirmed the wisdom of her earlier decision.

Maria Callas

Noam Chomsky

Jim Clark

Calvino, Italo 1923–85

Italian writer. Calvino's first novel, *The Path to the Nest of Spiders* (1947), written after his wartime experiences in the Resistance, examined war and Resistance through a child's eyes. Always exploring the various forms and conventions of communicational symbols, in *The Castle of Crossed Destinies* (1969) he uses Tarot cards to develop the plot. This also introduces elements of mystery, enigma, and traditional allegory, all typical of Calvino's work. *If on a Winter's Night a Traveller* (1979), a novel about novel-reading which consists of ten novel openings, increased his popularity outside Italy.

Carson, Johnny 1925–

American television personality. He worked as a magician in the 1940s and wrote comedy routines in the 1950s. His humorous monologues in *The Johnny Carson Show* led NBC to give him a spot on *The Tonight Show* in 1962, after which his naughty boy image and his "desk sofa" interview technique made him outstandingly popular.

Cartier-Bresson, Henri 1908–

French photographer. Cartier-Bresson took up photography in 1931, after studying painting and literature in Paris and Cambridge, UK. His first exhibitions took place in Madrid and New York in 1933. He assisted (1936–39) film director Jean Renoir, another powerful influence; and made two documentary films, one, *Return to Life* (1937) about the Spanish Civil War, and *Le Retour* (1945), on the postwar experiences of French prisoners-of-war. In 1947, with Robert Capa and others, he set up Magnum cooperative photographic agency. From 1948 to 1950 Cartier-Bresson worked in India, China, Indonesia and Egypt; in 1952 his collection, *The Decisive Moment*, appeared, and in 1955, another book, *People of Moscow. Photoportraits* appeared in 1983; his many exhibitions included one at New York's Museum of Modern Art in 1988. Cartier-Bresson was always concerned with the experience, and response to "great events" of ordinary people, rather than the spectacle of celebrities; he was instrumental in the acceptance of photo-journalism as an art form. In pursuing his art he showed courage, as on the streets of Paris in 1968, and integrity; he never intruded on what he saw to be "private" emotion.

Castiglione, Achille 1918–

Italian industrial designer. Born into a family of designers, he was a founder of the Italian Association for Industrial Design in 1966. His style is influenced by the theories of Marcel Duchamp. His "Toio" lamp for Flos used a car head-lamp. He made his name with the "Mezzadro" stool (1957) made of a tractor seat. His wit is also evident in the "Arco" lamp (1962), with its tiny arc-and-reflector light supported by a massive marble base.

Castro (Ruz), Fidel 1926–

Cuban revolutionary leader. After studying law, he practiced in Havana. He staged an unsuccessful rising against President Batista in 1953 and was sentenced to fifteen years' imprisonment. He was released after an amnesty in 1955 and continued his armed struggle against Batista's draconian regime until, with mounting support, he ended it in 1958. Castro was appointed prime minister in 1959, proclaiming a Marxist-Leninist program of reforms adapted to Cuban requirements. He undertook drastic reforms in industry and nationalized US-owned companies. Far-reaching reforms were also implemented in agriculture and education. A free welfare state system was established, employment was guaranteed and compulsory, ownership was centralized and the media government-controlled. The economy, ideologically soundly based but inefficient, has failed to cope with population growth. The ending of US economic dominance was coupled with the defeat of the attempted US-backed invasion at the Bay of Pigs in 1961. Cuba became dependent on Soviet economic and political aid, and this led to the Cuban missile crisis of 1962. In the late 1960s, under pressure from Moscow, he moderated his confrontational style and followed the Soviet line more closely. He continued to export revolution, particularly assisting pro-Soviet forces in Angola and Ethiopia, and by the 1980s had 40,000 troops stationed in some twenty-five countries. Domestic problems occurred in the production of sugar and tobacco, and thousands of Cubans left for the US. In the 1980s, Castro's disapproval of the Soviet leader Gorbachev's reforming policies cooled relations between their countries.

Chomsky, Noam 1928–

US linguist, writer and political activist. He studied math and philosophy at Pennsylvania University, became interested in linguistics, and developed as a research fellow at Harvard and M.I.T. his theories of generative grammar. Chomsky's theories led to the creation of a new school of linguistics and also had a profound impact on philosophy and psychology. Going against the dominance of structuralist thought, he argued that language is the result of an innate mental facility. Once this is fully discovered one could construct a grammatical framework to account for the vast range of sentence structures found in all languages (*Syntactic Structures*, 1957). *Aspects of a Theory of Syntax* (1965) develops his theory to link sound, syntax, and meaning. Chomsky is also known for his involvement with New Left politics and for his opposition to US foreign policy, especially in Vietnam during the 1960s and 1970s and in the Gulf Crisis and war (1990–91). His views on socio-political matters can be found in *American Power – The New Mandarins* (1969) and *At War with Asia* (1970).

Christo (C. Javacheff) 1935–

Bulgarian "wrapping" sculptor. Christo studied at the Academies in Sofia and Vienna, (1955–57), then went to Paris, where he joined the *Nouveaux Réalistes*, a movement deeply critical of the contemporary consumerist culture. He was also a founder member of the KWY. Opposed to materialist values, in 1958 Christo began wrapping objects, at first bottles and cans, and after moving to New York in 1964, larger and larger things. In 1968 he wrapped a public building in Italy, in 1969, a bay on the Australian coast, and in 1971, he made *Valley Curtain*, a long fence made of sheet plastic, in Colorado. Christo also produced, from 1961, assemblages made out of oilcans.

Clark, Jim 1936–68

Scottish racing driver. He won the world championship twice: in 1963 with a record seven of the ten events (equaled in 1984 by Alain Prost), and in 1965 with six, plus Indianapolis. Entering racing in 1956, he first competed on the international circuit in 1960 for the Lotus team. Both his victories were in Lotus-Fords.

Cohn-Bendit, Daniel 1945–

German Marxist/anarchist who became the figurehead of student uprising in France in the spring of 1968. Cohn-Bendit's family fled from the Nazis to France, where he was born. They returned to Germany (1958), and he took German nationality but returned to France to study sociology at the University of France (1964). The Marxist/anarchist theories he developed opposed all forms of authority and called for spontaneous action by and the granting of self-government to the masses. Cohn-Bendit became the leader of student activists who occupied University buildings. This unrest culminated in riots and Cohn-Bendit was seen as the compelling force behind them. However, he preferred to be considered merely as a spokesman rather than a leader. Expelled from France, he returned to West Germany where he rejected his earlier standpoint in the realization that such theories took no account of the ecological destruction of the planet, man's future. In the 1980s Cohn-Bendit became a Green Party member of parliament in Germany.

Conran, Terence 1931–

British retail entrepreneur. After setting up a holding company in the mid-1960s, he came to prominence after the foundation of the Conran Design Group and the Habitat Group, both in 1971. Habitat stores made available a well-coordinated collection of stylish articles for the home, forerunners of the "designer" items of the 1980s. In the mid-1980s his activities included the running of high-street stores, and he also became involved in the running of museums, being founder of the Boilerhouse Project in London.

▶ Sacha Distel

▶ Alexander Dubček

▶ Renato Dulbecco

Coppola, Francis Ford 1939–

US film director, screenwriter and producer. He got his first directing job from Roger Corman. The success of his second film, *You're a Big Boy Now* (1967), won him *Finian's Rainbow* (1968), which crashed. Another failure had his production company near bankruptcy, but then came *Patton* (1970), script only; *The Godfather* (1972); *American Graffiti* (1973), production only; *The Conversation* and *The Godfather*, Part II (both 1974); and *Apocalypse Now* (1979), crossing Conrad's *Heart of Darkness* with the Vietnam war. His policy of fostering young talent suffered when financial problems loomed again and thereafter success was fitful.

Courrèges, André 1923–

French couturier. He made his name in the mid-sixties with futuristic, mostly white designs after working for Balenciaga for 11 years. In 1961 he opened his own salon and by 1964 he had found youth-oriented style – a simple, trapezoid, short-skirted line. Other fashion originals include hipster pants, sequined jump suits and vinyl trimming on coats and suits.

Cronkite, Walter 1916–

American broadcast journalist. After dropping out of the University of Texas in 1935 to work for the Houston Post, he covered World War II and the Nuremberg Trials. He was taken up by CBS in 1950 and gained respect and popularity in the "You Are There" series. From 1962 to 1981 he was the anchor-man of his own nightly newscast, and his low-key broadcasting earned him the title of "The Most Trusted Man in America".

Davis, Miles 1926–91

US jazz trumpeter, keyboards and composer. He had a unique capacity for conceptual development. After three years with Charlie Parker (1945–48), he began leading nine-piece bands and found a sound epitomized by *Birth of the Cool* (1949/50). 1954–60 produced influential recordings from his five- and six-piece bands, including *Miles Ahead* and *Kind of Blue*, and established modal improvization. After 1965, his improvizations were more abstract; in 1968 he switched from song structures to extended pieces and launched jazz-rock with *In a Silent Way* and *Bitches Brew*. In the eighties his live performances gained new power.

De Beauvoir, Simone 1908–86

French novelist and feminist, de Beauvoir had an enormous impact on feminist thought. Privately educated, she attended the Sorbonne (1929) where her lifelong relationship with Jean-Paul Sartre began. Her most famous work is *The Second Sex* (1949) in which she argued for the rejection of the myth of women's feminity. In patriarchal society

the male and masculinity are held up as the norm, while the female and femininity are seen as abnormal or as "the other". Women's sense of "the other", of their alienation, is predominantly based upon their bodies and in particular their reproductive role. As a novelist, de Beauvoir's work focused upon existentialism and feminism (*All Men are Mortals*, 1955; *She Came to Stay*, 1954). *The Mandarins* won the 1954 Prix Goncourt. She also wrote a four-volume autobiography (1958–70). Eschewing marriage and motherhood and embracing independence, de Beauvoir was active in the women's movement, especially in the campaign to legalize abortion in France.

De Saint Phalle, Niki 1930–

French sculptor. De Saint Phalle became famous in the early 1960s for her assemblages featuring bags of paint, which she shot at so that they burst and splashed the whole piece. She moved on to gaudy, grotesque, blown-up female figures, such as *Nana*; she created, with Tinguely and Ultredt, the *Hon*, a sculpture large enough for people to walk on.

Distel, Sacha 1933–

French singer. A champion schoolboy swimmer, he went on to become the *Jazz Hot* magazine Guitarist of the Year from 1953 to 1958. But it was chiefly as a singer that he made his mark, recording more than 200 songs in several languages. Following the success of his song *Raindrops Keep Fallin' On My Head* (1970), he became one of Europe's most popular performers.

Dubček, Alexander 1921–92

Czechoslovakian politician. A member of the resistance movement in World War II, Dubček attained Slovakian Communist party leadership in 1963. He was voted Czechoslovakian party leader in 1968. Adopting the slogan "Socialism with a human face", he increased freedom of speech, removed Stalinists from high office and published a program of reform, "Czechoslovakia's Road to Socialism". The pace of change alarmed the Soviets, who feared the polarization of the Eastern bloc. After talks in which Dubček made only minor concessions, the Soviet army invaded Czechoslovakia in August 1968. Dubček was taken to Moscow, and forced to abandon his policies. He resigned in 1969, and was expelled from the party in 1970. He worked for the forestry administration until 1989, when he was appointed chairman of the new Czechoslovak parliament.

Dulbecco, Renato 1914–

Italian-US microbiologist. After studying medicine at the University of Turin and working in its anatomy institute, he went to the USA in 1947, first to the University of Indiana, and then the California Institute of Technology (1954–63). He was resident fellow at the Salk Institute, California

(1963–72) and was appointed distinguished research professor in 1977. He discovered the photoreactivity of phages inactivated by ultraviolet light, and he devised the patch test for the recognition of animal virus mutations. His research advanced knowledge of oncogenic viruses, polioma and simian viruses, and their action in cellular transformation. He was awarded a Nobel prize in 1975.

Dylan, Bob 1941–

US folk rock composer, singer and guitarist. The leader of American folk/protest in the sixties, he was, after the Beatles, the most influential person working in rock, and a poetic, political, passionate lyricist. Woody Guthrie was his own most formative influence. Early classic tracks include *A Hard Rain's A Gonna Fall* and *Blowin' in the Wind* (both 1963). *John Wesley Harding* (1968) was his comeback record after severe injury in a motorcycle accident in 1966. His rambling movie *Renaldo and Clara* (1978) flopped. The religious trend in *Slow Train Coming* (1979), *Saved* (1980) and *Shot of Love* (1981) was not popular with his fans.

Eastwood, Clint 1930–

US film actor, director and producer. One of the actor-producers of the seventies, he won fame by starring in Sergio Leone's spaghetti Westerns (1964–66). His image as the laconic hero under pressure brought worldwide popularity and in the eighties contributed to his election as mayor of his Californian hometown, Carmel. His credits include *A Fistful of Dollars* (1964), *Coogan's Bluff* (1968), *Magnum Force* (1973) *Escape from Alcatraz* (1978) and *Pale Rider* (1985).

Esaki, Leo 1925–

Japanese physicist. He did postgraduate research on semiconductors and then worked for the Sony Corporation (1956–60). He then joined IBM at their Thomas J. Watson Research Center, of which he was appointed director in 1962. From the outset of his career he investigated the so-called tunnel effect by which, in accordance with wave mechanics, a current carrier can penetrate a potential barrier which, in accordance with classical physics, it could not surmount. In 1960 he invented the tunnel (Esaki) diode, an important variation of Shockley's junction diode. Such diodes can be used as low noise amplifiers or as oscillators, up to microwave frequency. In 1973 Esaki was awarded a Nobel prize jointly with B.D. Josephson and I. Giaever.

Eysenck, Hans Jurgen 1916–

British psychologist (German born) who studied human personality and behavior. Eysenck stressed the importance of laboratory, statistical and questionnaire techniques. For example, he developed the Eysenck personality inventory and

▲ Leo Esaki

▲ Aretha Franklin

▲ John Kenneth Galbraith

questionnaire in order to measure the two personality dimensions of neuroticism and extroversion/introversion. Famous for his vigorous and controversial criticisms of psychoanalysis, he argued that its theoretical explanations were redundant, its therapy suspect and its results could be due to spontaneous remission or placebo effects. Instead, Eysenck advocated "behavioral therapy" which rejects traditional explanations of unconscious motives and childhood experiences and uses practical methods such as desensitization and relaxation in a process of unlearning and rearranging undesirable responses. He also believed that intelligence and personality are mainly influenced by genetic factors. He was the author of numerous books and articles on various topics, some for popular consumption and many of which fueled continuing debate, like *Causes and Cures of Criminality* and *Genes, Culture and Personality* (both 1989).

Fanon, Frantz (Omar) 1925–1961

West Indian psychoanalyst, social philosopher and revolutionary writer whose ideas influenced black leaders during the 1960s and 1970s. Fanon's work emphasized inter-racial conflict. In *Black Skin, White Masks* (1952) he analyzed the effects of white colonialism upon blacks and argued that the consequent racism was damaging for both. He also wrote extensively on the Algerian revolution and in *The Wretched of the Earth* (1961) he extended his analysis of struggle to cover the Third World. Fanon urged colonialized people to overthrow imperialism with violence, justifiable because violence had been used to enforce colonial rule. This action, he believed, would have a cathartic effect on those formerly oppressed. Fanon studied psychiatry in France and in 1953–56 was head of a psychiatric hospital in Algeria. He also joined the Algerian Liberation movement (1954) and served briefly as ambassador to Ghana for the rebel Provisional Government (1960).

Fellini, Federico 1920–

Italian director. An internationally famous director, many of whose films have a kaleidoscopic quality – part fantasy, part autobiographical – major credits include *I Vitelloni* (1953), *La Strada* (1954), *Le notti di Cabiria* (1957), *La Dolce Vita* (1960), (1963), *Giulietta degli Spiriti* (*Juliet of the Spirits*) (1965), *Roma* (1972) and *Amarcord* (1973). Work as a reporter, with a touring company of actors, and as a scriptwriter preceded collaboration with Rossellini (1945–48), and his début with *Luci dei Varieta* (*Lights of Variety*) (1951).

Foster, Norman 1935–

British architect. From 1956, Foster studied architecture at Manchester, and then Yale, where he met Richard Rogers. After working (1962–63) for Urban Renewal and City Planning Consultants,

Foster set up a practice in Britain with Rogers, and their wives. In 1967, he left to set up Foster Associates; from 1968–83 he worked with Buckminster Fuller. Foster's work includes the Willis, Faber and Dumas office-block in Ipswich (1974) featuring black mirror glass, curved to fit the street, and incorporating trees inside and a turfed roof-garden. Foster also designed an Arts Center in Nîmes (1984) and the Century Tower, Tokyo (1987). From 1987 he was based in Japan.

Franklin, Aretha 1942–

US singer. "Lady Soul" was steeped in gospel music in childhood, touring as a soloist with her evangelist father. At 18 she turned to blues and was signed by Columbia. It was with her Atlantic signing (1966) that she took off. She delivered eight consecutive million-selling singles – among them *I Never Loved a Man* and *Baby I Love You* (both 1967) and *I Say a Little Prayer* (1968) – the first female soloist to pull this off. After a period of illness in the 1970s, she made a comeback in the 1980s both as a soloist and in successful duets with pop stars Annie Lennox and George Michael.

Friedan, Betty 1921–

US feminist, regarded by many as the founder of the modern US women's movement. Campaigning for a wide range of women's issues, Friedan advocated an individualist and liberal form of feminism which was later rejected by more radical feminists. Her book *The Feminine Mystique* (1963) is one of the earliest and most influential books on the women's movement . It describes the discrepancy between the ideals to which women try to conform and the frustrated reality of their lives. Friedan called for women to reject the "mystique" wherein the highest achievement of a woman is fulfillment through domesticity and motherhood and to develop fully as individuals through education and work. Friedan herself had given up a career in psychology for marriage and a family. In *The Second Stage* (1981), she warned of the dangers of competing with men rather than insisting on the right to be different from them, and still cooperating. Friedan also founded the powerful National Organization for Women (1966).

Fuentes, Carlos 1928–

Mexican writer. Son of a diplomat, Fuentes, himself a diplomat and an international lawyer, pioneered the modern novel in Mexico. *The Death of Artemio Cruz* (1962), is a fine example, weighty, subtle, touched with eroticism, and bringing together the Mexican cultural/historical heritage and Western technical sophistication. The massive *Terra Nostra* (1975) is a brilliantly organized, fantastic, allusive, historically complex masterwork, with the magical quality so often found in the best Latin American writing. He also retold native myths and wrote literary criticism.

Fuller, Buckminster 1895–1983

American industrial designer and futurist. He was twice expelled from Harvard before becoming a self-styled "explorer in comprehensive anticipation design". He turned his immense inventiveness – he held over 2000 patents – to the solution of social problems, such as the "Dymaxion" house, designed to meet the housing shortage of the interwar years. Without formal training, he designed the famous geodesic dome, providing the maximum of space with the minimum of materials, most notably in his construction of the translucent US pavilion at Expo 67 in Montreal. A brilliant and visionary thinker, Fuller was passionately committed to conservation and always aimed to achieve the minimum weight in his structures, so that the minimum of scarce resources would be used. He wrote prolifically.

Gajdusek, Daniel Carleton 1923–

US virologist. After studying medicine at the University of Rochester and Harvard Medical School he held a number of overseas research appointments. In 1958 he was appointed director of a program – sponsored by the National Institute of Health, Bethesda – to study child growth and disease patterns in primitive communities. He visited Papua New Guinea and came in contact with the Fore people, among whom a fatal disease called kuru is endemic. He identified the cause as a kind of virus previously unknown. This is the "slow" virus, which takes up to a year to develop. Gajdusek was awarded a Nobel prize in 1976.

Galbraith, John Kenneth 1908–

Leading US economist. After teaching at Harvard, he ran the Price Section of the Office of Price Administration. In 1949, Galbraith became Professor of Economics at Harvard University and from 1961 to 1963 was US ambassador to India. In 1952 *A Theory of Price Control* and *American Capitalism: The Concept of Countervailing Power* were published. The former advocated the use of price control and rationing in peacetime as well as during war. In the latter Galbraith contended that giant monopolistic organizations dominate modern advanced economies, contrasting with accepted economic theory and its assertion of the efficiency of competition. In *The Affluent Society* (1958) Galbraith argued that demand for luxury goods is artificially created by the producer; at the same time, funding for public services decreases, because taxation is seen as a disincentive to economic growth. This results in a society with private wealth but public poverty. *The New Industrial State* (1967) protested the domination of "big business". These controversial propositions are now accepted as an alternative to traditional economic theory. He wrote prolifically on other subjects as well as economics, producing a novel in 1990, and in 1992, *The Culture of Contentment*.

159

▲ Billy Graham

▲ Gunther Grass

▲ Jimi Hendrix

Gomulka, Wladyslaw 1905–82

Polish political leader. Gomulka joined the Communist party in 1926. He was a union activist, and was imprisoned several times before World War II. He then moved to the Soviet-occupied east of the country, and organized resistance against the Germans after they had invaded the Soviet Union in 1941. In 1942, he became a member of the central committee of the newly formed Polish Workers' party, and in 1943 was made its general secretary. In 1945 he was deputy premier of the provisional government in Lublin, and went on to serve as minister for the recovered territories. In the same year, he became a member of the Politburo and general secretary of the central committee. He suppressed the Peasants' party, and supported a forced merger with the Socialist party. He remained skeptical about the collectivization of agriculture, and in 1947 opposed the creation of the Cominform. In 1948 Stalin engineered his dismissal as party secretary and Politburo member, and in 1949 his expulsion from government and the party. He was imprisoned from 1951 to 1954, but rehabilitated by Khrushchev in 1956. A national hero, he was installed as first secretary. He curbed the role of the secret police, and abandoned the persecution of the Catholic Church and the collectivization of agriculture. However, he did not introduce freedom of speech or economic reform, and came to be regarded by many as still ultimately under the control of Moscow. In 1968, intellectuals spoke out against the regime, and students rioted in major cities. Gomulka then tried to introduce economic reforms, but in 1970 a drastic increase in food prices led to more rioting, and he resigned.

Graham, Billy 1921–

US evangelist known for his large-scale, highly organized revivalist campaigns which led to the conversions of thousands and the re-energizing of the Christian movement. Converted at the age of sixteen, in 1939 Graham was ordained as a Southern Baptist minister. In 1949 he began his preaching tours in America and was soon regarded by many as the main spokesman for the Fundamentalists. He went on to preach throughout the world including Europe (1954–55), Africa and the Holy Land (1960), and Korea (1973). His support widened to include all the major denominations. Graham used modern communications, especially television, to reach vast audiences and by the 1990s controlled one of the largest electronic churches in the USA. He also adopted modern business production methods and established the Billy Graham Evangelistic Association, Inc. to communicate with his followersHis preaching style remained simple, direct, energetic and popular. He also produced religious films, published books and developed friendships with several US presidents.

Grass, Günter 1927–

German writer. A member of Hitler Youth, and a prisoner of war, Grass took various jobs before studying art in Düsseldorf and Berlin. In 1956 he moved to Paris. *The Tin Drum* (1959), the first of a trilogy exposing Hitler's grip on ordinary people, affronted many with its obscenity, and despite its intractability, was internationally acclaimed. As a playwright, he was influenced by Absurd theater and Brecht. He wrote speeches for Willy Brandt and proselytized for the Social Democrats. *The Flounder* (1977) is arguably his masterpiece. Seen as "the nation's conscience", he called himself rather "the court jester".

Guevara, Che (Ernesto) 1928–67

Professional revolutionary. Born in Argentina, Guevara mixed with revolutionaries throughout Latin America. He became Castro's advisor and trained his guerrillas. When Castro came to power in 1959, he conferred Cuban citizenship on Guevara and gave him a series of important posts, including directorship of the National Bank. As minister of industry in 1961 Guevara implemented mass nationalization and in the same year wrote an influential manual on guerrilla warfare. In 1965, after writing *Man and Socialism in Cuba*, he disappeared. It was revealed in 1967 that he had been captured and executed while leading revolutionaries in Bolivia. His works inspired many student radicals in the late 1960s.

Hassel, Odd 1897–1981

Norwegian chemist. He did postgraduate research in Copenhagen and Berlin before returning to Oslo, where he later became professor of physical chemistry (1934–64). His main focus was the investigation of crystal structure using X-ray and electron diffraction techniques. He also investigated electrical dipole movements (the segregation of charge within molecules) and the stereochemical configuration of organic molecules.

Hayek, Friedrich August von 1899–1992

Austrian economist. Studied law, psychology and economics at the University of Vienna, then at New York University (1923–24). He was the first director of the Austrian Institute for Economic Science (1927). From 1931 to 1950 he was Tooke Professor at the London School of Economics. In *Price and Production* (1931) Hayek argued that in a boom rising prices cause a fall in real wages and increased capital investment in equipment to replace labor. As the demand for capital goods rises faster than supply, interest rates rise, investment falls and the economy turns down. The converse occurs in a slump. This directly opposed the Keynesian viewpoint. Involved in the major economic debates during the 1930s concerning monetary, business cycle and capital theories, he also argued against government intervention in

modern economies, as politically undesirable and ultimately ineffective. After the war he took up psychology and social, political and legal philosophy, holding professorships at Chicago (1950), Freiburg (1962), and Salzburg (1969). Awarded the Nobel Prize for Economics (1974), he continued publishing in the 1980s.

Hendrix, Jimi 1947–70

US rock guitarist, and composer. An appearance on British TV gave the Jimi Hendrix Experience its first hit single, *Hey Joe*, and his impact was phenomenal. The power of his blues playing seemed to re-create the electric guitar – it was the heaviest rock around – yet his vocals were cool. In 1969 he disbanded the group and formed Band of Gypsies. His most highly rated albums include *Are You Experienced* (1967), *Band of Gypsies* (1970) and *Soundtrack from Jimi Hendrix* (1973).

Henze, Hans Werner 1926–

German composer. Henze began to compose around 1938; from 1946 to 1948, he studied counterpoint with Fortner; the success of his *Kammerkonzert* gained him a publishing contract. He worked in several opera houses; his *Piano Concerto* (1951) won the Schumann prize, and the radio opera *Ein Landarzt* won the 1953 Prix d'Italia. In 1953, Henze settled in Italy – his music acquired a new warmth and lyricism, and he continued to produce fine operas and orchestral works. *The Bassarids* (1965) had a libretto by Auden and Kallmann. *Das Floss der "Medusa"* (1968), a requiem for Guevara, shows his increasing preoccupation with the politics of the left; he worked with Edward Bond on the opera *We Come to the River* (1976), and all his later dramatic work is socialist in import. Henze's music is eclectic and highly organized, influenced by Stravinsky, Weill, and Berg, as well as Italian opera. His opera *Das Verratene Meer* (1990) received much adverse criticism.

Hess, Harry Hammond 1906–69

US geologist. After graduating at Princeton he joined Loangwa Concession, Northern Rhodesia, as geologist in 1928. In 1934 he returned to Princeton, later becoming professor of geology. From the 1930s he carried out gravity measurements and echo sounding experiments with the US navy which gave him a keen interest in submarine geology and gravitational anomalies. In 1957 W.W. Ewing demonstrated the global distribution of deep central rifts in the mid-ocean ridges, associated with anomalously young deposits in the ocean depths. Hess suggested that material rose constantly from the earth's mantle to form the mid-ocean ridges and then spread out sideways until it reached the continental margins, sank below the lighter continental crust and eventually found its way back to the mantle.

Ho Chi Minh

David Hockney

Enver Hoxha

Hewish, Antony 1924–

British radio astronomer. He graduated in Cambridge in 1948 and did postgraduate research there before going to the Royal Aircraft Establishment, Farnborough (1943–46). Returning to Cambridge, he was a lecturer in physics until appointed professor of radio astronomy in 1971. He designed a special form of radio telescope, completed in 1967, to examine a variation in radio signals from space analogous to the twinkling of stars, noticed after the war. He and his research assistant S.J. Bell picked up unusual signals in the 3.7m waveband; they fluctuated steadily. The source proved to be a tiny neutron star within our own galaxy. It was the first pulsar. For this Hewish was awarded a Nobel prize in 1974.

Ho Chi Minh 1890–1969

Vietnamese revolutionary and president. In 1911, Ho fled a background of poverty to become a seaman. In 1917, he settled in France, where he joined the newly-formed French Communist party (PCF). He went to Moscow in 1923 and attended the 1924 Communist International there, and spoke on the importance of the peasantry in revolution. From 1923 to 1924 he was in the Soviet Union, and then, as a representative of Comintern, in China until 1927. He helped to found the League of Oppressed Peoples, the Vietnamese Revolutionary Youth League, and, in 1930, the Indochinese Communist party. He returned in 1940 to Japanese-occupied Indochina, and formed a resistance force, the Vietminh. He later established a government in Hanoi with himself as president. In 1946 he waged a war against the French, who had occupied southern Vietnam, finally defeating them at Dien Bien Phu in 1954, and so bringing about the partition of Vietnam. Abroad, Ho maintained good relations with China and the Soviet Union. In 1959 he agreed to help the Vietcong guerrillas in South Vietnam to overthrow their own government and resigned as party secretary, but remained president.

Hockney, David 1937–

British artist. In 1961, Hockney won the Royal College of Art Gold Medal, the Guinness Award for etching, and two other prizes; and, still a student, he won international success with his series of etchings "The Rake's Progress". With the resulting income he visited California, later his home, and, inspired by the light, painted many pictures of swimming pools. He has also lived and exhibited in Paris. In 1962 Hockney taught in England and at three US universities. In 1966 he designed *Ubu Roi*, at London's Royal Court theater; in 1978, he designed *The Magic Flute* at Glyndebourne. A brilliant draftsman, he has received many international awards. In his pursuit of simplicity and realism, his work has become more conventional.

Hoffa, James Riddle 1913–75

US labor leader. Began union activities in the 1930s. Became president of the Local International Brotherhood of Teamsters (IBT) in 1937. Helped organize the Central States Drivers' Council in 1937, became its chairman, then president of the Michigan Conference of Teamsters in 1942. Was elected IBT vice-president in 1957. In the same year Hoffa was charged with attempted bribery, but acquitted. He accelerated the centralization process within the IBT that allowed him to negotiate and sign the first national freight-handling contract in the trucking industry in 1964. Under him the IBT became the largest labor union in the US. In 1967 he began a 13-year prison term for jury tampering, fraud and conspiracy in the disposal of union benefit funds. Hoffa remained president of the Teamsters until 1971, when his sentence was commuted by President Nixon with the provision that he would not participate in any union affairs until 1980. In July 1975 he mysteriously disappeared and was officially declared dead in 1982.

Hounsfield, Godfrey Newbold 1919–

British physicist. After studying in London at the City and Guilds College and Faraday House he served in the Royal Air Force (1939–46). He returned to Faraday House (1947–51) and then joined EMI (Electrical and Musical Industries), becoming initially head of medical systems and later, senior staff scientist (1977). His early work was on radar and computers: in 1958–59 he led the design team for the first large fully transistorized computer to be built in the UK (the EMIDEC 1100). Later he developed the technique of X-ray computerized tomography or CAT (1969–72). If soft tissues are scanned with X-rays the differences in absorption are too small to be very revealing: in the CAT technique these slight differences are accentuated to give an effective degree of contrast by means of a computer. In 1979 Hounsfield shared a Nobel prize with A.M. Cormack, who independently developed a similar system.

Hoxha, Enver 1908–85

Albanian politician. In 1941 Hoxha was a founder member of the Albanian Communist party. In 1943 he took charge of the party's military wing, leading the resistance against the Germans and Italians. In 1946 he deposed King Zog, and Albania became a Communist state, effectively under Yugoslav control. Hoxha served as prime minister (1945–54), and minister of foreign affairs (1946). In 1954 he became first secretary of the central committee. In 1948, after the Soviet- Yugoslav split, Albania broke away from Yugoslavia and in 1961 Hoxha severed relations with the Soviet Union, and aligned his country more closely with China. However, in 1978, after Hoxha's criticism of their regime, China severed ties with Albania.

Hulanicki, Barbara 1936–

British fashion designer and retailer. Born in Palestine of Polish parents, she moved to England in 1948 and worked as a commercial artist, illustrating fashions for magazines such as *Vogue* and *Tatler*. She set up the Biba boutique in 1964 in London's Kensington, and her glamorous yet inexpensive designs – from vamp dresses to demure sweet-heart neck-lined T-shirts – together with the lush 1930s' romanticism of the store's furnishings, made her boutique a mecca for fashion-lovers of the 1960s.

Hundertwasser (Stowasser), Fritz 1928–

Austrian painter. He traveled extensively in Europe and N. Africa before settling in Rome in 1957. By 1952, when he had a one-man show in Vienna, he had evolved the abstract decorative style he is known for, using vivid, luminescent colors including gold and silver – see *The Hokkaido Steamer* (1961) – and from 1953 using spirals extensively in his, mostly watercolor, work. His major influences are Klimt and Schiele. In 1959 he became a visiting lecturer at Hamburg Art College.

Jagger, Mick 1943–

British rhythm & blues vocalist. The charismatic lead vocalist of the Rolling Stones could claim to have made androgyny fashionable. He was spokesperson when press cast the group as anti-establishment trouble makers and later fronted their long-running career of "jet-set debauchery and chic demonic postures". The group's greatest albums include *The Rolling Stones* (1964) and *Beggars' Banquet* (1968). His film career's greatest success is *Performance* (1970). Jagger was also renowned for the beautiful women in his life; including his Nicaraguan wife Bianca and the Texan model Jerry Hall. He continued performing with frenetic energy throughout his forties.

John XXIII (Angelo Roncalli) 1881–1963

Italian pope. Ordained priest in 1904, Roncalli served as an army chaplain in World War I and afterward as a Vatican diplomat (1925–52). Appointed patriarch of Venice in 1953, he was elected pope in 1958 and was viewed by many as a "caretaker". However, in 1959 he announced the summoning of an ecumenical council, the first for almost a century, in order to reinvigorate Catholic Christianity and promote Christian unity. Pope John took an informal approach to the papacy and emphasized his pastoral role. In his encyclicals *Mater et Magistra* (1961) and *Pacem in Terris* (1963) was a reminder not to confuse error with the erring person; for example, the philosophy of Marxism with the governments that espoused it. The former was to be rejected, the latter understood. An obviously humble and compassionate man, he won the respect and affection of millions, Catholic and non-Catholic.

▲ Shashi Kapoor

▲ Jomo Kenyatta

▲ Har Gobind Khorana

Johnson, Lyndon B. 1908–73

36th US president. In 1937, Johnson entered the House of Representatives as a Democrat and strong supporter of Roosevelt. In 1948, he was elected to the Senate, where from 1951 to 1953 he was majority whip, and party leader from 1953 to 1961, ensuring the smooth passage of the first civil rights bills of 1957 and 1960. In 1960 he unsuccessfully challenged Kennedy for the presidential nomination. He became Kennedy's running mate, and was elected vice-president in 1960. He oversaw equal employment opportunities and space research, and in 1961 toured Southeast Asia. He became president in 1963 after Kennedy's assassination and ensured continuity, passing Kennedy's civil rights and voting rights bills. Reelected by a large majority in 1964, he undertook a large program of social legislation aimed at creating what he termed the "Great Society". His popularity waned when American involvement in the Vietnam war escalated. He stepped down in 1969.

Josephson, Brian David 1940–

British theoretical physicist, discoverer of "tunneling" between superconductors (Josephson Effect). After graduating in physics at Cambridge he remained there in the Cavendish Laboratory as, successively, director of research in physics (1967–72), reader (1972–74) and professor (1974). The two discoveries by which he is known was made in 1962 while he was still a research student. If two superconductors are separated at very low temperatures by a narrow insulating gap, current will pass from one to the other without an electric potential being applied. Conversely, if an electric potential is established across such a gap an alternating current will flow in proportion to the potential. The effects find application in various high-speed switching devices. Such applications led Josephson to interest himself in the theory of intelligence. In 1973 he was awarded a Nobel prize jointly with Leo Esaki and Ivar Giaever.

Kadar, Janos 1912–1989

Prime minister of Hungary (1956–58, 1961–65) and First Secretary of Hungary's Communist Party (1956–88). Kadar was instrumental in the transition from Nagy's antiSoviet government of 1956 to the ensuing proSoviet regime. Despite being installed by Moscow, he did achieve independent reform within the Soviet bloc and presided over a communist regime of a liberality unparalleled in Eastern Europe. However, he achieved this after violent suppression of the 1956 revolutionary government, of which he was once a member, and of subsequent unrest. A member of the Communist Party from 1931, Kadar was arrested several times before the communists came to power. Appointed Minister of the Interior (1949), he clashed with the Stalinists and was imprisoned

as a "Titoist" (1951–53) before being rehabilitated (1954). He was ousted from leadership in 1988 and from all party functions in 1989 after failing to respond to demands for more reforms.

Kapoor, Shashi 1938–

Indian film actor and producer. Hailing from a family with a strong cinematic tradition, he worked for the Prithvi and Shakespeareana theatrical companies before appearing in his first film, *Char Diwari*, in 1960. He came to international notice through a series of films by James Ivory and Ismail Merchant, beginning with *The Householder* in 1963. He began producing in 1978, with the award-winning *Junoon*.

Kaunda, Kenneth 1924–

Zambian president. Kaunda joined the ANC in 1949, and became secretary for Northern Rhodesia (Zambia) in 1952. He became head of the organization in 1953, but broke away in 1958 to found the Zambian ANC. He began a campaign of civil disobedience against the federation by Britain of Northern Rhodesia, Southern Rhodesia (Zimbabwe), and Nyasaland (Malawi). The federation was eventually abandoned. Kaunda was imprisoned in 1959 and released in 1960. Now regarded as a national hero, he headed the rapidly growing United National Independence party (UNIP) and in 1960 helped negotiate independence for Northern Rhodesia. The large European and Asian populations attempted to delay the process, and Kaunda managed, by and large, to defuse the ensuing tension. UNIP was victorious in the 1962 elections, and in 1964 Kaunda became chief minister. Zambia gained independence in 1964, and President Kaunda averted civil war. From 1965, he provided bases in Zambia for the anticolonial forces of Southern Rhodesia (Zimbabwe) and Namibia, and boycotted the former's railways. In 1972, Zambia became a single-party state. His economic policy was disastrous, taking Zambia into the world's highest per capita foreign debt. After an attempted coup in 1990 Kaunda restored multi-party politics in 1991.

Kennedy, John F. 1917–63

35th US president. A naval officer in World War II, in 1947, as a moderately liberal Democrat, he entered the House of Representatives, where he campaigned for the underprivileged and supported the Cold War. In 1952 he was elected to the Senate, and in 1960 he was selected as the Democratic presidential candidate campaigning for internationalism and civil rights. In 1961, he became the youngest ever and first Roman Catholic US president. Domestically he introduced a program of radical reform, and spoke of the "New Frontier". Abroad, he established the Alliance for Progress between the USA and several Latin American countries for the development of the

latter, and the Peace Corps, through which volunteers supplied Third World countries with skilled labor. In 1961, exiles attempted a US-backed invasion of Cuba, planned during the previous administration, but were routed at the Bay of Pigs. Kennedy accepted full responsibility. In 1961, he had a meeting in Vienna with Khrushchev. Kennedy's firmness prevented Khrushchev from signing a separate peace treaty with East Germany. In 1962 Kennedy demanded the removal of Soviet nuclear bases being installed in Cuba, the US navy blockaded Cuba, and the world seemed close to nuclear war. The Soviet Union agreed to remove the weapons in return for an American assurance that Cuban territorial integrity would be respected. Relations between the two superpowers improved, and in 1963 at Kennedy's initiative the United States, the Soviet Union and Great Britain signed a limited nuclear test ban treaty. On 22 November 1963, Kennedy was assassinated while campaigning in Dallas, Texas.

Kennedy, Robert F. 1925–68

US politician. Kennedy graduated in 1948 from Harvard and in 1951 from the University of Virginia law school; he became attorney, and managed his brother John's successful presidential campaign. In 1961 the new president made Robert attorney-general, and his chief advisor on all matters, domestic and foreign. Robert was a pillar of the civil rights movement, and was admired by disadvantaged Americans for his championship of the poor and the oppressed. Grief-stricken at his brother's assassination in 1963, he resigned as attorney-general in September 1964, to be elected senator for New York a month later. The voice of liberalism, he criticized US policy in Vietnam, and continued to protect the civil rights movement. in 1968 he ran for the presidency, winning five out of six primaries in twelve weeks; on June 5, after the fifth victory, he was shot dead by an Arab immigrant. Kennedy wrote *The Enemy Within* (1960) and a book on the Cuban missile crisis.

Kenyatta, Jomo 1890s–1978

First prime minister of independent Kenya. In 1922, Kenyatta joined the campaign for the return of Kikuyu tribal lands from the British, conducted by an organization called from 1926 the Kikuyu Central Association. In 1928, Kenyatta became its general secretary. He spoke in London against the proposed union with Uganda and Tanganyika and in 1930, in a letter to *The Times*, he demanded the return of tribal lands, representation in the legislature, educational opportunities, and freedom to follow tribal customs. In 1932, he got some compensation for the loss of lands. He then traveled extensively, writing and studying. In 1946, he attended the fifth meeting of the Pan-African Congress, and became its president. He returned to Kenya in 1946, became president of the Kenya

◄ Nikita Khrushchev

◄ Billy Jean King

◄ Henry Kissinger

African Union (KAU) in 1947, and made it into an influential power. In 1952, falsely accused by the British of leading the Mau Mau terrorist organization, he was imprisoned. In 1960, the British agreed to majority rule, and in 1961, Kenyatta was released, became president of the Kenya African National Union (KANU) and negotiated a new constitution. KANU won the 1963 elections, and Kenyatta became prime minister. In 1964, Kenya became a single-party state. Domestically, Kenyatta developed the economy and attracted foreign investment, though there remained much inequality. Internationally, he pursued a policy of nonalignment, but was always sympathetic to the West.

Khan, Mohammad Ayub 1907–74

Pakistani president. In 1951, Ayub Khan was appointed commander-in-chief of the army, and went on to serve as defense minister during 1954–55. In 1958, after a military coup, he became chief administrator under martial law, and later in the same year replaced Mirza as president. In 1959, he created the electoral college of Basic Democracies, and in the same year was promoted to field marshal. He also pursued economic reforms, and attempted to improve relations with East Pakistan. In 1962, he introduced a new constitution, with a powerful president and assemblies elected by the college of Basic Democrats. Martial law was lifted, and two years later he was returned as president. His support declined, however, particularly in East Pakistan, after the war with India in 1965 and during the increasing severity of his rule which followed it. He resigned in 1969.

Khorana, Har Gobind 1922–

Indian-US molecular biologist, the first to synthesize a gene. After studying science at the Universities of the Punjab, Liverpool, Zurich (ETH) and Cambridge, UK, he did research at Simon Fraser University, Canada (1952–60); then at the Institute for Enzyme Research, University of Wisconsin; and finally at MIT. Much of Khorana's research was devoted to the synthesis of nucleic acids and, ultimately, to the synthesis of a gene. In 1968 he shared the Nobel Prize for Physiology or Medicine with R.W. Holley and M.W. Nirenberg.

Khrushchev, Nikita Sergeyevich 1894–1971

Soviet political leader. Khrushchev joined the Communist party in 1918, and rose rapidly until becoming a member of the Politburo in 1939. After the outbreak of World War II, he consolidated Soviet power in eastern Poland, and after the German invasion in 1941 he organized the Ukrainian resistance movement. In 1944, he reasserted Soviet control of the Ukraine and presided over its reconstruction. In 1949 he resumed his post as first secretary of the Moscow

City party, and became a specialist in agricultural matters, but was unsuccessful in his plan to create agricultural towns. In 1953 Khrushchev replaced Malenkov as first secretary of the all-union party, and in 1955 ousted him as chairman of the council of ministers, installing his own protégé Bulganin in his place. In 1956 Khrushchev condemned Stalin, and argued for peaceful coexistence with the West. He introduced a degree of liberalization into Soviet society, and allowed the eastern bloc parties more independence. However, he resorted to military intervention in Hungary, after Imre Nagy had announced withdrawal from the Warsaw Pact. In 1957 Khrushchev survived an attempt to oust him, and in the following year succeeded Bulganin as chairman of the council of ministers (head of state). Khrushchev traveled widely throughout his career, and in 1959 met Eisenhower during a tour of the United States. A proposed summit was abandoned, though, after an American aeroplane was shot down over Soviet airspace. In 1961 he met Kennedy, but they failed to solve the Berlin problem, and later that year Khrushchev ordered the building of the Berlin Wall. In 1962 he attempted to install nuclear missiles in Cuba, and this led to a major confrontation with the United States. In 1963, the Soviet Union, the United States and Britain agreed the nuclear test ban treaty. Relations with China had deteriorated. The Soviet Union also suffered agricultural failures, and he was ousted in 1964.

Killy, Jean-Claude 1943–

French skier. Top male international alpine skier from 1965 to 1968, his irreverent attitude and good looks won wide popularity. Success came quickly: in 1964 he won the French alpine events, in 1965 the European championship, and in 1966 the combined world title. He held the World Cup for the most international wins in 1966–67 and 1967–68 and in 1968 was the second skier to win all the alpine events at the Olympics. In all he won eight world championships, two world cups, and three Olympic gold medals. He retired from amateur competition in 1968 and turned professional in 1972, becoming the world professional champion.

King, Billie Jean 1943–

US tennis player. Her campaigning and play raised the status of women's tennis. Winner of the most Wimbledon titles, she took the singles six times (1966–68, 1972–73, 1975), women's doubles nine times (1961–62, 1965, 1967–68, 1970–73 and 1979) and mixed doubles four times (1967, 1971 and 1973–74). She also won the US singles four times (1967, 1971–72 and 1974) and the French title in 1972. Turning professional in 1968, she was the first woman athlete to win more than $100,000 in a season. She helped form a separate tour for women and was co-founder of the Women's Tennis Association.

King, Martin (Michael) Luther Jr 1929–68

US clergyman and civil rights leader. While studying for a PhD in theology, King was profoundly influenced by Gandhi's principle of *satyagraha*. In 1955–56 he led a boycott against racial segregation on local buses. After a year, this segregation was abandoned, and King became a national figure. He then helped to found and became president of the Southern Christian Leadership Conference, which oversaw civil rights organizations throughout the area. In 1960 he returned to his native Atlanta, supported demonstrations and was imprisoned. The civil rights movement under King was at its height during 1960–65, orchestrating generally successful demonstrations against localized examples of racial discrimination. In 1963 while in jail, King wrote his famous Letter from Birmingham, spelling out the principles of nonviolent noncooperation. In the same year, he helped to organize the March on Washington of more than 200,000 people, after which he delivered his powerfully moving "I have a dream" speech. In 1964, the Civil Rights Act was passed, and King was awarded the Nobel Peace Prize. In 1965 the Voting Rights Act was passed. King's campaign then moved to the turbulent north, where the Black Power movement was attracting support, and was marginally successful in protesting against segregated housing in Chicago. King broadened the civil rights agenda, and in 1967 publicly condemned the Vietnam War, tried to unite the poor of all races, and committed himself to the restructuring of society. In 1968 he planned a Poor People's Campaign, but was assassinated on 4 April.

Kissinger, Henry (Heinz) A. 1923–

US politician. In 1957 Kissinger wrote *Nuclear Weapons and Foreign Policy*, advocating a strategy of graduated "flexible response". He was security advisor to Eisenhower, Kennedy and Johnson. In 1969, Nixon appointed Kissinger assistant for national security and executive secretary of the National Security Council, and he became the architect of both Nixon's and Ford's foreign policies. He specialized in diplomacy, and pursued a policy of détente with the Soviet Union, culminating in the SALT 1 treaty in 1972. He also restored relations with China. In the Vietnam War, Kissinger ordered the bombing and invasion of Cambodia, oversaw the process of "Vietnamization" (the replacement of US combat troops with South Vietnamese), and in 1973 helped to negotiate a ceasefire and was awarded the Nobel Peace Prize. In the same year, he became Secretary of State, mediated a ceasefire in the Arab–Israeli "Yom Kippur" war, and restored US relations with Egypt. Kissinger also backed CIA operations to destabilize Allende's socialist government in Chile, and to give support to anti-Cuban forces in Angola. He resigned in 1977.

▲ Rod Laver

▲ Claude Lévi-Strauss

▲ Roy Lichtenstein

Kosygin, Aleksey 1904–80

Soviet politician. Kosygin fought in the Russian civil war, and joined the Communist party in 1927. In 1938 he was elected to the Supreme Soviet. In 1939, he became textiles minister, and joined the party's central committee. From 1940 to 1953, he was deputy chairman of the Soviet of People's Commissars. He was also premier of the Russian Republic during World War II, finance minister in 1948 and light industry minister (now including his old ministry of textiles) (1948–53). He became a full Politburo member in 1948. After the death of Stalin, however, Kosygin lost both his place on the Politburo and his position as deputy chairman. He regained the latter position a short time later, lost it again in 1956, but returned in 1957. During 1959–60 he was chairman of Gosplan. In 1960, he was restored as a full member of the Presidium (Politburo), and was also appointed as first deputy chairman of the Council of Ministers (head of state). In 1964, after the fall of Khrushchev, he became chairman of the Council of Ministers, and the moderate influence in the dual leadership comprised of himself and Brezhnev. Kosygin traveled widely, meeting Lyndon Johnson in 1967, and Zhou En Lai in 1969, after the Sino-Soviet border conflicts. In the mid-1970s, Brezhnev became prominent, and in 1980 Kosygin retired.

Kubrick, Stanley 1928–

US film director. A meticulous worker who latterly took years to make each film, he kept tight control at every stage. His first two features were almost one-man shows; the next two critical successes. It was with *Dr Strangelove* (1964) that his mordant vision really found expression. Even his detractors cannot deny that his later films – *2001: A Space Odyssey* (1968), *A Clockwork Orange* (1971), *Barry Lyndon* (1975), *The Shining* (1979) and *Full Metal Jacket* (1987) – were visually stunning.

Laver, Rod 1938–

Australian tennis player. He was the second man to win the Grand Slam and the first to win twice (1962 and 1969). He began taking major titles in 1959 and won seven Wimbledon titles: the singles (1961–62 and 1968–69); the mixed doubles (1959–60) and the men's doubles (1971). Turning professional in 1963, he dominated the game. In 1971 he broke a record by taking over $1 million in prize money.

Lean, David 1908–91

British film director. He made his début (co-directing with Noel Coward) on *In Which We Serve* (1942), but is perhaps best known for lavish landscape epics: *The Bridge on the River Kwai* (1957), *Lawrence of Arabia* (1962), *Doctor Zhivago* (1965), *Ryan's Daughter* (1970) and *A Passage to India* (1984). Earlier work included several skillful adaptations, such as *Brief Encounter* (1945), *Great Expectations* (1946) and *Hobson's Choice* (1954).

Lennon, John 1940–80

British pop composer, singer, guitarist and writer. One of the legendary group the Beatles, he and Paul McCartney were brilliant co-writers. Many rate *Strawberry Fields Forever/Penny Lane* and *Sergeant Pepper's Lonely Hearts Club Band* (both 1967) the group's best single and album. His career after the break-up (1970) was the most innovative, and the *Imagine* album (1971) its high point. He was murdered by a "fan".

Leone, Sergio 1921–

Italian film director and screenwriter. The originator of the spaghetti Western spent years assisting other directors before making *Il Colosso di Rodi*, in 1961. His highly successful series of Italian Westerns began in 1964 and comprised *A Fistful of Dollars*, *For a Few Dollars More* (1965), *The Good, the Bad and the Ugly* (1966) and *Once Upon a Time in the West* (1968). *Once Upon a Time in America* (1983) was an impressive return to direction.

Lévi-Strauss, Claude 1908–

French social anthropologist. As well as introducing a new analytical method in anthropology, his work has profoundly influenced western thought. Lévi-Strauss's approach, drawing on Saussurean linguistics and in particular structuralism, viewed a social structure as a "model" rather than a concrete set of social relationships. This approach was used with regard to kinship, myth and primitive classification in an attempt to uncover underlying patterns, regularities and types. In much of his work the driving force behind much human behavior is seen to be communication, since it is this which structures how we perceive the social world. A Paris University graduate in philosophy and law, Lévi-Strauss taught in Brazil, New York and later at the Collège de France. His works include *The Elementary Structures of Kinship* (1969); *The Savage Mind* (1966); *The Raw and the Cooked* (1969); *Totemism* (1962); *The Naked Man* (1971); *The Distant Gaze* (1983); and *Lynx Story* (1991).

Lichtenstein, Roy 1923–

US artist. In 1949, after studying art, he had his first one-man show. He worked as a commercial artist until 1957, when he took a teaching post in New York. He was producing Abstract Expressionist work, until in 1961 becoming a leading Pop artist, producing, most notably, blown-up copies of strip cartoon images, like *Whaam!* (1963). In 1962 his was the first Pop one-man show. He also produced ceramics and enamelwork, and from 1977, bronze sculptures also using dots and the same Pop images. He also imitated Art, as in *Artist's Studio: The Dance* (1947), a Cubistic still life including Matisse's *The Dance*. Lichtenstein's work holds its subjects up for reassessment; it does not presume to assess.

Ligeti, György 1923–

Hungarian composer. After studying composition in Kolozsvàr (1941–43), and postwar, at the Budapest Academy, Ligeti became a professor at the Academy in 1950. Under the Communist regime, Ligeti was unable to work as experimentally as he wished, or to publish or perform his innovative material. In 1956 he escaped to Vienna, where he worked in electronic music, with Stockhausen and Boulez. The orchestral *Atmosphères* (1961) brought recognition, and fame came with *Requiem* (1965), used by Stanley Kubrick in his blockbusting movie *2001; a Space Odyssey*. He produced humorous work, like *Trois Bagatelles* (1961), satirizing Cage. *Lux Aeterna* (1966), is a choral work, famous for its use in *2001: A Space Odyssey*, which develops further the tonal experiments of the *Requiem*. Ligeti's work is characterized especially by what he has named "micropolyphony" – a sound carpet of numerous interweaving melodic lines often causing aural illusions – and by an impressionistic approach to harmony and orchestral color.

Lumumba, Patrice H. 1925–61

Congolese prime minster. A Liberal party and union activist, Lumumba founded the Congolese National Movement (MNC) in 1958. In 1959 the Congo's Belgian rulers announced a five-year buildup to independence, beginning with local elections, which the nationalists, however, boycotted. A Belgian clampdown ensued, culminating in a violent confrontation, and Lumumba's imprisonment for incitement to riot. In 1960, Lumumba was released to attend a Round Table conference in Belgium, to set a date for independence. The MNC won the general elections of the same year, and Lumumba became prime minister. A short time later, a section of the army mutinied, the Katanga province seceded, and Belgian troops returned. UN troops arrived at Lumumba's request, but would not intervene in Katanga. Lumumba turned to the Soviet Union for help, alienating the West. He prepared to invade Katanga, and was then dismissed by President Kasavubu, but disputed the legality of this action. The army intervened against him, and the UN recognized Kasavubu's government. Lumumba was killed by Katangan secessionists in 1961.

McLuhan, Marshall 1911–80

Canadian communications theorist. He became Professor of English Literature at Toronto University in 1952 and director of its Center for Culture and Technology in 1963. He prophesied that printed books would become obsolete, killed off by television and electronic information technology, and that our thought processes would be reshaped by these phenomena. His books include *Understanding the Media* (1964) and *The Medium is the Message* (1967).

Patrice Lumumba

Mao Zedong

Steve McQueen

McNamara, Robert Strange 1916–

US businessman and Democrat politician. Hired as one of a young team to rejuvenate the Ford Motor Company in 1946, he worked his way up with successful plans such as introducing rigorous cost-accounting methods, until in 1960 he became the first non-Ford family member to be president of the company. In 1961 he resigned to join the Kennedy adminstration as secretary of defense, continuing his service under Johnson. McNamara modernized the armed forces, restructured budget procedures and introduced cost-cutting. Initially supporting US military involvement in Vietnam, by 1966 he came to question its escalation. He tried to initiate peace negotiations in 1967 and carried out a major investigation into US involvement which concluded against continued bombing. In 1968 he resigned to become president of the World Bank, a post he held until his retirement in 1981 and in which he showed a great sensitivity toward Third World needs.

McQueen, Steve 1930–80

US film actor. One of the most popular stars of the sixties and seventies, his supercool, loner, pragmatic style suited the times. A drifter until 1958 there was TV stardom in *Wanted: Dead or Alive*, and the film part that gave him his break, *Never So Few*. He did well in *The Magnificent Seven* (1960), but *The Great Escape* (1963) confirmed his stardom. The best of his later credits were *The Cincinnati Kid* (1965) and *Bullitt* (1968).

Magistretti, Vico 1920–

Italian industrial designer. Graduating from the Milan Polytechnic in 1945, he became one of Italy's leading furniture designers, creating the first Italian plastic chair, the "Selene", which was manufactured by Artemide in 1968. His best-known chair is perhaps the "Modello 115", with its classic frame and traditional rush seating. His work won many awards; in the 1980s it became quieter in style. An important design consultant in Italy, he also taught at London's Royal College of Art.

Maiman, Theodore Harold 1927–

US physicist. After military service with the US Navy, he studied engineering physics at Colorado University; he gained his PhD at Stanford University and joined the Hughes Research Laboratories in Miami in 1955. The principle of the laser (Light Amplification by Stimulated Emission of Radiation) had been illustrated in 1958. Working on and improving the maser (Microwave Amplification by Stimulated Emission of Radiation) principles, in 1960 Maiman perfected such a device, capable of producing pulses of very intense monochromatic light. He left Hughes in 1962 to found the Korad Corporation and other industrial firms to develop and manufacture lasers.

Malcolm X 1925–65

US black militant leader who advocated racial pride and black separatism during the early 1960s. In direct contrast to Martin Luther King, Malcolm X advocated violence and argued against racial integration. His reputation grew at a time when many blacks were dissatisfied with the slow pace of reform and turned to Malcolm for an alternative, more direct approach. After his assassination in 1965, his intellectual influence increased and for many young blacks he became an ideological hero. Converting to the Black Muslim faith (Nation of Islam) while in prison, he was assigned to lead a mosque in Harlem after his release (1954). Malcolm was suspended from the movement when he described the assassination of John F. Kennedy as "the chickens coming home to roost" – an example of the type of violence whites had been using against blacks for a long time. Having amassed a large personal following, he established his own religious organization in 1964 and reaffimed his conversion to orthodox Islam in the same year. He won the support of African and Arab states but clashed with the Black Muslims.

Mao Zedong 1893–1976

Chinese head of state, revolutionary leader, and Marxist thinker. In the 1911 revolution, Mao fought with Sun Yat Sen's nationalist forces in the overthrow of the Manchu dynasty, and in 1919 became politically active with the May Fourth Movement. In 1921 he was a founder member of the Chinese Communist party (CCP), and later its leader. In 1927 he led the Communists in a civil war against the forces of Jiang Jieshi, and in the following year founded a soviet republic in southeast China. In 1934 to 1935, the period of the Communists' Long March and relocation in the northwest, Mao emerged as leader. After this he wrote his chief works of political philosophy. He finally achieved victory in 1949, and became chairman both of the CCP and of the newly founded People's Republic of China. Maoism differs from Marxism-Leninism in its emphasis on the peasantry as the driving force of the revolution, in its fight against the rise of bureaucratic and technocratic elites. These ideological differences with the Soviet Union, and Khrushchev's lack of support in China's 1962 border war with India, damaged Sino-Soviet relations, and Mao later cultivated the United States. In 1957 he initiated the "Great Leap Forward" to decentralize the economy and encourage continued economic growth. It was a failure, and Mao retired as chairman of the republic in 1959, remaining chairman of the CCP. He reasserted his power in the "Cultural Revolution", a violent attempt to halt ideological revisionism. Mao's theories of mass revolutionary fervor as a spur to economic growth, and of a paramilitary way of life, were replaced by an emphasis on managerial competence.

Marcos, Ferdinand E. 1917–89

Philippine president. In 1939, Marcos was convicted of the assassination of a political opponent of his father, but was acquitted on appeal a year later. He escaped from Japanese capture during World War II, but there is no evidence for his claim that he then became a Philippine resistance leader. He was elected to the House of Representatives in 1949, and to the Senate in 1959. He left the Liberal party in 1964, after failing to gain the presidential nomination, and in the same year, was elected president as the Nationalist party candidate. In 1969, re-election made him the first Philippine president to serve a second term. He introduced economic and social reform, but growing political unrest led him in 1972 to impose martial law, and imprison opposition leaders, including Benigno Aquino. The Catholic Church opposed his regime, and guerrilla warfare was waged against it by Maoists and Muslim separatists. In 1973 a new constitution was introduced, further extending the president's powers. In 1981, the constitution was amended, martial law lifted, and Marcos reelected. During the next two years, government corruption, the poverty gap, and Communist guerrilla activities all increased, while the economy declined. Opposition to Marcos grew, and in 1983 Aquino returned, to be shot dead on arrival. The government were widely believed to have been responsible, and Marcos's support fell still further. He was opposed in the presidential elections of 1986 by Aquino's widow, Corazon Aquino, and though Marcos was officially declared the winner, he was suspected both at home and abroad of having perpetrated massive electoral fraud. The army split, and Marcos fled to Hawaii.

Matthews, Drummond Hoyle 1931–

British geologist, codiscoverer of anomalies in the magnetism of the ocean bed. After graduating and doing postgraduate research at Cambridge he was appointed geologist to the Falkland Islands Dependencies Survey (1955–57). He returned to Cambridge to do further research in geophysics and was appointed reader in marine geology (1971–82). He then joined the British Institutions Reflection Profiling Syndicate, Cambridge, which uses seismic reflection techniques to study the earth's crust at depths up to 75km (45.6mi). In 1962 H.H. Hess had put forward his seafloor spreading hypothesis. Matthews produced experimental evidence in support of this by showing (with F.J. Vine) that the earth's crust on either side of the ridges is magnetized in different directions in bands running parallel to the ridges. This is in accordance with the fact that the direction of the Earth's magnetic field has reversed many times over geological ages and the alternations of remanent magnetism correspond to the magma's having solidified at different times.

Golda Meir

Eddy Merckx

Paul Newman

Matuyama, Motonori 1884–1956

Japanese geologist. After studying at the Imperial University, Kyoto, and at Chicago, he became professor of geology in Kyoto. Studying the remanent (frozen-in) magnetism of basalts he discovered that over approximately the last 5 million years the Earth's magnetic field has reversed in polarity at least 20 times, mainly between one and two million years ago. This total reversal is quite different from the continuous wandering of the north magnetic pole. This is known as the Matuyama reversal epoch.

Meir, Golda (Goldie Myerson) 1898–1978

Israeli prime minister. Born in Russia and brought up in the United States, in 1921 Meir emigrated to Palestine, where she held various executive positions in the Histadrut. During the war, she helped negotiate independence from the British, and in 1946 became head of the Jewish Agency's political department. She worked for the release of illegal immigrants and political prisoners. In 1948, after independence, Meir became ambassador to Moscow, and in 1949 was elected to parliament as a member of the Mapai party. From 1949 to 1956 as labor minister, she organized the building of houses and roads. From 1956 to 1966, as foreign minister, she worked to develop good relations with nonaligned African countries. In 1966 she became general secretary of the Mapai party, and after the six-day war in 1967 was involved in the creation of the Labor party. She became prime minister in 1969, traveled widely, tried to negotiate peace in the Middle East, and in 1973 received Willy Brandt, the West German Chancellor. Israel found itself unprepared for the Yom Kippur war in 1973, and in 1974, Meir resigned.

Merckx, Eddy 1945–

Belgian cyclist. He became the amateur world champion in 1964, winning the professional title three years later and again in 1971 and 1974. He dominated the world of cycling in the early 1970s, taking first place in the Prix de France in all but one of the six races between 1969 and 1974. Six times awarded the title of Sportsman of the Year in his native Belgium, he did much to bring cycling to public attention throughout Europe.

Newman, Paul 1925–

US film actor, director and producer. A graduate of the Actors' Studio, he is intelligent, athletic, handsome and he has intensely blue eyes. Hollywood snapped him up after a Broadway hit and despite a terrible debut in *The Silver Chalice* (1955) he was soon getting good roles, giving good performances. In the sixties and early seventies he was America's top male lead. Credits include *The Hustler* (1961), *Hud* (1963), *Cool Hand Luke* (1967), *Butch Cassidy and the Sundance Kid* (1969) and *The Verdict* (1982).

Nicklaus, Jack 1940–

US golfer. With natural talent, power, astuteness and iron nerve, he dominated world professional golf in the sixties and seventies. Turning professional in 1962, he won the Masters six times (1963, 1965–66, 1972, 1975 and 1986), the US Open four times (1962, 1967, 1972 and 1980), the PGA championship five times (1963, 1971, 1973, 1975 and 1980) and the British Open three times (1966, 1970 and 1978). He was the first golfer to win over $300,000 in a year (1972).

Nixon, Richard M. 1913–

37th US president. In 1946 Nixon was elected as a Republican to the House of Representatives, where he was a member of the Un-American Activities Committee. He was elected to the senate in 1950, and in 1953 became vice-president. He ran unsuccessfully for the presidency in 1960 and for the governorship of California in 1962, and in 1968 was elected president. He cut federal expenditure, twice devalued the dollar, and then introduced the New Economic Policy, instituting wage and price controls. He reestablished relations with China, which he visited in 1972, in the same year visiting the Soviet Union, and agreeing the SALT I treaty. In Indochina he followed the Nixon Doctrine of US disengagement from foreign wars, and by 1973 had withdrawn from Vietnam. He was criticized when it was later revealed that Cambodia had been secretly bombed during 1969–70. His political career came to an end with the Watergate affair. After an order of the Supreme Court, transcripts of conversations between Nixon and his staff were made public. They revealed that Nixon had tried to cover up a break-in to Democratic headquarters by several of his close aides. Threatened with impeachment, he resigned in 1974 and was succeeded by Gerald Ford, who granted him a pardon. He regained a sort of respect in the 1980s as an elder statesman with some insight into world affairs.

Nkrumah, Kwame 1909–72

Ghanaian president. In 1945, Nkrumah helped to organize the Fifth Pan-African Congress, and in 1947 he became general secretary of the proindependence United Gold Coast Convention (UGCC). In 1949 he helped to found the more radical Convention People's Party, and in 1950 he initiated a campaign of nonviolent noncooperation. He was then imprisoned for encouraging strikes, and in 1951, while still in prison, he was elected to parliament. Upon his release, he became Leader of Government Business, and in 1952 was made prime minister. In 1957, the Gold Coast gained independence as Ghana. Nkrumah introduced social reforms, while taking a hard line on potential subversives. In 1960, Ghana became a republic, and Nkrumah its president. He played a key role in the Charter of

African States (1961). Economic recession led to domestic social unrest, to which Nkrumah responded by increasing the authoritarianism of his rule, and by turning to the Communist nations for assistance. In 1964, a single-party system was installed, and in 1966, while Nkrumah was on his way to help negotiate a settlement of the Vietnam War, the military seized power. He was given asylum in Guinea, and spent the rest of his life writing.

Noguchi, Isamu 1904–

US sculptor and designer. He studied in New York, then worked as Brancusi's assistant in Paris, where he was influenced by abstract sculptors and the Surrealists. His first exhibition was in New York in 1929. His sculpture often represents elegant, abstract organic forms, and his instinctive awareness of the interrelationship of bone and rock evolved into a sense of "oneness with stone." As a designer, he worked on several environmental projects, including the UNESCO garden (1958), a Hawaiian playground and a fountain for the Detroit Civic Center (1975).

Nyerere, Julius Kambarae 1922–

President of Tanzania. A graduate of Edinburgh University, Nyerere helped form the Tanganyika African National Union (TANU) in 1954, as its president. TANU won the 1958 and 1960 national elections and Nyerere became chief minister in a limited self-government. He became prime minister in 1961, shortly before full independence, and in 1962 when Tanganyika was declared a republic he was elected President. After 1964 Nyerere developed the new Republic of Tanzania as a one-party state, with elections for MPs. Recognizing the need for economic independence and the poor response to requests for aid, he made the Arusha Declaration in 1967. It stated that TANU leaders should not accumulate personal wealth and power; that economic growth to industrial revolution was inappropriate for Tanzania; and that the country was not to be run for the benefit of the urban population. He nationalized major enterprises and created *ujamaa* villages. He resigned as state president in 1985, but remained party chairman till 1990.

Okita, Saburo 1914–

Japanese economist. Educated at Tokyo University, he joined government service as an engineer in 1937. In 1947 he joined the chief research section of the Economic Stabilization Board and was a member of the UN Economic Commission for Asia and the Far East (1952). Appointed director general of the Planning Bureau (1957) and of the Development Bureau (1962–63), he moved to become president of the Japanese Economic Research Center in 1964, and its chairman in 1973. He was a member of numerous committees on

▼ Richard Nixon

▼ Julius Nyerere

▼ Gary Player

national and international economic policy, including the Pearson Commission on International Development (1969–80) and the UN Committee on Development Planning (1965–80) and was Special Advisor to the International Development Center of Japan (1973–79). Foreign minister from 1979 to 1980, he became chairman in 1981 of the Institute of Domestic and International Policy Studies. From 1984 he was president of the Japanese Worldwide Fund for Nature (WWF). Okita was president and chancellor of the International University of Japan. Recipient of several honors, he published many works on the Japanese economy and economic policies.

Oldenburg, Claes 1929–

Swedish-born US artist. Son of a diplomat, Oldenburg's childhood was nomadic; in self-protection he created, in detail, an imagined island he called Neubern. After studying art and literature at Yale, Oldenburg became a crime reporter, and took art evening classes. From 1956 he painted, and wrote poetry, prompted by the New York slums – *The Street* (1960) – and began to create "Happenings", working with Jim Dine, Allan Kaprow and others, and staging such events, from 1961, in "The Store" a Pop Art gallery selling replicas of food and everyday items. He continued this theme with a series of *Soft Typewriters*, *Soft Toilet*, giant hamburgers, and other larger-than-life consumer fantasies.

Ono, Yoko 1933–

Japanese-born artist and singer. Raised in Tokyo by her wealthy family, in 1953 she went to New York where she experimented with avant-garde conceptual art. In 1966 she met John Lennon. In 1969 they married and held their first "Bed-in for Peace" at the Amsterdam Hilton, and a year later began releasing their *Plastic Ono Band* LPs.

Palme, Olof 1927–86

Swedish prime minister. Palme entered parliament as a Social Democrat in 1958, and in 1963 he became minister without portfolio. In 1969, after two ministerial posts, he became party leader and prime minister. A pacifist, he spoke against US policy in Vietnam, and permitted the immigration of deserters, though he would not grant them refugee status. During 1976–82, while out of office, he chaired both the Nordic Council and the Independent Commission on Disarmament and Security (in Geneva), and was UN mediator in the Gulf War. He returned to power in 1982, and was assassinated in 1986.

Palmer, Arnold 1929–

US golfer. The leading figure in world golf from the late fifties to the mid sixties, he became a professional in 1954. He was the first to win the US Masters four times (1958, 1960, 1962, 1964) and to win $100,000 in prize money in one year. Other titles include the US and the British Open (1960), (1961–62). He built a business empire and arranged the construction of China's first golf course.

Papanek, Victor 1925–

American design theorist. As professor of design at the University of Kansas, he wrote his polemical study, *Design for the Real World*, in 1967, a book which attacked the preoccupation of modern designers with "concocting trivia" and their neglect of the more pressing needs of good design for the Third World. His energetic lecture-touring and his emphasis on the need to use diminishing resources wisely made him a cult figure in the ecology movement of the 1970s.

Pasolini, Pier Paolo 1922–75

Italian film director. A novelist and essayist, he began writing screen plays in 1954. *Accattone!* (1961), his first feature, was based on one of his novels and brought instant recognition. He mined world literature and the contemporary scene, often exciting charges of blasphemy. A committed Marxist, a profoundly mystical Christian and a Freudian, he always produced controversial work. Credits include *The Gospel According to St Matthew* (1964), *Teorema* (1968), *The Decameron* (1971), The *Canterbury Tales* (1972) and *Saló: le Centoventi Giornate di Sodoma* (1975).

Paz, Octavio 1914–

Mexican writer. Paz, after attending the University of Mexico, produced *Forest Moon*, his first book of poetry, aged 19. In Spain in 1937 he published the excellent *Beneath your Clear Shadow and Other Poems*; he was deeply influenced by the Surrealists. *On Parole* (1949) made his name as a brilliant Latin American poet. He wrote several other volumes of poetry, and some of prose, the best of these being *The Labyrinth of Solitude* (1950); he also edited and set up several literary journals. In 1962 he became ambassador to India, resigning in 1968 in protest against the government's brutality toward radical students. He lived in Europe and in the US, lecturing at Harvard in the 1970s. Paz's poetry has a strong metaphysical-mythological flavor, is inquiring and sometimes whimsical. He received the 1990 Nobel Prize for Literature.

Pedersen, Charles John 1904–89

Norwegian-US chemist. Born in Korea of Norwegian-Japanese parents, in 1921 he went to the USA and studied chemical engineering at the University of Dayton, Ohio, and MIT. In 1927 he joined the company Du Pont, where he worked until retirement in 1969. There he did research in many fields, but his outstanding discovery (1962) was that of a range of new complexing agents, both natural and synthetic, which have the surprising property of making alkali metal salts soluble in nonaqueous solvents such as chloroform. They produce their effect by wrapping themselves round the metal ion, effectively "hiding" it from the solvent. For this reason the complexes have been called cryptates. He was awarded the Nobel Prize for Chemistry in 1987.

Penn, Arthur 1922–

American director. After acting and university he became an NBC floor manager in 1951 and by 1953 was writing and directing drama. In 1958 he had a Broadway success, *Two for the See-Saw*, and directed his first film, *The Left-Handed Gun*, with little impact. Other Broadway hits followed before he filmed one of them, *The Miracle Worker* (1962). His subsequent sixties films – *Mickey One* (1965), *Bonnie and Clyde* (1967) and *Alice's Restaurant* (1969) – were socially and/or stylistically influential, especially for his theme of violence. Other credits include *Little Big Man* (1970) and *Night Moves* (1975).

Penzias, Arno Allan 1933–

US astrophysicist, discoverer of universal background radiation in the microwave band. After studying physics he joined Bell Telephone Laboratories in 1961, eventually being appointed vice-president, research in 1981. Concurrently he held some academic appointments, including that of professor of astrophysics in Princeton University. In the 1960s, with R.W. Wilson, he was investigating radio noise in the 7cm band emanating from the Milky Way. This was more intense than expected; it came equally from all directions; and no terrestrial source could be identified. It corresponded with radiation from a black body at 3.5°K. This was in accordance with, and gave experimental support to, the "big bang" theory of the origin of the Universe. In 1978 Penzias and his colleague Wilson were jointly awarded the Nobel Prize for Physics.

Player, Gary 1935–

South African golfer. After turning professional in 1953, he won the British Open six years later and became a leading competitor of the 1960s and early 1970s. A small and slightly-built player, he relied on fitness, diet, and a somewhat mechanical technique rather than the traditional qualities of power and swing.

Poitier, Sidney 1924–

US actor and director. Hollywood's "token" black star for almost two decades, he was a charismatic personality with an impressive acting talent. He first made Broadway in 1946 in an all-black production of *Lysistrata*. He made his first film appearance in 1949; major credits include *The Blackboard Jungle* (1955), *The Defiant Ones* (1958), *To Sir With Love*, *In The Heat of the Night* and *Guess Who's Coming to Dinner* (all 1967).

Georges Pompidou

Bridget Riley

Pompidou, Georges 1911–74

French president. As De Gaulle's aide, in 1958–59 Pompidou helped to draw up the constitution of the Fifth Republic, and to make plans for economic recovery. De Gaulle assumed the presidency in 1959 and Pompidou became a member of the Constitutional Council while continuing his outside business activities. In 1961, he helped to negotiate a ceasefire in Algeria, and in 1962 became prime minister. In 1968, he helped end the student–worker revolt, and then resigned. Elected president on De Gaulle's resignation in 1969, Pompidou strengthened the economy, maintained good relations with Arab nations, kept the French military independent of NATO, and reversed de Gaulle's veto on UK entry into the EEC.

Popper, Karl 1902–

Austrian British philosopher. After taking a PhD in psychology at the University of Vienna, he taught math and physics. *The Logic of Scientific Discovery* (1934) was published by the Vienna Circle, whose views he opposed, stating the source of scientific discovery to be imagination, not experience, so that all theories must become acceptable as quasi-fact only, and only in the face of repeated attempts to disprove them. In 1937, with the rise of Nazism, he left to teach philosophy in New Zealand; fame followed on the publication of *The Open Society and its Enemies* (1945), delineating a society valuing truth above dogma; and condemning Plato, Hegel and Marx, and any totalitarian society. He moved to the UK and taught at the London School of Economics until 1969, continuing as a professor emeritus. In *Objective Knowledge: an Evolutionary Approach* (1972) he treated the acquisition of knowledge. Popper did not reject metaphysics, but asserted human freewill, although untestable. His influence on scientific methodology was massive.

Prelog, Vladimir 1906–

Yugoslav-Swiss organic chemist. After graduating in chemistry at the University of Prague, he taught there (1929–34), and then became professor in the University of Zagreb (1935–41). From there he went to the Swiss Federal Institute of Technology, Zurich, latterly as professor of organic chemistry (1950–76). His interest was almost wholly in the molecular constitution and stereochemistry of natural products. Internationally he received many honors. In 1975 he shared the Nobel Prize for Chemistry with the Australian-British organic chemist John Cornforth.

Prigogine, Ilya 1917–

Russian-Belgian physical chemist. He moved to Belgium from Russia in 1929 and graduated in physics in the University of Brussels in 1941. He was appointed professor of physics there in 1951 as well as holding chairs at Chicago (1961–66) and

Austin (Texas) (1967–). The equilibria posited in classical thermodynamics are rarely encountered in real life. Living organisms achieve a regular confirmation from disorganized materials: inanimate systems tend to run down and become increasingly disorganized. Prigogine devoted himself to the investigation of nonequilibrium systems and devised mathematical models to account for them. These have significance also in the wider sphere of ecosystems generally. He was awarded a Nobel prize in 1977.

Quant, Mary 1934–

British dress designer. The leader of the sixties youth-oriented fashion movement which usurped the power of the couturiers, she set up a cosmetics business in 1955 and spent two years designing millinery before opening a boutique in the King's Road, London, in 1957. In seven years she was mass-producing designs which sold throughout Europe and the USA. The miniskirt and hot pants were her most original designs. Early in the seventies she ceased manufacture but continued to design clothes, furs, linen and spectacles and to run her cosmetics business. In 1990 Quant was awarded an OBE.

Redford, Robert 1937–

US film actor and director. The most popular Hollywood star of the seventies, his strong- jawed, blond looks commended him to all. He made Broadway in 1959 and won the lead in *Barefoot in the Park* in 1963. From 1965 he had regular film work but it was *Butch Cassidy and the Sundance Kid* (1969) which hit gold. Credits include *The Candidate* (1972), *Three Days of the Condor* (1975) and *All the President's Men* (1976). He ventured into directing with *Ordinary People* (1980) and *The Milagro Beanfield War* (1988).

Reed, Lou 1942–

American singer, song-writer, guitarist. It was with the formation of the Velvet Underground in 1964 that he first made his mark. His songs depicted the empty debauchery of New York street-life with a mixture of lyricism and violence. He found more solo success with *Transformer* (1972) and *Rock and Roll Animal* (1974).

Rhine, Joseph Banks 1895–1980

US psychologist and "father of parapsychology". Rhine gained his PhD, in botany, in 1925, and taught in West Virginia, until developing a strong interest in extra-sensory phenomena on seeing Sir Arthur Conan Doyle lecture. He studied psychology with W. McDougall at Duke University, where he taught from 1928 to 1965, in 1930 cofounding the parapsychology laboratory there and directing it from 1940. He pioneered experiments in telepathy, using the (extremely boring) Zener cards he had designed, in

clairvoyance and in psychokinesis – moving objects by mental force. He named and popularized extrasensory perception (ESP), and in 1964 founded the Institute of Parapsychology in N. Carolina, which he directed until 1968. He wrote several books on the subject, including *Extra-Sensory Perception* (1935).

Riley, Bridget 1931–

British painter. Riley studied art from 1949 to 1955, and had her first solo show in 1963. She was influenced by Vasarely, but concerned herself in her work solely with optical effect; she was the major proponent of Op Art. At first using only black and white, she moved through grey and blue until, in 1967, employing full color, as in *Late Morning*. Although her technique is mechanistic, the presentation her work makes of the subjective nature of perception gives it a unique place in modern art history.

Rogers, Richard 1933–

British architect. Born in Italy of Anglo-Italian parents, Rogers worked for an Italian architect before studying in London, and at Yale University, where he won several scholarships, and met Norman Foster. From 1963 to 1967 he worked with Foster in Team 4, then went into practice with his wife. From 1971 he worked with Renzo Piano. They shared a conviction that technology must be used to solve social and ecological problems. They won a competition to design the famous Paris *Centre Georges Pompidou* (1977). Rogers also designed the Lloyd's Bank HQ in London (1986). Rogers' work is responsive to environmental and human needs. He is intensely concerned with the interface of public and private space. Later chairman of Richard Rogers and partners, he has lectured at universities, and received many awards, including (1986) the Légion d'Honneur.

Rostow, Walt W. 1916–

US economist. Educated at Yale and Oxford, he taught at Harvard University during the 1940s and became professor of economic history there in 1952. He left Harvard in 1961 to become Deputy Special Assistant in National Security Affairs to President Kennedy. Rostow was Chairman of the Policy Planning Council at the State Department (1961–66) and a US member of the Inter-American Committee to the Alliance for Progress. Appointed Special Assistant in National Security Affairs to President Johnson in 1966, he left in 1969 to become professor of economics and history at the University of Texas. In Rostow's most famous publication *The Stages of Economic Growth: A Non-Communist Manifesto* (1960), he postulated that, having examined the historical records of now industrialized countries, there were definite phases in the relationship between savings rates and capital–output ratios (the productivity of new

▲ Abdus Salam

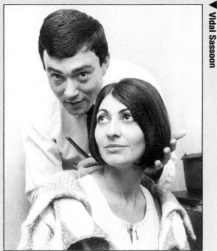

▲ Vidal Sassoon

▲ Jean Shrimpton

investment), in which, given the prevailing capital–output ratio, savings rose to levels that facilitated "take-off" to steady and increasing economic growth. This theory was heavily criticized and is now regarded as naive. Rostow also wrote the important *The Growth and Fluctuation of the British Economy, 1790–1860* (1953).

Salam, Abdus 1926–
Pakistani theoretical physicist. He studied at Government College, Lahore, and Cambridge, UK. After returning briefly to Pakistan he returned to Cambridge as lecturer in mathematics (1954–56) and was then appointed professor of theoretical physics at Imperial College, London. His background made him very conscious of the problems of scientists in the Third World and this led him to found the International Center of Theoretical Physics in Trieste in 1964. Four basic forces are now recognized in nature: the long-familiar forces of gravity and electromagnetism and the much more recently discovered "strong" and "weak" intranuclear forces. Salam made an important advance by formulating a theory linking the electromagnetic and the weak nuclear forces, although these differ by a factor of about a million. This theory was independently put forward also by S. Weinberg (1967) and developed by S.L. Glashow. Salam, Weinberg and Glashow were jointly awarded a Nobel prize in 1979.

Salinger, J.D. 1919–
US writer. After distinguished military service in World War II, he wrote several short stories based on his wartime experiences. Then in 1951 his only novel, *Catcher in the Rye*, took young America by storm. Its hero, Holden Caulfield, was the original model for disaffected youth, promoting the romantic alienation which persisted throughout the century, in varying forms. Salinger wrote little else, mainly using the story form to present the neurasthenically brilliant Glass family in books like *Franny and Zooey* (1961) and *Seymour: An Introduction* (1963). Salinger himself had a privileged upbringing resembling that of Holden Caulfield, was not academically successful, but always wanted to write. Self-indulgence, or indulgence toward his self-absorbed characters, and a lack of humor verging on the paranoiac mar his work. He lived reclusively, granting only one interview.

Sandage, Allan Rex 1926–
US astronomer and first optically to identify a quasar. After graduating from the University of Illinois and the California Institute of Technology, he joined the staff of the Hale Observatories in 1952, at first as assistant to E.P. Hubble, who had provided experimental evidence for the concept of an expanding Universe. In 1960 Sandage turned

his attention to radio astronomy and the mysterious remote bodies known as quasars (quasi-stellar objects). At that time they were known only as cosmic sources of radio waves. Concentrating on quasar 3C48 with a powerful optical telescope he – in collaboration with T. Matthews – discovered it to correspond with a visible material object. Observation of the optical spectrum by the Dutch astronomer M. Schmidt showed a peculiarity in the red band indicating that it was receding at around one-fifth of the velocity of light. Sandage subsequently detected other similar quasars, and he also observed quasars which do not emit radio waves.

Sapper, Richard 1932–
German-born Italian industrial designer. Having studied mechanical engineering, he went to work for Mercedes-Benz in Stuttgart, but in 1958 moved to Milan to collaborate with Marco Zanuso. Together they produced a number of prized cult objects, such as the Brion Vega folding radio in 1965 and the Italian "Grillo" telephone in 1969. On his own account, he designed the stork-like "Tizio" low-voltage lamp in 1978, a triumph of Italian elegance and German engineering – the current runs through the slim flexible screwless bodywork. Later work showed a tendency toward formalism. His stylish kettle for Bollitore in 1983 could not be used because the handle became too hot to hold before the water boiled.

Sassoon, Vidal 1928–
British hair-stylist. He opened his first salon in Bond Street, London, at the age of 26 and soon became the favorite of British pop stars and models. After developing techniques such as blow-drying and the blunt cut, he created numerous new styles for women, such as "The Shape" (1959), the "Nancy Kwan" (1963), the geometric "Five-Point-Cut" (1964), and later the "Feather Cut" (1977), for men and women.

Shrimpton, Jean 1942–
British fashion model, "La Shrimp" was discovered by the rising star of British fashion photography, David Bailey, whose first pictures of her appeared in *Vogue* in 1961. Three years later, her face had appeared on the cover of 17 Condé Nast glossies within a year and her earnings had risen to £25,000 per annum.

Sihanouk, Norodom 1922–
Cambodian monarch and prime minister. Sihanouk ascended to the throne in 1941, under French control. In 1944, the Japanese, who had recently invaded Cambodia, endorsed his declaration of independence, but French rule resumed in 1945. In 1952 Sihanouk began a campaign for independence, which was effectively granted by the Geneva agreements in the following

year. In 1955, he founded the People's Socialist Community party and abdicated in favor of his father. His party then won the elections, and Sihanouk became prime minister. He also served as representative to the UN, and became head of state in 1960. Cambodia's relations with China improved, and in 1965 relations with the US were terminated. His government followed a policy of nonintervention in the Vietnamese war, but the Vietcong established bases in Cambodia. Consequently, the United States backed Lon Nol's coup in 1970, and Sihanouk fled abroad. He supported the Khmer Rouge, and returned after their victory in 1975. He was arrested, and released in 1979 in an attempt to gain UN support after the Vietnamese invasion, which he condemned, at the same time refusing to give support to the Khmer Rouge. In 1982 he became president of a government in exile.

Smith, Ian D. 1919–
Rhodesian prime minister. In 1948, Smith was elected to the South Rhodesian Assembly as a member of the rightwing Liberal party. In 1953 he joined the governing Federal Party. Representation for blacks was proposed, and in 1961 Smith broke away to found the ultra-rightwing Rhodesian Front, who won a majority in the 1962 elections; in 1964 Smith became premier of Southern Rhodesia. He opposed majority (black) rule, and called for immediate independence from Britain. Negotiations failed, and in 1965 Smith made a unilateral declaration of independence. A further round of talks broke down, and the United Nations applied economic sanctions. Smith extended discriminatory legislation and in 1970 declared an "apartheid-style" republic. Protest and guerrilla war escalated, forcing Smith to attempt to incorporate blacks into government, without however, conceding to effective majority rule. He resigned as prime minister in 1979 and attended the Lancaster Constitutional Conference, which conceded the principle of majority rule.

Smithson, Robert 1938–73
US sculptor and "land artist". After studying art in New York, Smithson spent two years hitch-hiking around the USA and Mexico. He had his first one-man show of paintings and assemblages in 1959; he retired from 1962 to 1964, then worked as a sculptor and wrote essays on art. He embarked in the 1970s on the massive al-fresco projects for which he is chiefly known, *Partially Buried Woodshed*, *Spiral Jetty* (1970), and *Broken Circle – Spiral Hill* (1971) using naturally-occurring materials like boulders to produce an art form whose effect on life was his main consideration. After many rejections for industrial design projects, Smithson was commissioned to execute a pond project, *Amarillo Ramp* (1973) but died in a plane crash while photographing the site.

▲ Wole Soyinka

▲ Kenzo Tange

▲ Hendrik Verwoerd

Solzhenitsyn, Alexander 1918–

Russian writer. Solzhenitsyn graduated in mathematics, and fought in World War II. From 1945 to 1956 he was in labor camps, then exile, for criticizing Stalin in a letter. A math teacher, he then began writing, and *One Day in the Life of Ivan Denisovich* (1962) appeared in the journal *Novy Mir*. Its account of a day in a labor camp caused a sensation in Russia and abroad. He was criticized, his work banned and *The First Circle* (1968), dealing with the dilemma of scientists working for repressive governments, and *Cancer Ward* (1968), both drawn from his own experience, were published abroad. He was awarded the 1970 Nobel Prize. The three-volume *Gulag Archipelago* (1973–78) is a compendious chronicle of the network of prison and labor camps, using historical accounts and personal testimonies, held in memory from the writer's incarceration. In 1974 Solzhenitsyn was arrested and exiled for "treason". He settled in Switzerland, then, from 1976, the USA, where he continued to work on his vast novel-sequence (begun with *August 1914*) about the 1917 Revolution.

Soyinka, Wole 1934–

Nigerian playwright and novelist. Soyinka graduated in English at Leeds University in 1958. *A Dance of the Forests* (1960), written for the Nigerian independence celebrations, was unpopular because it deglamorized the past. He edited the literary magazine *Black Orpheus* until 1964, and taught drama and literature at several universities. From his early comic, village pieces, he progressed to more experimental work, developed with actors; *Madmen and Specialists* (1965) and *Death and the King's Horseman* (1975), a study of the clash between Yoruba tradition and colonial imposition, achieve the universality he sought. Soyinka used Brechtian alienation techniques. He also wrote poetry, much of it while in prison (1967–69) for supporting Biafra's secession. He won the 1986 Nobel Prize.

Spector, Phil 1941–

US record producer. Originally with Atlantic, he set up Philles Records in 1961, creating a uniquely rich orchestral rhythm & blues sound using massed pianos, strings and percussion and cascading riffs in a style which recalled gospel singing. His early recordings were with the Crystals and the Ronettes: notably *Then He Kissed Me* and *Be My Baby* (both 1963). But the Righteous Brothers single *You've Lost that Loving Feeling* (1964), and Ike and Tina Turner's *River Deep, Mountain High* (1966) sum up his mature style.

Steinberger, Jack 1921–

US particle physicist. A chemist, during World War II he worked in the Radiation Laboratory at MIT and then took a doctorate in physics at Chicago, doing research on cosmic rays. In 1959 he took a post at Columbia University, moving to CERN in Geneva in 1968. At Columbia he worked closely with L. Lederman and M. Schwartz: they shared a Nobel prize in 1988. Steinberger had shown at Chicago that a particle known as a muon decays to give two neutrinos and an electron. They surmised that neutrinos should be of two kinds – muon neutrinos and electron neutrinos, and confirmed this experimentally with the aid of a new high-energy particle accelerator. While at CERN Steinberger continued his work on neutrinos and contributed to the development of a "standard" model for particle physics.

Stella, Frank 1936–

US painter. Stella studied art, then worked as a house painter, while painting Abstract Expressionist pieces. Throughout his career, he worked in series, and his first series, 23 black canvases with bare canvas forming fine stripes was shown in 1960. He then painted three series in aluminum, copper and magenta, using geometric shapes. Stella began in the sixties to introduce the issue of the interaction of shape and color into structure. In the 1970s he produced a *Polish Village* series, of painted wood reliefs, a Brazilian series, in aluminum and steel, and *Exotic Birdsong*, incorporating found shapes attached straight to the canvas, and scribbled lines. Stella's work is consciously and rigorously formally developed, yet has strong feeling and decorative qualities.

Tange, Kenzo 1913–

Japanese architect. After completing his architecture studies at Tokyo University in 1945, Tange worked with Mayekawa and Sakakura, who had worked with Le Corbusier; they pioneered International Style (often called "Brutalism") in Japan. Tange became Professor of Architecture at Tokyo University, wrote extensively on architectural theory, and achieved international fame with his winning design for the Hiroshima Peace Center, completed 1955. His plan (1960) to reduce Tokyo's traffic congestion by extending the city on stilts into Tokyo bay was not executed. In 1961 he founded URTER, Urbanists' and Architects' team, following Gropius. His buildings and his writings – such as *Function, Structure and Symbol* (1966) – have been very influential.

Tshombe(-Kapenda), Moise 1919–69

Congolese politician. In 1959 Tshombe became president of the Katangan Conakat party, who wanted a federalist system. In the 1960 elections, Conakat won a majority in the Katanga provincial assembly, and Tshombe declared independence from the rest of the Congo. Lumumba was ousted as premier by the military, and Tshombe was allegedly involved in his subsequent murder. After unsuccessful negotiations with President Kasavubu, the Katangan secessionists were finally defeated in 1963 by UN forces, and Tshombe fled abroad. He was rehabilitated in 1964, and appointed premier to subdue leftwing insurrectionists; he used white mercenaries to do so. In 1965 he was sacked amid rumors of a plot to overthrow Kasavabu. He went abroad again, and after rumors of his imminent return, was kidnapped in 1967 and taken to Algeria, where he remained for the rest of his life under house arrest.

Twiggy 1949–

British model and performer. Born Lesley Hornby, she was called "Twiggy" on account of her slender, boyish figure. Under the tutelage of entrepreneur Justin de Villeneuve, she was launched as "The Face of 1966" appearing in fashion magazines such as *Elle* and *Vogue*. She was Britain's most adulated model for five years. Later, she appeared in films, notably *The Boy Friend* (1971).

Ulbricht, Walter 1893–1973

East German head of state. A member of the Social Democratic party, in 1919 Ulbricht helped found the German Communist party. He joined its central committee in 1923, and was elected to the Reichstag in 1928. After Hitler's rise to power in 1933, Ulbricht fled abroad and worked as a Comintern agent. He settled in Russia, and during World War II was involved in propaganda work with German prisoners of war. Returning home in 1945, he helped to form an administration in the Soviet zone. He was also involved in the forced merger with the Social Democrats. In 1949 he became deputy premier of East Germany, and in 1950 general secretary of the ruling Socialist Unity Party (SED). A harsh ruler, in 1953 he resisted, with Soviet help, attempts to overthrow him. In 1960 he was elected chairman of the council of state, a post which replaced the presidency. He successfully resisted pressure for reform after Stalin's death, but permitted some liberalization after the construction of the Berlin Wall at his behest in 1961. In his foreign policy he regarded West Germany with deep suspicion, and opposed détente. In 1968 he was one of the chief advocates of military intervention in Czechoslovakia. He retired as general secretary in 1971, but kept his post as chairman of the council of state.

Verwoerd, Hendrick Frensch 1901–66

South African politician and chief architect of apartheid, a policy which legalized the separation of races and has perpetuated white domination. He introduced the Promotion of Bantu Self-Government Act (1959) whereby blacks were resettled in eight separate "Homelands" with empty promises of eventual independence. He also removed the last nonwhite representatives in parliament. Such policies provoked demonstrations by blacks to which Verwoerd

John Vorster

Andy Warhol

Zhou En Lai

responded with increasing repression, including the Sharpeville shootings of unarmed people, including children (1960), banning the African National Congress and Pan-African Congress, and introducing imprisonment without trial. He became professor at Stellenbosch (1927–37) before editing the nationalist newspaper *Die Transvaler* (1938–48) where he made his racist views known. Appointed senator after the nationalists won the 1948 elections, he became minister of Native Affairs (1950–58), was elected to parliament (1958), and became prime minister (1959). He survived an assassination attempt in 1960 but was eventually stabbed to death in parliament.

Vine, Frederick John 1939–88

British geologist. A Cambridge graduate, he worked at Princeton University (1965–70) before returning to the UK as reader, later professor, in Environmental Sciences at the University of East Anglia. In 1963, as a postgraduate research student working with D.H. Matthews, he showed that the magnetism of the ocean bed on either side of the midoceanic ridges alternates in direction as one moves out from the source. This accords with known reversals of the Earth's magnetic field over time and supports the hypothesis of seafloor spreading advanced by H.H. Hess in 1962.

Vorster, John (B. Johannes) 1915–83

South African prime minister. During World War II, Vorster was a member of the neo-Nazi Ossewa Brandwag (Oxwagon Guard), and was imprisoned in 1942. In 1953 he was elected to parliament as a member of the Nationalist party, and promoted in 1960 to minister for justice, police and prisons. He took a hard line in the drafting of the apartheid system, created a new security police force, and introduced the power of detention for 90 days without trial in cases of suspected subversion. Having gained the premiership in 1966, he introduced minor reforms to apartheid and severely restricted antiapartheid movements. Abroad, he pursued dialog with black African leaders, but in 1975 sent troops to oppose the Angolan liberation movement. He was later instrumental in persuading Ian Smith to share power in Rhodesia, but totally rejected a similar policy for South Africa. He resigned the premiership in 1978, and assumed the principally ceremonial position of president. He resigned in 1979, after it became known that he had tried to cover up the Muldergate scandal, in which large amounts of government money had been misappropriated.

Warhol, Andy 1930–87

US artist and film-maker. After attending the Carnegie Institute of Technology, in 1949 Warhol settled in New York and worked as an advertising illustrator. In 1957 he won the Art Director's Club

medal. He became known as the supreme Pop Artist with the production, in 1962, of works like *Campbells Soup Cans 200*, which became icons of the consumer society. His screen-prints of *Marilyn Monroe* (1962) revealed the star as another cleverly packaged commodity. Warhol also used violent subject matter, distancing it by an ordinary, precise representation. The studio where he began to mass-produce silk-screened copies of media images was called The Factory. Warhol also made films, attempting to remove the element of creative choice by leaving a camera in one position for hours – as in *Empire* (1965). He cultivated inconsequentiality and banality in whatever he did, and his enduring achievement is to have elevated these qualities into art.

White, Patrick 1912–90

Australian novelist. White was born in England, and brought up on an Australian sheep station until 13, when he was sent to school in England. He read modern languages at Cambridge, then settled in London, where he wrote the early, untypical novels *Happy Valley* (1939) and *The Living and the Dead* (1941). During the war he served as an R.A.F. intelligence officer in Greece. *Voss* (1957) the tragedy of a German immigrant's epic attempt to traverse Australia, made him famous. *Riders in the Chariot* (1961) concerns four disparate characters who share a vision of the chariot, symbol of the inner life, one of White's main concerns. He was often savagely satirical, in highly wrought and resonant prose. His interest in Jung and myth led him to write *The Solid Mandala*, about two complementary brothers unable to escape each other. *The Eye of the Storm* won the 1973 Nobel Prize.

Whitman, Marina Bon Neumann 1935–

US economist. She graduated from Radcliffe College in 1956, received an MA in 1959 and a PhD in 1962, both in economics at Columbia University. She then taught economics at the University of Pittsburgh (1962–72), becoming a full professor in 1971. In 1971 Whitman became senior staff economist in international affairs to the Council of Economic Advisors and was appointed by President Nixon to the US Price Commission, the commission's only female member and its youngest. A member of the Council of Economic Advisors (1972–73), she played a key role in producing the economic forecast for 1973. Returning then to the University of Pittsburgh, she was appointed Distinguished Public Service Professor of Economics. In 1979 she resigned to become vice-president and chief economist of General Motors. She was on the overseas board at Harvard College (1972–78); economic advisor for the the US Department of Commerce from 1979; trustee of Princetown University from 1979; member of committees on national and

international monetary policies; recipient of many honors and member of the Royal Economic Society and American Economic Association. She received numerous academic grants and wrote several books.

Wilson, (James) Harold 1916–

British prime minister. During World War II Wilson worked at the ministry of fuel and power, where he produced the basic plan for the nationalization of the coal industry. He became a Labour MP in 1945 and in 1947 president of the Board of Trade, initiating deregulation and negotiating a trade agreement with the Soviet Union. He resigned in 1951, in protest over the introduction of medical prescription charges. Party leader from 1963, he promoted Labour as the party of technology and efficiency. In 1964, he became prime minister; he failed to prevent Southern Rhodesia's unilateral declaration of independence in 1965, and subsequent negotiations and economic sanctions proved ineffective. Wilson was returned with a greatly increased majority in 1966, but soon met with economic problems; and in 1967 the pound was devalued. In 1968, he visited the United States and the Soviet Union in a vain attempt to help solve the crisis his Vietnam. In 1969, he abandoned plans to introduce trade union reform. The economy began to recover and Wilson's popularity revived, but Labour lost the 1970 elections. He regained the premiership in 1974, during a period of rising inflation and a miners' strike. Inflation rose sharply, and in 1976 Wilson resigned as premier and party leader.

Zhou En Lai 1898–1976

Chinese politician. Zhou was active in the Chinese Communist party in Paris from 1921, and fought with Jiang Jieshi in China against the warlords, but was sentenced to death in 1927 during Jiang's purge of the Communists. Now a Politburo member, he continued to spread revolutionary propaganda until 1931, when he became political leader of the Chinese Red Army. After the Communists' Long March, he became their chief negotiator, and in 1936 saved Jiang from execution by his own generals by securing his promise to make war against the Japanese his first priority. In the ensuing Communist- Nationalist coalition Zhou was Jiang's military advisor. In 1949, on the foundation of the People's Republic of China, Zhou became prime minister and foreign minister. In 1950 he secured the Sino-Soviet alliance, and at the 1954 Geneva conference negotiated concessions for Korean and Indochinese Communists. He attended the Bandung Conference of neutral countries in 1955, and in 1971 engineered President Nixon's visit to China. Zhou was a stabilizing influence during the Cultural Revolution; and helped to suppress the Red Guards.

ACKNOWLEDGMENTS

Picture credits

1 Dead student following demo at Kent State University l970: AP
2–3 Boy meets girl: HDC/Bettmann Archive
4–5 Beach at Ostende: HDC
6 Vietnamese civilians displaced by war: M/Philip Jones-Griffiths
8 Andy Warhol and friends enjoy 15 minutes of fame: M/Burt Glinn
10–11 Antiwar demo, Washington: M/Charles Harbutt
44–45 Advertising the latest model, l959: M/Henri Cartier Bresson
80–81 An illegal political meeting in South Africa: M/Ian Berry
118–119 The Pranksters' Psychedelic Bus: Gene Anthony

15 M/Henri Cartier-Bresson 16 CP 17c Chicago Sun Times, Mauldin 17b CP 18t PF 18b AP 19t,19b CP 21 CP 22–23 M/Marc Riboud 23 CP 25t M/Philip Jones-Griffiths 25b M/Marc Riboud 26t, 26b M/Ian Berry 27t, 27b M/Don McCullin 28 M/Leonard Freed 29 M/Micha Bar Am 30t M/Robert Capa 30b M/Fred Scianna 30–31 AP 31bl, 31bc RF 31br AP 33 M 34t IKON 34b M/Roger Malloch 35 M/Bruno Barbey 36t PF 36b M/Elliott Erwitt 37t PF 37b Los Angeles Times 38–39 M/Philip Jones-Griffiths 38b M/Don McCullin 39 IKON 40t, 40b PF 40–41 M/Don McCullin 42t IKON 42b RF 42–43 M/Bruno Barbey 43tl Arthur Lockwood 43tr AP 43br RF 49 HDC 50t HDC 50b, 51t BPL 51b HDC 52 CP 53 TPS 54 CP 55 BPL 56t, 56b PF 56–57 HL 57tr, 57bl CP 57br ME/SP 59 BPL 60t Japan Information Centre 60b HL/M MacIntyre 60–61, 61 Japan Information Centre 62t, 62b CP 63t Korea National Tourism Office 63b HDC 65 N/Barry Lewis 66, 67 Society for Cultural Relations with the SSR 68–69 Society for Cultural Relations with the USSR 70t HL 70b PF 71t, 71b HL 72 M/Steve McCurry 72–73 FSP 73tl M/Erich Hartmann 73tr Art Direction/Craig Aurness 73bl, 73br N/Mike Goldwater 75 HL 76 ME/SP 77 United Nations 78 F/Maggie Murray 78–79 RF 79 BPL 85 HL/Sarah Errington 86 LC 87 HL/Crispin Hughes 88 M/Henri Cartier-Bresson 90–91 ME/SP 91 HL 92t, 92b PF 92–93 M/Martine Franck 93tl Sally and Richard Greenhill 93tr Euan Duff 93b South American Pictures/Tony Morrison 95 F/Brenda Prince 96 CP/Armand Latourre 97 CP/Klaus Lehnartz 98t CP/John Launois 98b M/Henri Cartier-Bresson 100 BPL 101t AA 101b TPS 103 HDC 104 M/Henri Cartier-Bresson 104–105 Paul Trevor 105 M/Henri Cartier-Bresson 106 SV 107 M/Gilles Peress 108 M/Bruce Davidson 109t Bettmann Archive 109b M/Burt Glinn 110t RF 110b Courtesy of Tupperware Home Parties 111 Bettmann Archive 112t AA 112 John Webb 113 M/Leonard Freed 114t PF 114b M/Alex Webb 114–115 FPG International 115t M/Jean Gaumy 115c Culver Pictures 115b Juhan Kuus 116–117 SPL/Dr G M Rackham 116t SPL/CNRI 116b SPL/NASA 117t US Navy 117c OSF/Owen Newman 117b SPL/Simon Fraser 123 Pictorial Press Limited 124l TPS 124r PF 125t PF 125b Victoria and Albert Museum, Fashion Department/John French Estate 126t Telegraph Colour Library 126b Whitmore-Thomas 127t AA 127b Architectural Press/Malcolm Lewin 128l Arcaid/Richard Einzig 128r John Rose and John Doyle 129t Rosenthal Group 129b Bang and Olufsen 131 AA 132tl KC 132tr APL 132b KC 133 KC 134t Pictorial Press 134b AP 135t RF 135b AP 137 Novosti Press Agency 138t M/Raymond Depardon 138b RF 139t TPS 139b Colorsport 140–141 RF 141t AP 141cr PF 141br Allsport UK Ltd 143b FPG International/Mary Englander 143r AP 144 Pictorial Press 145t Retna/Bob Freeman 145b Val Wilme 146t Retna/Joel Axelrod 146b Pictorial Press 147l Michael Ochs Archives/Venice, California 147r Retna/Barron Wolman 148 HDC 148–149 RF 149t AA 150t Michael Ochs Archives/Venice, California 150b Lisa Law 150–151 RF 151tr,151cr Michael Ochs Archives/Venice, California 151cl Jack Kilby 152t Museum of Modern Art, New York 152b FSP/Gamma/Bertrand Laforet 152–153 TPS 153t Richard Bryant 153b FSP/Liason/Ferry 154l United Press International 154c PF 154r

M/Elliott Erwitt 155l RF 155c Jocelyn Bell Burnett 155r PF 156l RF 156c PF 156r HDC 157l PF 157c PF 157r RF 158l RF 158c M/JK 158r HDC 159l HDC 159c RF 159r HDC 160l PF 160c HDC 160r Val Wilmer 161l PF 161c PF 161r PF 162l RF 162c PF 162r PF 163l Mirrorpic 163c RF 163r PF 164l PF 164c M/Henri Cartier-Bresson 164r PF 165l HDC 165c RF 165r PF 166l PF 166c Colorsport 166r APL 167l M/Elliott Erwitt 167c PF 167r Colorsport 168l Syndication International 168r HDC 169l HDC 169c PF 169r Cecil Beaton Photography, courtesy of Sotheby's, London 170l PF 170c M/Henri Cartier-Bresson 170r PF 171l CP 171c RF 171r M/Marc Riboud

Abbreviations

AP	Associated Press, London
APL	Aquarius Picture Library, Sussex
BPL	Barnaby's Picture Library, London
CP	Camera Press, London
F	Format, London
FSP	Frank Spooner Pictures, London
HDC	Hulton Deutsch Collection, London
HL	Hutchison Library, London
KC	The Kobal Collection, London
LC	Library of Congress, Washington
M	Magnum Photos Limited, London
ME/SP	Mark Edwards/Still Pictures, London
N	Network Photographers, London
PF	Popperfoto, Northampton
RF	Rex Features, London
SPL	Science Photo Library, London
SV	Suddeutscher Verlag, Germany
TPS	Topham Picture Source, Kent

t = top, tl = top left, tr = top right, c = center, b = bottom etc.

Editorial and Research Assistance

Steven Chapman, Mary Davies, Jackie Gaff, Jane Higgins, John Horgan, Louise Jones, Nick Law, Andy Overs, Mike Pincombe, Maria Quantrill, Graham Speake, Michelle von Ahn

Artists

Alan Hollingberry, Ayala Kingsley, Kevin Maddison, Colin Salmon, Dave Smith, Del Tolton

Design Assistance

Cyndy Gossert, Nicholas Rous, Dave Smith, Del Tolton, Michelle Von Ahn

Photographs

Shirley Jamieson, David Pratt

Typesetting

Brian Blackmore, Catherine Boyd, Anita Wright

Production

Stephen Elliott, Clive Sparling

Cartography

Maps drafted by Euromap, Pangbourne; Alan Mais (Hornchurch); Sarah Rhodes

Color Origination

J. Film Process, Bangkok; Scantrans, Singapore

INDEX